Dubai

Footprint • *Zee Gilmore*

Contents

Listings

About the author

Born in Dubai and brought up in England and Saudi Arabia, Zee's family has a long history of service in the Middle East. Her grandfather was in the Levant Consular Service, her father served with two Arab armies during his military career and her mother was born in Baghdad. Her own extensive travels have seen her fleeing from charging elephants in Namibia, escaping organ donors in Cambodia and being washed down a waterfall in South Africa. With degrees in English and Criminal Justice, she has taught underprivileged children in the Drakensberg Mountains, worked as a travel trade journalist and has also contributed to the Footprint Laos and Thailand books. She now lives and writes in Dubai.

Acknowledgements

Thanks to David Bulleid for making all this possible; Doctor Samia Rab, Peter Jackson and Rashad Mohammed Bukhash for their advice and help on architectural matters; Martin Patterson for acting as interpreter when needed; Magrudy's for their guidance on books; Nabeel for opening up the world of Dubai's fabulous restaurants and Nabeela and Peter Bennett for their discerning comments on the same; Mike Chapman for his words of wisdom on Dubai's better bars; Ian, Toni, Natalie for their never-ending hospitality; Sophie and Tom for the use of their flat and their awesome knowledge of the city; Sarah McQueen for her midnight communications about Al-Ain; Billy and Manisha for being complete saviours despite trying to end my life once by chilli and once by desert; Annisa, my fellow-explorer at times; Fran and Liz for G&Ts; Claire Malcolm for her insights about the region; and Janice Cunningham for opening my eyes to Karama's phenomenal 'designer' bag culture. But most of all, thanks to Mark Lynch for his indefatigable help and support.

'If we build it, they will come.' So runs the audacious Al-Maktoum family mantra, and so they built. A sleepy fishing village not half a century ago, before the discovery of oil and subsequent building boom, the dust of the desert is now clearing to reveal a thriving metropolis with a sophisticated network of highways and high-rises, a plethora of glittering malls and an awesome concentration of top-notch hotels and attractions, all beautifully greenified by gallons and gallons of de-salinated water. The limitations of environment, geography and history were not going to get in the way of global recognition and acclaim!

This is a city built on the visionary determination of its rulers, whose zeal has attracted entrepreneurs and adventurers from around the globe in search of a slice of the action. And with over 70 different nationalities calling Dubai 'home', the city is a cultural crossroads – a bit of a microcosm surrounded by its traditionally Arab and inward-looking Middle Eastern neighbours. For the tourist, this rich mix of cultures has created a feast for the eyes, spirit, stomach and shopping bag.

Supersonic city

Think Dubai, think superlative. The words 'first, tallest, deepest, most expensive, lavish, outlandish' could have been created for this city. Where else would you find a hotel that out-classes (at whichever end of the spectrum your personal preference puts it!) the world's hotel classification system? The ever-employable builder is in the process of drilling the world's first underwater luxury resort, along with a series of 200 man-made islands in the shape of the countries of the world, not to mention the world's tallest building, proving that not even the sky is the limit to this city's ambitions. And in the midst of all this modernity, as you zoom from a swim in the sea to a round of golf, to a top teppanyaki restaurant, the age-old souks still attract the haggling masses and camels still delight those who venture into the nearby desert.

United colours of Dubai

It's entirely possible to lose yourself in a whirlwind of fine dining, hedonistic activities, designer shopping and other Gucci pursuits, but a little time out from this frenetic activity can reveal another side to Dubai, appealing in quite a different way. Coursing through this open-minded society is an undercurrent of Islamic tradition in which tolerance and hospitality are key. This accounts for the careless cosmopolitanism of Dubai; its willingness to accept all nationalities and all cultures, and the way the *abras* plying the Creek carry a kaleidoscope of sun-tinted tourists sitting cheek by jowl with colourful, sari-wrapped Indians and locals sporting spotless *dishdashas*. It's noticeable further afield, too, as you head out of town to explore the barren beauty of the mountains, or rolling beaches of the East Coast. Almost without exception, everyone you meet will be friendly, unassuming, and willing to enter into conversation, blithely ignoring the lack of a common language.

At a glance

The Creek

Despite the bulldozing and building that's swiftly giving Dubai its trendy new face, 'Khor Dubai' has managed to hang on to its original character, and remains much as it ever was – a busy trade thoroughfare around which the rest of this thriving community arranges itself. Running several kilometres inland from the Arabian Gulf to culminate in what is now the Khor Dubai Wildlife Sanctuary, it neatly divides the city in two. As Deira (to the north) and Bur Dubai and Oud Metha (to the south) fight to contain their ever-expanding selves, many sights and attractions can be easily spotted from the Creek serving as a natural compass. Bridging the gap between north and south is Al-Shindagha Tunnel near the mouth of the Creek, as well as Al-Maktoum and Al-Garhoud bridges further inland.

Deira

Framed by the Creek to the south and the Arabian Gulf to the north, Deira's eclectic mixing of the traditional with the trendy encapsulates Dubai's ability to make the old rub shoulders with the new. To the west is the heart of Dubai's souk land, a rabbit warren of narrow alleys and overflowing shops, where old Dubai is preserved in shelves, racks and sacks bursting with goods, glittering with gold and wafting pungent spices. To the east along the Creek bank lies a row of striking buildings marking Deira's burgeoning business district, the dhow wharfage and that popular tourist retail magnet, Deira City Centre. Further east yet, Dubai Creek Golf & Yacht Club hugs the Creek and signifies the location, further inland, of the Tennis Stadium, Century Village and Airport. Dubai Festival City is currently under construction further east still, along the bank.

Bur Dubai

Home to the greatest concentration of Dubai's tourist sights and heritage areas, each painstakingly renovated by a very determined

Dubai Municipality, Bur Dubai is also known as a bustling business hub with a strong concentration of residential apartment blocks. The area stretches south from the mouth of the Creek, encompassing Al-Shindagha's many attractions before curling around to encircle the electronics area, Textile Souk, and major sights including the old merchant community HQ, Bastakia and the pretty corniche running east along the Creek. Most of the action falls Creekside of Khalid bin Al-Waleed Road, although the area does stretch out further towards Karama and ultimately Jumeira and Satwa to the southwest.

Oud Metha

Bordered by the Creek to the north and by Karama and Bur Dubai to the west beyond Za'abeel Road, Oud Metha's southern stretch is neatly contained by the sweep of Route 11 before it loops around to cross the Creek at Al-Garhoud Bridge. It's a largely residential area, with a variety of recreational, educational and retail facilities, though all but a few have a distinctly deserted, tumble-weed air about them. The lovely grassy stretch of Creekside Park remains popular, arching along the bank of the Creek opposite the Dubai Creek Golf & Yacht Club on the other side of the water. Within its grounds is the excellent interactive museum, Children's City, while the main event is the glorious reincarnation of ancient Egypt that is Wafi City – a retail and dining Mecca.

Sheikh Zayed Road

Heading southwest from Trade Centre Roundabout towards Abu Dhabi, the infamous eight-lane Sheikh Zayed Road runs parallel to the coast, with Jumeira and Satwa sandwiched in the middle. The road itself is sometimes fringed with the odd smoking body shell, signalling the impossible driving you'll sometimes encounter. That first strip, between the roundabout and the first Intersection, is the main attraction: modern buildings of varying architectural designs and merit line the roadside in a striking avenue of high-rise hotels,

apartments and offices. For a long time, only the Dubai World Trade Centre stood surveying the area, but since the 1990's the steady addition of more and more trendsetting buildings.
The second strip is less dramatic but continues with high-rises, offices, residential apartments reaching the districts of Umm Suqeim, Al-Sufouh and Marsa Dubai.

Jumeira and Satwa

Running parallel to the coast along the Jumeirah Beach Road from the beautiful Jumeirah Mosque, Jumeira stretches 10 km south towards Jebel Ali. Peppered with beaches, desirable residential properties, galleries, scenic parks and a proliferation of shopping malls to cater for the every whim of the bold and the beautiful who live here, it's an American society soap opera neighbourhood in the making. The well-heeled female residents have even been dubbed the 'Jumeira Jane' set. Keeping pace geographically with Jumeira is neighbouring Satwa, although there the similarities end. To Jumeira's cool sophistication, Satwa is earthy, Arab and atmospheric, best known for its array of textile shops and excellent tailors, although Al-Dhiyafah Road on Thursday and Friday nights is a catwalk for the world's hottest wheels.

The Southwest

Further along the Jumeirah Beach Road, Umm Suqeim, Al-Sufouh and Marsa Dubai together boast more five-star beach hotels than you can shake a stick at. The area's potential for development has already been clocked and as Dubai's population swells and seeps increasingly in this direction, a host of luxury residential projects and resorts look set to breathe new meaning into the term 'ground-breaking'. Al-Sufouh and Marsa Dubai are currently in the grip of a development frenzy, so do bear this in mind if you're looking for a quiet, peaceful retreat in which to relax while on holiday – construction noise can be formidable as the labourers work around the clock.

Trip planner

Summer, June to September, can be oppressively hot, with humidity sometimes hitting 90 per cent and the sea feeling like soup. However, the dramatic reduction in room rates at many hotels is a tourist magnet, as is the Dubai Summer Surprises (DSS), see p174.

October to April sees the finest weather, with temperatures ranging between the early 20s and 30s, and this is when Dubai receives the majority of its visitors. Dubai Shopping Festival (DSF), see p173, is a big hit, and hotels often hit peak capacity, so serious advance booking is necessary.

The holy month of Ramadan, during which Muslims fast from dawn till dusk, has a significant impact on the entire city. Dubai's nightlife takes a bashing – bars don't open until about 1900, and clubs are left to gather cobwebs all month in deference to the ban on live music. Many restaurants won't serve alcohol, and food and even water, can be hard to find during the day. Everyone, regardless of their religion, is required to abide by the fast in public. Abstention includes not just eating and drinking, but smoking too!

24 hours

To make the most of Dubai in a day, you'll need to get up early and head off into the heart of Bur Dubai, stopping to appreciate the traditional architecture of Bastakia and a sublimely good lemon mint drink at XVA Gallery. The intriguing displays in the Dubai Museum are a must, after which turn your footsteps towards the rainbow hues of the Textile Souk. Al-Shindagha is your next port of call, to dive in and out of Sheikh Saeed Al-Maktoum's House and the Heritage and Diving Villages. Nearby Kanzaman Restaurant is an excellent place to break for a leisurely lunch. Then it's over the river via Al-Shindagha Tunnel to the famous Gold, Spice and Covered souks in Deira. When you're haggled out, head to the nearby *abra* station and charter a boat for an hour's spin up and down the Creek to see the sights and investigate the ant-like activity that characterizes the busy dhow

Ten of the best

1 **Bastakia** Winding lanes, silent walls and breezy courtyards reveal echoes of yesteryear, p42.

2 **Dubai Museum** Learn about life in the pre-oil era and chart Dubai's meteoric rise to world prominence over the last 40 years, p40.

3 **Desert safari** There's no better place to climb on a camel, ski down a sand dune, capture the sunset, feast like a sheikh, learn how to belly dance and sit back with a shisha, p27.

4 **The Creek** Stroll along the Creek and hop aboard an *abra* or dhow to soak up the bustling atmosphere and cement your understanding of Dubai's heritage, p31.

5 **Gold Souk** The best place on earth to 'go for gold', p35.

6 **Big Bus Company** Conquer the city in a day, hopping off en route to shop and explore before racing back to resume the running commentary, p25.

7 **Burj Al-Arab** Built like a billowing sail and shamelessly lavish, stop off for tea at the world's only seven-star hotel, and then hand over just Dhs5 to sun yourself on the beach here, p62.

8 **Rooftop Lounge & Terrace** Kick off your heels on these wonderfully comfortable cushions or sit back elegantly sipping cocktails whilst watching the sun set and the stars come out over the deepening blue waters of the Gulf, p161.

9 **Wild Wadi** Hours of fun for everyone at one of the world's most sophisticated water parks; enjoy 12 acres of pools, and masses of sun-decks, fast-food joints and sophisticated rides including 'master blasters', p59.

10 **Sharjah** Cultural (and carpet!) Capital of the Arab World, the excellent museums and heritage areas stand as testimony to its commitment to promoting art and preserving its heritage, p67.

wharfage. Once back on dry land, it's worth knowing that the shawarmas carved up at Al Abra restaurant by the *abra* station are amongst the best you'll find anywhere. If you're wanting something more substantial, Hatam Restaurant in Deira won't disappoint with its cheap and cheerful Iranian fare. Once refuelled, a post dinner foray into Deira City Centre mall is the perfect way to end the day.

A long weekend

Having seen some of the city, gear yourself up to hit the shops on your second day at any one of Dubai's countless malls. If your ability to resist temptation, or indeed your abhorrence of 'things retail', means you have free time in the afternoon, try heading for one of the beaches (via the notorious Sheikh Zayed Road to gawp at some of the architecture) to recover from your morning ordeal. As the shadows lengthen, make your way to the impossibly romantic Rooftop Lounge & Terrace at the One&Only Arabian Court for a sundowner, stopping off en route at the peaceful Majlis Al-Ghorfat Um Al Sheef to drink in the beauty of this historic building. The world is your oyster for dinner venues, although the views from any of the Madinat Jumeirah outlets will round off your Dubai experience nicely. A third day at Wild Wadi will keep your grin in place, while a sundowner desert safari can't be topped in the evening entertainment stakes. For your final day, leave Dubai behind and go to Sharjah's Heritage and Arts Areas or the Central Market (Blue Souk) for the morning coming back after lunch to avoid evening rush hour. Round off your trip with a relaxing stroll and leisurely dinner around one of Bur Dubai's bustling evening venues.

A week

A week would allow you to do all of the above and also to spread your wings and head off to explore the scattered ruins, stunning scenery and teeming marine life over on the East Coast, or the mysterious rock pools at Hatta, or the remarkable Hanging Gardens and oases found in and around Al-Ain.

Contemporary Dubai

Rome wasn't built in a day, but Dubai wasn't far off. It may have been an important trading post for years, the liberal attitudes of its rulers attracting a growing number of settlers from other trading nations, but it has only recently come of age. Sheikh Rashid bin Saeed Al-Maktoum, the universally-acknowledged architect of modern Dubai, ruled from 1958-1990 with a clear vision of what was required to transform his windswept, sandy backwater into what is now one of the great cities of the twenty-first century.

The discovery of oil in 1966 was the kick-start the Maktoum family needed to breathe life into their more visionary development plans for infra-structure, trade and tourism. The desert sands were transformed. Up sprang schools, hospitals, roads, a huge port, a new airport terminal, the first five-star hotels and the city's original free zone, where foreign investors could enjoy 100 per cent business ownership and tax-free trading conditions.

Dubai's metamorphosis was also a result of the new sense of unity emerging between the neighbouring (and traditionally warring) emirates, and the ultimate formation, on 2 December 1971, of the United Arab Emirates (UAE). It was agreed that Abu Dhabi with its rich oil reserves would hold the greatest sway within the federation, followed by Dubai, although each emir would retain a large degree of autonomy over his own emirate. The federation has weathered over 30 years of cooperation, and the region has benefitted from a new stability, although it hasn't all been political plain sailing; border disputes caused great storms for years and constant debates still rage about the level of integration the seven emirates would do best to pursue. Dubai has fought the hardest to safeguard its independence so it can be free to pursue its liberal policies and ambitions with minimal interference.

Such negotiations take place very much behind the scenes, and tourists are likely to reap only the rewards of the Maktoum family's ability to dance the delicate political quickstep: indeed, is there anywhere else on earth that can claim to be so attuned to the whims of tourists, so wholly dedicated to the entertainment of its guests and so completely accomplished in the pursuit of pleasure? Dubai's transformation into one of the world's most talked about tourist destinations almost has to be seen to be believed. The construction boom is drilling and bulldozing the city into the record books, pulling no punches and taking no prisoners as its lust for global recognition and love of the limelight ensures project after project beggars belief in terms of scale, innovation and grandeur.

The powers that be are capitalizing on every imaginable opportunity to make sure they've filled every gap and covered every corner of the tourist market. The city's thirst for prestige is comprehensively addressed by the facilities and events on offer. In the middle of the desert, a golf course was created. Such was its popularity that there are nearer 10 now, despite astronomical watering costs which can never be recouped. Their success in putting Dubai's name on the map means they're considered excellent investments and have only prompted the even greater excess of the electricity gobbling Nad Al-Sheba floodlit course. The much-feted Dubai Desert Classic heralds the arrival of the big guns in the golfing world every March. There's also no ignoring the legendary Dubai Cup, which holds rank as the richest horse race in the world, its US$6 million prize money attracting crowds of designer-clad celebrities pouting and pirouetting for the world's press. The Rugby Sevens is perhaps the most social fixture, when Dubai opens its arms to a deluge of around 20,000 fans from across the world; the Tennis Open brings in top seeds and plenty of groupies, and if football is still very much a fledgling sport out here, the wealth and celebrity of the footballer himself is not stranger to Dubai. No fewer than 11 members of the England squad now own properties on The Palm.

Architecturally, as long as it's eye-catching, it seems that anything goes, from the sublime to the ridiculous, and sometimes a combination of the two (just look at the opinion-dividing Burj Al-Arab, described by Canadian architectural theorist Trevor Boddy as

'Versace on steroids'!). What's interesting is Dubai's extraordinarily short building cycle; while cities over 100 years old like Harare and Johannesburg are on their third and fifth rebuild respectively, Dubai, at less than 40 years old, is already demolishing buildings created in the 1970s. It's remaking its own image faster than any other city in the world, and the architectural recycling is about fashion, prestige and – to a certain extent – boasting a striking superficial façade rather than holding much intellectual depth. Buildings are demolished not because they're functionally redundant, but because Dubai's aspirations have outgrown them.

Running alongside this determination to out-manoeuvre all rivals in increasingly modern and outlandish projects is the relatively new desire to preserve Dubai's earlier heritage. That said, architecturally, Dubai still appears to be lost in its preoccupation with the new, and hasn't yet mastered the art of accurate historical restoration – the current trend is quite heavy-handed rebuilding rather than sympathetically repairing what's already there. But the good news is that the American University of Sharjah has just introduced a new Graduate Certificate in Heritage Resource Management, which will hopefully bring about a distinct improvement in the sensitivity with which some of the region's older buildings are preserved.

As for the locals themselves, Dubai is a melting-pot of so many different communities and individuals, every one of them carving out their own peculiar niche in a safe, clean, vibrant society that caters for all, that this relentless modernization of their city is just something residents – locals and expats alike – take in their stride. Civic pride runs high, and while what's best about the city lives on for some in the unmatchable character of the Creek, the souks and the desert, they can still be proud of the towering achievements, overflowing malls and sophisticated haunts so much appreciated by their fellow Dubaians and world neighbours. In the most extraordinary and wonderful way, Dubai is emerging as a city with one foot rooted in the past, one foot firmly in the future.

With most visitors arriving by air, Dubai presents no problems in terms of its accessibility. Most of the world's major cities have direct flights as there's no other major tourist destination in the Gulf. The road network, though excellent, is limited by the UAE's coastal position. There aren't any rail connections.

Plenty of car hire firms, combined with good road surfaces, mean that, in theory at least, getting around the city is easy. That said, the road system itself is a bit of a tangle, and takes considerable getting used to, so a decent map is a necessity rather than a luxury. Depending on your agenda, though, it may be just as convenient to gad about by taxi, or by the very inexpensive local bus service, which is steadily (and necessarily!) improving. Getting to the sights outside the city is an adventure in itself. Either be prepared for Wacky Races or else go by public transport or take a tour.

Dubai offers a fantastic range of intriguing city tours and action-packed desert safaris that are well worth signing up for, especially if time is limited and your inner tourist is trying to break free.

Getting there

Air

From Europe There are multiple daily direct flights (seven hours) with **British Airways** and **Emirates** from London, Birmingham, Glasgow and Manchester, departing either early morning or late evening and costing something under £400, although Christmas and summer holidays see the prices rise. A host of other carriers will complete the journey in two legs. **Lufthansa** is often the cheapest, although **Qatar Airways** and **Al Italia** sometimes run excellent deals, which mean you could travel for around £250 return. If you're happy taking a more roundabout route, the new national carrier of the UAE, **Etihad Airways**, offers the best standard rates, flying direct to Abu Dhabi from where they bus you to Dubai (£250 return). The papers are a good source of discounted flights and last-minute deals.

There are daily services to Dubai from most major European hubs, including direct flights from Amsterdam with **KLM**; from Germany with **Emirates** and **Lufthansa**; from Paris with **Air France**, **British Airways** and **Emirates** and from Rome with **Emirates**. Amongst the cheaper airlines servicing Europe are **Kuwait Airways**, **Olympic Airways** and **Turkish Airlines**.

From North America The first direct flight to the USA was introduced by **Emirates** in June 2004 with a Dubai-New York route (14 hours). Otherwise, North America is served by a variety of carriers all of which stop off en route in Europe, including **Air France**, **BA** and **Swiss** to name but a few. **Malaysian Airlines** also operates a service to Los Angeles and New York that flies via Kuala Lumpur. Prices vary, but expect to pay around US$1,500.

Airport information **Dubai International Airport**, T 2245555 (switchboard), **T** 2166666 (flight information), www.dubaiairport. com, located 4 km from the city centre, is state of the art and its

→ Airlines and agents

Airlines
Air France, T 0845-3591000, www.airfrance.com.
Al Italia, T 0870-5448259, www.alitalia.com.
British Airways, T 0870-8509850, www.britishairways.com.
Emirates, T 0870-2432222, www.emirates.com.
Etihad, T 0870-2417121, www.etihadairways.com.
KLM, T 0870-5074047, www.klm.com.
Kuwait Airways, T 020-74120007, www.kuwait-airways.com.
Lufthansa, T 0845-7737747, www.lufthansa.com.
Malaysian Airways, T 0870-6079090, www.malaysiaairlines.com.
Olympic Airlines, T 0870 - 6060 460, www.olympicairlines.com.
Qatar Airways, T 020-78963636, www.qatarairways.com.
Swiss, T 0845-6010956, www.swiss.com.
Turkish Airlines, T 020-77669300, www.thy.com.

Agents
www.cheapflights.com; www.expedia.com;
www.flightcentre.com; www.nouvelles-frontieres.com;
www.statravel.com; www.travelocity.com.

consistently top-notch service explains its host of industry accolades. Most visitors currently arrive at Terminal 1, where round-the-clock facilities include visa collection, duty free, hotel and apartment reservation, a tourist information kiosk, ATM and money exchange, car rental, taxis, café and a special lounge where minors or passengers with special needs can be received. At the individual hotel counters you can either make a booking on the spot or pick up pre-arranged transport. Terminal 2 offers similar facilities. Terminal 1 is easily reached by car, just off Airport Road, and parking costs up to Dhs5 per hour. The departure halls offer an eye-watering array of duty free, complete with special bulk purchasing desks! A third terminal is currently under construction and will expand the airport's already excellent capacity to handle whatever the future throws at it.

There are bus stations outside both terminals where the 401 Deira service and the 402 Bur Dubai route both run every 30 minutes through two of the most popular corridors of the city. Tickets, bought on boarding the bus, cost Dhs3. Buses depart (and arrive) 24 hours a day, and journey time is around half an hour. The main pick up/drop off points in town are the Al-Sabkha bus station in Deira and the Al-Ghubaiba bus station in Bur Dubai. The journey into the centre of town in one of the (metered) cabs will take about 10 minutes and cost around Dhs35-40.

Car

With most visitors arriving by air, relatively few arrive in Dubai by road, despite the excellent state of the highways. There are, however, numerous bus companies clustered around the DNATA Airline Centre on Al-Maktoum Road, Deira, each operating daily services to Muscat, Oman (five hours, Dhs100 return). Departure times vary between outfits, but the morning exodus is from 0630-0730, while afternoon departures run from about 1530-1730.

Ferry

Dubai's lavish Cruise Terminal, straddling two massive berths in Port Rashid, opened its doors for business in 2001, but the world's raised eyebrows at the stability of the Middle East has contributed towards relatively few cruise lines making use of its intelligently designed facilities. There appear to be plans afoot to introduce a high-speed ferry between Dubai and Abu Dhabi, although for the time being this project lives only as part of the rumour mill.

Currently, there's a passenger service operating out of Dubai to Um Qasser in Iraq. Contact Naif Marine Services, **T** 3457878, for more details. There's also service to Bandar Lengeh in Iran. Contact Sharaf Travel, **T** 2725026, for details.

Travel extras

Clothing Loose-fitting cottons suit the year-round sunny climate best, with hats for the heat of the day. Winter evenings can be surprisingly cool, and it's best to come equipped for ferocious air-conditioning. A healthy respect towards local sensibilities means reserving short shorts and bikinis for the beaches, and dressing more modestly around town. Dubai is by far the most permissive Arab states, so baring flesh when venturing further afield is a definite no-no; long skirts/trousers and short sleeves are advisable.

Currency UAE dirham £1: Dhs6.7. See p226 for money exchange.

Duty free Inbound: 1,000 cigarettes or 400 cigars or 2 kg loose tobacco; a reasonable amount of perfume; four bottles of wine or spirits if arriving by air. Outbound (to UK): 200 cigarettes or 50 cigars or 250 g loose tobacco; 50 g perfume; two litres of wine or spirits. Duty is paid on over £145 worth of gifts. NB spirits are laughably cheap to buy on the Dubai side and there's a shop conveniently situated right by the baggage reclaim belts.

Safety Dubai's low crime rate makes it a very safe place. Women should have no trouble exploring the city alone; even the vendors in the souks are nothing like the aggressive breeds found elsewhere.

Vaccinations No special injections are needed to enter the UAE.

Visas GCC nationals do not require a visa. Citizens from the UK, USA, Canada, Australia, New Zealand and most Western European and Far Eastern countries are entitled to a free extendable visit visa on arrival. Others must obtain a visa through a local sponsor.

Drugs and alcohol Drugs are absolutely forbidden, and while alcohol is served at licensed restaurants, bars and clubs, it cannot be bought around town. Drinking and driving is another absolute no-no, with very heavy penalties for the drink-driver.

Mosques With the exception of Jumeirah Mosque, which hosts tours every Thursday and Sunday (see p27), non-Muslims are not permitted to set foot over the threshold of any UAE mosque.

Getting around

Bus

Travelling by local bus is a wonderfully cheap option, although admittedly that's where the good news ends. Goodness knows where they find some of their drivers, but hang on to your hats! Buses operate from the two major stations on either side of the Creek; Al-Ghubaiba Bus Station, off Al-Ghubaiba Road, Bur Dubai, and Deira's main station, known as Gold Souk Bus Station thanks to its handy position nearby. Buses run daily from around 0545-2300 (although Friday lunchtime is a quiet period, coinciding with the week's most important prayer time). Tickets are bought from the driver, and most of the routes around town cost a couple of Dirhams. Free timetables, fares and route maps are available at the bus stations, although actual departure times bear little correlation to the printed schedule. Passengers can obtain bus information from Dubai Municipality, **T** 8004848, www.dubaipublictransport.ae.

Departure details from Dubai to the following destinations are as follows: Jebel Ali buses (nos 90, 91 and 91A) depart Gold Souk and Bur Dubai stations regularly, Dhs4.50, one hour; Fujairah buses depart from Gold Souk station every hour on the hour, 0700-2200, Dhs25 (for other East Coast destinations you'll have to get negotiate with taxi drivers here, as there's still no public transport); Sharjah services depart Gold Souk and Bur Dubai stations every 20 minutes from 0630-2330, Dhs5, 15 minutes to two hours; Hatta buses (no 16) depart the Gold Souk bus station (in theory) from 0600-2135, Dh7, two hours; Al-Ain buses depart from Al Ghubaiba station, Dhs30, 1½ hours. Services to the other emirates run from both bus stations, and are normally in full swing by 0700, running until 2200 and sometimes later.

! The original airport terminal was the first public place here to be air conditioned. As a consequence it would be packed in the evenings, not so much with travellers, but with anyone who could squeeze in to escape the heat and humidity.

Car

Driving is the best way to cover the turf in and around the city; petrol is cheap, costing a mere Dhs4.75 per imperial gallon, and parking usually costs around Dhs5 for two hours around town. See Directory p226 for a list of car hire companies.

However, visitors should beware: Dubai is no place for nervy or inexperienced drivers; the signs can be very confusing for newcomers and the roads can get horribly congested at peak times (0700-0900, 1300-1430 and 1800-2030), especially around the approaches to Al-Maktoum and Al-Garhoud bridges. What's more, you should be prepared for other vehicles to cut in front of you, turn without indicating (often from an inside lane), wander in and out of lanes (especially at roundabouts) and ignore red lights and zebra crossings. If you must drive, then exercise extreme caution and good humour. Do not succumb to a fit of road rage, no matter what the provocation and, under no circumstances make any gestures *whatsoever* to other road users. Whereas this might not provoke a huge reaction back home, in Dubai hand gestures are considered deeply offensive – far more so than even the most extreme breaches of driving etiquette. If you have an accident, the police must be alerted immediately (**T** 999). The police should be treated with respect and will treat you decently in return, as long as you keep your cool.

Walking

The best way to drink in the bustling dhow wharfage and explore the souks, heritage areas and museums is on foot. That said, beware of the higher summer temperatures, which can soon make any outside activity exhausting. The rest of Dubai is too sprawling a city to conquer without wheels.

Tours

The more conventional packages are run by a huge variety of agencies – try the half-day 'Dubai by Night' or 'City Tour' for a quick culture fix, or head off into the desert for a day or overnight.

Aerial tours

Fujairah Aviation Centre, Fujairah International Airport, **T** 0922 24747, www.fujairah-aviation.ae. Plane tours constitute a fabulous (and again pricey) way to absorb the beauty of the East Coast, with trips lasting from 30 minutes to anything up to several hours.

Umm Al-Quwain Aeroclub, 16 km north of Umm Al-Quwain, **T** 067681447, www.uaqaeroclub.com. Competitively priced plane tours in Cessna aircraft, costing Dhs300 per half hour, make this a stunning, if pricey, way to get your bearings.

Birdwatching tours

Colin Richardson (author of the definitive birdwatchers' bible for the area, *The Birds of the United Arab Emirates* (1990), Hobby), **T** 0506503398, colinr@emirates.net.ae, has been organizing birdwatching tours in Eastern Arabia since 1992. May to August is the best time of year for migrant birds, but most birders come when the heat is easier to cope with from October to April. Tours can last from half a day to a full week or more, prices starting at Dhs250. The Crab Plover, Grey Hypocolius and White-collared Kingfisher are just three of the 200 or so birds you'd be likely to see on a week's trip.

Bus tours

The Big Bus Company, Wafi City, Umm Hurair, **T** 3244187, www. bigbus.co.uk. An excellent way to absorb bags of mainstream and anecdotal information about Dubai in a single day. Jump on board and listen to the running commentary before hopping off at up to 10 of the city's top tourist spots along the way. You'll have an hour

→ Hands off

Sharjah's close relationship with Saudi and its subsequent intensifying conservatism is reflected in the decency laws introduced in 2001. In brief, the message is clear: conservative, flesh-covering clothes are a must; alcohol is universally banned, even in hotels and restaurants, and there's little freedom for men and women who are not married or 'connected by a legally acceptable relationship'. Forbidden to be alone in public 'or in suspicious times or circumstances,' it remains a bit of a grey area as to quite how these guidelines are interpreted, but it certainly means no room-sharing between unmarried members of the opposite sex. Remember that Dibba, Kalba and Khor Fakkan on the East Coast are all territories of Sharjah Emirate, and subject to these laws.

to explore before the next double-decker comes trundling along and you can resume the tour. It costs Dhs120. Recommended. **Wonder Bus Tours**, BurJuman Centre, **T** 3595656, www.wonder busdubai.com. For a different experience altogether, these two-hour tours take in both Creekside and land-based sights – from the vantage point of an amphibious vehicle. Commentary dwells on the landmarks and general background of Dubai. Weekends can be busy. Tours cost Dhs95.

Creek tours

Creekside Leisure, opposite the Sheraton, Creekside, Deira, **T** 3368406. A daytime cruise up and down the Creek (Dhs35) is a great way to soak up the scenery and appreciate the architecture. Alternatively, charter an *abra* (Dhs65 or so per hour) and make the trip independently.

Desert safaris
Arabian Adventures, Sheikh Zayed Rd, **T** 3034888. Although most tour operators offer desert safaris, Arabian Adventures do it particularly well. They'll tip you down towering dunes, take you to a camel farm, wine and dine you with a fabulous desert feast and entertain you with an exceptionally good belly dancer and deft-handed henna artists until you come away with a real sense of the romance of Arabia. Recommended.

Dhow tours
Al-Marsa Travel & Tourism, **T** 00968836550, www.musandam diving.com, run by Lamjed El-Kefi, member of the Dubai Natural History Group, offers excellent weekend, day or half-day dhow trips. The route starts at Al-Mina port in Dibba Bayah on the East Coast and takes you up along the stunning Mussandam Peninsula, stopping off to snorkel along the way.

Mosque tours
Sheikh Mohammed Centre for Cultural Understanding, Bastakia, **T** 3536666, 0900-1700. As part of its 'Open Doors, Open Minds' policy to promote greater understanding between different cultures, this non-profit organization runs guided tours of Jumeirah Mosque at 1000 every Thursday and Sunday, making this the only mosque in the UAE to allow non-Muslims inside.

Stable tours
Nad Al Sheba Club, Nad Al Sheba, **T** 3363666, www.nadalsheba club.com, from 0700-1100 every Monday, Wednesday and Saturday. Dhs130 will buy you breakfast and a tour of this famous club. Visit the stables to watch the training in progress, then move on to the Godolphin Gallery where all the trophies are kept...

Tourist information

The Department of Tourism & Commerce Marketing (DTCM) is Dubai's official tourism board, and there are several outlets dotted over the city. Don't expect great things from a conversation with any of the staff that usually man the desks and phones though. Unless you're lucky enough to hit the jackpot, you'd be better off talking to some of the bigger tour operators, or one of the larger hotels. The following maps are recommended for the city centre and getting around the sights outside the city respectively:

Street Map Explorer (Dubai) (2003), Motivate. An easy to read, essential accessory for anyone determined to conquer the confusing road system which snakes throughout the city.

Off-Road Explorer (UAE) (2002), Explorer Publishing. Arguably the best guide for adventurous souls to grab before they go it alone off the beaten track amongst the region's wilder *wadis* and mightier mountains.

! Trying to find your way around Fujairah without a map can be confusing, and in Sharjah down-right suicidal. Maps are easily obtained in bookshops throughout Dubai.

The Creek

Dubai owes a great deal to the long, lazy S of the Creek. 'Khor Dubai' has been the artery around which the city has grown and prospered. It washed in first fishermen, pearl divers and traders, then a prosperity that now attracts the attention of international businessmen and pleasure-seeking tourists.

Much of the city's vitality and character is embedded in the Creek, and a single glance can provide a snapshot of the factors shaping the nature of contemporary Dubai. An intriguing mix of vessels constantly ply its waters carrying traders with their wild variety of goods, fishermen servicing the demands of the city's restaurants and tourists wielding their newly bought cameras. All this bustle is set against the ever-developing backdrop of traditionally renovated buildings and modern towers of glittering glass.

The surprisingly clear, green waters also effectively divide the city in two: Bur Dubai seeping ever further to the south to accommodate the growing population, and souk-filled Deira to the north. A tunnel connects the two sides near the mouth of the Creek, and Al-Maktoum and Al-Garhoud Bridges provide crossing points further inland.

▸▸ *See Eating and drinking p123, Sports p203*

◉ Sights

★ **Dhow Wharfage**
Off Baniyas Rd. *Map 2, C6, p251*

This is just fabulous. Steeped in Emirati history and stretching gloriously along the Creek bank north of Al-Maktoum Bridge are countless creaking dhows, some well over 100 years old, moored in time-honoured tradition to load and unload their diverse cargos before setting off once again for the high seas and the next trading post, be it Kuwait, Iran, India or elsewhere. Bursting with colour,

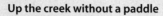

Up the creek without a paddle

By far the most romantic method of hopping from one side of the Creek to the other is to jump into an *abra*, one of the local water-taxis that have been noisily chugging passengers back and forth for years. It costs 50 fils each way, or you can push the boat out (forgive the pun) and exchange around Dhs60 for an hour's chartered spin up and down the Creek – you just can't beat it for an authentic Emirati experience. It's a wonderfully inexpensive way to sit back and soak up the colour and character of the dhow wharfage, compare the modern contours of the newly emerging Deira skyline with the careful renovations of Bur Dubai's heritage sites, and take in the myriad activities that constitute the ceaseless, ant-like industry of those whose lives revolve around the Creek. For the best understanding of what's going on on the Creek, it's well worth signing up for one of the various Creek cruises on offer. See Tours, page 25.

activity and character, this whole area is home to a way of life that has remained a constant from Dubai's earliest days. It's worth visiting on foot, too, as the friendly Iranian sailors are usually very happy to invite you on board for cups of sweet Arabic tea and a tour of their vessels.

Al-Jaddaf dhow building yard
On the Creek after Al-Garhoud Bridge. *Map 2, off H11, p251*

Budding photographers will find plenty to quicken the pulse here. Several dhows in various stages of construction or repair lean nonchalantly along the river bank, their sculpted timbers bleaching quietly in the sun when not being administered to by the friendly *qalaleef* (dhow builders). Happily, and despite the advent of

(side margin) Dubai

modern boat-building technology, the powers that be have already swooped to ensure the protection of Dubai's marine heritage. Construction is therefore very much as it always was; using only hammer, chisel, saw, plane and drills, the long teak or shesham planks of the hull are shaped and fitted together first, only after which a frame of ribs and beams is added on the inside, with any gaps stopped by oil-soaked material.

Deira

Deira's warren of winding streets plays host to the tread of innumerable feet, and the ebb and flow of daily commercial and residential life reflects better than anywhere else in the city the stew of different nationalities that have come to call Dubai 'home'. At the heart of the area, out to the west, the streets are lined with all manner of shops which burst at the seams, spilling their wares onto the pavements to tempt you inside. The unmistakable glister of gold is a magnet to some, while the breezes that glide down the narrow alleys, uncorking scents of perfumes and spices, tempt others further into the maze of stalls, or to the oldest souk in Dubai.

Here, too, on the bank of the Creek are ancient dhows, constantly loading and unloading their various cargos as they have for over 100 years. As a backdrop, the glittering glass and steel towers of modern banks and hotels speak eloquently of Dubai's recent economic and tourism successes.

▸▸ *See Sleeping p96, Eating and drinking p124, Shopping p177*

 Sights

Al-Ahmadiya School

Off Al-Ras Rd and 19 St, **T** 2260286. *Sat-Thu 800-1930, Fri 1430-1930. Free. Map 3, E5, p252*

Established in 1912 by philanthropic pearl merchant Ahmed bin Dalmouk, this was the first regular school in Dubai. Teaching initially only a limited range of subjects – basic maths, Islamic studies and Arabic language and grammar – to around 200 boys seated at desks (an altogether different set up from the traditional classes at the Qur'an schools), Sheikh Rashid himself was one of its early pupils. By the 1920's three other schools had been set up by wealthy pearl merchants, but the subsequent decline in the local pearling industry meant they all had to shut down. Al-Ahmadiya was reopened in the late 1930's, and flourished as a school until its relocation to larger premises in mid 1960's, after which the building soon fell into disrepair until 1995 when Dubai Municipality took it in hand. Since its restoration it has been open to the public as a museum of education, with touch screens and sound tracks guiding visitors around.

Heritage House

Next to Al-Ahmadiya School, off Al-Ras Rd, **T** 2260286. *Sat-Thu 0800-1930, Fri 1430-1930. Map 3, E5, p252*

The original building – two bedrooms overlooking a wide courtyard framed by numerous *barasti* rooms – was constructed in around 1890, and belonged to a number of people including Sheikh Ahmed bin Dalmouk, then Dubai's most famous pearl merchant. It was bought in 1935 by Ibrahim Al-Said Abdullah, under whose close supervision the house really came into its own, with painstaking extensions and modifications made involving the finest materials and decorative motifs. Restored

Saffron – the red stigmas from a small purple crocus – is the world's most expensive spice. Each flower provides only three stigmas, and one ounce of saffron comprises around 14,000 of these tiny threads. Dubai's spice souk is one of the cheapest places in the world to buy saffron.

in 1994, it's now an excellent example of a traditional, two-storey Emirati family home, built around the courtyard, but differing from the houses in Bastakia in that it has no wind tower. Great little booklets, published by DTCM, are available free of charge at the house.

★ Souk area
East from Heritage House. *Map 3, p252-253 See also p196*

Deira is alive with souks from the world-renowned **Gold Souk** to the ancient **Covered Souk** to each of the other **Electronics**, **Fish**, **Meat**, **Veg**, **Perfume** and **Spice souks**, all housed within this vibrant part of the city. Once a labyrinthine tangle of stalls laid out in ordered chaos under patchy, corrugated iron roofing, the old souks have long since been spring cleaned and spruced up to encourage the greatest possible flow of human traffic and exchanging of Dirhams. Happily, while these traditional markets may look enormously different from their younger selves of 40 years ago, the change is mainly cosmetic, as the essence of hospitable trading and good-natured bartering remains a constant even today.

● *A stone's throw from the Gold Souk you'll find a scattering of snack kiosks dispensing delicious fruit juices, ice creams, crisps, dates, and, after 1800, shawarmas and popcorn.*

Baniyas Road
Map 2, B5, p250

The sheer diversity of buildings running alongside Baniyas Road to frame the Creek is worth stopping to gawp at for a bit, although the view is perhaps seen to best advantage from the Bur Dubai corniche on the opposite side of the bank. Unquestionably modern towers of shimmering glass and chrome rub shoulders with some pretty dated looking 1960's and 1970's blocks which all enjoyed their hour of glory during Dubai's lightning transformation from windswept desert to the modern face presented to the world today. Setting the pace at the moment are the identical oval towers of the **Twin Towers** office block and shopping centre; **Etisalat Tower**, HQ to Dubai's telecommunications company and easily distinguished by the massive 'golf ball' perched on top; the striking **National Bank of Dubai**, with its convex glass front that captures and reflects the comings and goings of life along the Creek; and the glittering glass wedge of the **Dubai Chamber of Commerce** which when seen from certain angles looks like a huge blue monolith rising skywards. Further south, past Al-Maktoum Bridge, are the distinctive sail-shaped contours gracing the roof of the **Dubai Creek Golf & Yacht Club**, see p38, sitting pretty as it has for over a decade like a miniature Sydney Opera House, now boasting newly revamped grounds.

● *Off Baniyas Road is Dhow Wharfage, one of the most fascinating sights in Dubai, see p31.*

Century Village
Next to the Tennis Stadium, Al-Garhoud. *Map 2, F11, p251*
See also p219

Moving southwards, downtowards the area classed as Al-Garhoud, you arrive at Century Village. This is a fantastic social or family spot for a bite to eat. Numerous restaurants sprinkled around a central courtyard mean the whole area is thick with crowded tables, racing waiters, the clink of cutlery on china and chink of glasses as the hordes flock here to enjoy a leisurely lunch or balmy evening meal whenever the weather permits. And when it gets too hot,

! Such is the speed of construction out here that between the day the plans for the Chamber of Commerce were handed over to the construction company to the day the keys were handed over for use, a mere nine months had elapsed.

All around you, a new world is taking shape on a scale that makes Disneyland look like a Mickey Mouse operation.

Rory Bremner

everyone just moves inside. A stone's throw from the Tennis Stadium, the Aviation Club and the ever-popular Irish Village, lunch and supper times are never quiet here.

Deira City Centre

At the airport end of Baniyas Rd, Al-Garhoud, **T** 2954545, www.deira citycentre.com. *Sat-Thu 1000-2200, Fri 1400-2200. Map 2, D9, p251 See also p190*

Dubai's favourite mall features as a 'must see' stop on every tourist bus itinerary. It's huge and caters for shoppers of every description, with an excellent range of high street and designer clothes outlets, a huge Cineplex, Magic Planet to keep the kids happy, Virgin Megastore, an excellent ground floor electronics area, and, best of all for culture vultures, a wonderful (if relatively pricey) pocket of shops known collectively as Arabian Treasures – where you can find some genuine antiques as well as the usual array of souvenirs and curios. Hold onto your hats at the weekend, when the crush can be merciless.

★ Dubai Creek Golf & Yacht Club

Map 2, F9, p251 See also p211

This club is an oasis of greenery in the middle of the city. It became the second of the two venues for the Dubai Desert Classic golf tournament, partially on account of its happy location on the Creek which means that, in making their way here, visitors necessarily see much of the surrounding city in all its magnificent diversity. Recent improvements to the course and surrounding area will be finished in December 2004, but quite apart from these enhancements, it's a wonderful place to come to feel cocooned by the enviable levels of wealth that characterize so much of Dubai's leisure and social scenes.

Mushrif Park

Past Dubai Airport on Al-Khawaneej Rd, **T** 2883624. *0800-2300. Dhs10 per car or Dhs3 pedestrians.* Map 1, H12, p249

Coated in grass and peppered with all sorts of trees, bushes and flowers, this park is vast and best manoeuvered in a car. There are camels and ponies (rides Dhs2), a train winds through the park (Dhs2), and there are separate male and female pools (Dhs10 adults, Dhs5 children). Musical performances are staged at the theatre during public holidays.

Mamzar Park

Past Al-Hamriya Port, Al-Mamzar, www.dm.gov.ae, **T** 2966201. *Sat-Wed 0800-2300, Thu-Fri 0800-2330. Women and children only (boys under 8 years) on Wed. Dhs5 per person, Dhs30 per vehicle. Pools: Dhs10 adults, Dhs5 children (under 15).* Map 1, B13, p249

A quiet alternative to the busy beaches along the Jumeirah strip, there are four beaches, two pools, grass galore, chalets, barbecues and decent picnicking areas, making this a good family option.

Bur Dubai

A windswept, sandy backwater until 1833, the arrival of the Al-Maktoum family marked the beginning of Bur Dubai's transform into today's modern city. From a smattering of barasti *dwellings guarded by **Al-Fahidi Fort**, the area has emerged as a bustling district, home to some of the city's most historic buildings. Wind-towered **Bastakia** is the most obvious example, and the government's zeal in renovating these old houses illustrates Dubai's civic pride and determination to preserve its heritage.*

*Ever the administrative hub of the emirate, Bur Dubai still houses the **Diwan** (Ruler's office) where matters of state are decided. The old* *fort, now a museum, traces the city's development from humble fishing village and convenient trading post to economic success story and tourism magnet. Most of today's commercial activities are centred around the streets near the Creek. Jammed with countless textile and electronics shops, they offer very reasonable deals to the constant flow of human traffic. Further east, eateries and shisha joints have sprung up along the Creek. People gather here to watch the sunset burnishing the glass buildings on the opposite bank as the day winds to a close.*

▸▸ *See Sleeping p104, Eating and drinking p130*

◉ Sights

★ Dubai Museum
Al-Fahidi Fort, Al-Fahidi St, **T** 3531862, www.dubaitourism.ae.
*Sat-Thu 0830-2030, Fri 1430-2030. Dhs3 adults, Dhs1 children.
Bus no 25. Map 3, H6, p252*

A far cry from the dust-covered exhibits and oppressive atmosphere of some museums, this place is alive with interest, and even culture-phobes come away pleasantly surprised. Built in 1787 to guard the city from invasion, Al-Fahidi Fort is probably the oldest building in Dubai and has served time as palace, garrison and prison. First renovated as a museum in 1971, it underwent more extensive cosmetic surgery in 1995.

Creativity screams at you from every angle, and the exhibits have been designed so that walking away without a new burst of knowledge just isn't an option. From the aerial photographs charting the growth of Dubai from the 1950's, to the displays of traditional weapons, dances, musical instruments (the most obscure being the *shekhlelah* – a sort of 'skirt' made of goats' hooves!), to the slick multi-media presentation of the city through the decades, to the labyrinth of exhibits depicting traditional

Slices of yesterday

Dubaian life, archaeological finds and much more, the museum surpasses itself in content, presentation and ability to fascinate.

Grand Mosque

Off Ali bin Abi Taleb St. *Entry to non-Muslims is not permitted.*
Map 3, H6, p252

As the largest mosque in Dubai, the Grand Mosque is very much at the heart of the city's religious and, therefore, cultural life. Once the town's *kuttab* (Islamic elementary school frequently attached to mosques where boys were instructed in the Qu'ran, reciting it daily from memory), it's a great place to visit during the Friday midday prayers. Stand outside and absorb a sense of the city's underlying culture as hundreds of Muslims arrive to pray.

From its convenient location near the Ruler's Court the multi-domed (nine large and 45 smaller) edifice might be grand, but old it is not. Built as recently as 1998 with an impressive 70-metre minaret (the city's tallest), today's building does nevertheless adhere to the style of the original Grand Mosque. In 1960 the initial mosque was demolished to be supplanted by another model. The current building is, however, a good example of the care taken by the government to resurrect the buildings of yesteryear, and its tall, mud-coloured walls and inscrutable wooden shutters complement the recent restorations completed in the Bastakia quarter a stone's throw away.

Shri Nathje Jayate Temple and Sikh Gurdwara (Sikh shrine)
Map 3, G6, p253

In an alleyway just Creekside of the Grand Mosque is the Shri Nathje Jayate Temple. Easy to miss until prayer time (0630, 0830, 1015, 1700, 1800), when the collection of shoes on shelves outside is a dead give away, visitors are allowed into this Hindu temple, although not to take photographs. Nearby, atop a flight of steps, is the Sikh Gurdwara (Sikh shrine), where again it will be a collection of shoes that denotes you're in the right place.

● *The narrow alleys that wind throughout the whole area are worth exploring, as this hotbed of Hindu culture reflects Dubai's multi-faith, cosmopolitan face.*

★ Bastakia
Map 3, H8, p253

One of the oldest heritage sites in Dubai and the last wind tower quarter left on the Arab side of the Gulf, this area has been restored over recent years to try and capture some of its former glory. Bastakia's very name is derived from the Iranian town of Bastak, from where many of Dubai's first trading immigrants hailed in the early 19th century. Sophisticated houses with rough, discreet walls shielding the privacy of the wealthy families within, became a trademark of the area. Wind towers topped these walls, trapping the wind and funnelling it down into the bowels of the house as an early and effective means of air-conditioning. Inner courtyards, shady and highly decorated, provided a sharp contrast to this outer impenetrability.

! ● Unlike some other Arab states where you're not allowed to practise any faith other than Islam, Sheikh Rashid believed that a happy community worked best, and subsequently laid the foundation stone of several foreign churches built in Dubai.

Shisha venues

Best

- Aroma Garden, Oud Metha Road near Al-Maktoum Bridge.
- Fatafeet, off Al Seef Rd, Bur Dubai.
- Mazaj, Century Village, Al-Garhoud.
- QD's, Dubai Creek Golf & Yacht Club, Al-Garhoud.
- Shimmers, Mina A'Salam (winter only).

The Bastakia you see today is only half the size of the original settlement, much of which was demolished to make way for newer buildings in the 1980's, including the Diwan. Wondering around these restored walls, narrow alleyways, open courtyards and ornately carved doors, it's easy to transport yourself back to a bygone era. Numerous buildings have now been renovated along traditional lines, including the Sheikh Mohammed Centre for Cultural Understanding (see p226). Basta Art Café (see p132) is a popular stop for a refreshing drink, Local House (see p132) provides the only truly authentic Dubaian food in the city, the Majlis Gallery is a must for art-lovers, and XVA (see p105) has a handful of bedrooms for those wanting to stay in authentic surroundings.

Majlis Gallery, Al-Fahidi St, **T** 3536233, majlisga@emirates. net.ae, Sat-Thu 0930-2000, is a great favourite with residents and visitors alike, set around the whitewashed courtyard of a beautiful old Arabic house in historic Bastakia. It is a really lovely gallery. Framed by numerous rooms awash with all sorts of exciting artwork, you'll find everything from traditional watercolours to whackier oils and acrylics, from ancient ammonites to contemporary handmade glass and plenty more besides filling every nook and cranny.

XVA, 15a St, **T** 3535383, xva@xvagallery.com, Sat-Thu 0930-2000, is great spot for culture vultures. This gallery is housed in one of Bastakia's beautiful old buildings with several rooms opening off a central courtyard. The artwork is usually searingly modern, and generally by resident artists or those with a strong affinity with the area. If you don't round off your visit by sampling some of the truly superb vegetarian food they rustle up, or at the very least try one of their lemon mint drinks or iced-teas with apple, XVA regulars might argue you've not experienced the true glory of this gallery.

The Diwan
Opposite Dubai Museum. *Not open to the public.* *Map 3, G7, p253*

Although the original town palace has long since been demolished, the Diwan, where Dubai's government sits and decides matters of state, is today perched in a prime location overlooking the Creek. Enclosed by a black iron fence, this large white building with arched windows lies immediately to the northwest of Bastakia, blending with the architecture of this historic area. Built in 1990 on land that used to belong to this once-thriving and considerably larger merchant stronghold, Sheikh Maktoum now has his office here, so it's often referred to by people and signposts alike as the Ruler's Office.

Textile Souk
Near the abra landing station. *Daily 0900-1300, 1600-2200.*
Map 3, H4, p252 See also p177

Walking eastwards along the Creek from the Diwan you will meet with a large wooden gateway which ushers you into a kaleido-scope of colour. Carefully renovated, the old souk comprises avenues of stalls containing bolt after bolt of rainbow-hued materials of every description, shipped in all over Asia. Evenings are perhaps the best time to soak up the atmosphere, when the constant throng of human traffic weaves its way through.

● *In front of the souk, on the Creek, is Dubai's first office building, Bait Al-Wakeel. Built in 1934, restoration work was completed in 1995 so it now sits rather less precariously on its Creekside foundations.*

★ Sheikh Saeed Al-Maktoum's House

On the corniche, Al-Shindagha, **T** 3937139. *Sat-Thu 0730-2100, Fri 1500-2130. Dhs2 adults, Dhs1 children.* Map 3, C1, p252

This modest, two-storey dwelling was home to the visionary and much-beloved Sheikh Saeed Al-Maktoum, ruler of Dubai from 1912-1958 and grandfather of the present ruler. Dating back to 1896, it was built by Sheikh Saeed's father, Sheikh Maktoum bin Hasher Al-Maktoum, to preside over the to-ings and fro-ings of the Creek. Serving originally as a communal residence for Sheikh Maktoum's extended family, Sheikh Saeed then chose to live here until his own death, after which it lay abandoned and increasingly derelict until it was demolished, rebuilt next to its original site and opened to the public as a museum in 1986. Today, it forms part of the Shindagha heritage area, standing as a proud reminder of Dubai's pre-oil era. It houses some truly fascinating historical photographs (some dating back to the late 1800s) and documents that breathe life into many aspects of the social, cultural and educational life of yesteryear. Official documentation from 1822 in the form of letters, maps, treaties, coins and stamps will delight history buffs with the light they shed on the development of the emirate through the years. The gift shop sells a handy guide to the house (Dhs5).

Heritage and Diving Villages

On the corniche, Al-Shindagha, **T** 3937151. *Sat-Thu 0800-2200, Fri 0800-1100, 1600-2200.* Map 3, C2, p252

The Heritage and Diving Villages are living testimony of the government's zealous reclamation of Dubai's past. Modelled along the same lines as traditional buildings, visitors are invited to explore Dubai's architectural, cultural and maritime heritage. Within the Diving Village are exhibitions illuminating Dubai's historical significance as a pearling nation, while potters and weavers practice their traditional crafts at *barasti* stalls set up in the Heritage Village. There are usually a couple of camels waiting patiently to take visitors on a short spin, making this a good family stop. The place really comes into its own during public holidays, and the Dubai Shopping Festival (DSF) in particular is a livley time when you can enjoy a host of demonstrations ranging from traditional cookery training to desert life exhibitions, parachuting shows to ship building.

● *The best time to visit this area is from 1800 onwards, when the cooler temperatures and Creekside restaurants nearby attract a healthy evening trade happy to meander around tasting the snacks and rooting about for bargains in the little curio shops in Heritage Village.*

Oud Metha

*Oud Metha is home to an array of recreational and educational facilities suitable for all ages. There are classy shops at **Wafi City Mall**; some excellent eateries at the nearby **Pyramids** and additional retail opportunities at **Lamcy Plaza**. You'll find bowling and iceskating at **Al-Nasr Leisureland**; grassy knolls, barbecue pits, a mini falaj (traditional irrigation system) and cable-car rides at **Creekside Park**; excellent interactive learning opportunities for five to 15 year olds at **Children's City**; plenty of rides at **Wonderland Theme and Water Park** and dinner dhow cruises setting off every evening from **Al-Boom Tourist Village**. Dig a little deeper, though, and it quickly becomes apparent that, with the notable exception of Wafi City and the Grand Cineplex, the crowds are now being enticed elsewhere as Dubai's rapid expansion sees the birth of newer, more exciting venues. On weekdays in particular, you can find yourself rattling around these once popular haunts as if in a ghost town. It's great as far as lack of queues go, but you can hardly call the atmosphere electric.*

▸▸ *See Eating and drinking p133, Bars and clubs p152, Kids p221*

◉ Sights

★ Wafi City

On the corner of route 11 heading towards Al-Garhoud Bridge and Oud Metha Rd (Route 79), Umm Hurair, **T** 3244426.
Map 2, H6, p250

Keep your eyes peeled for the brown signs, as getting to here can be quite confusing. Very much alive and kicking, Wafi City, with its ancient Egyptian influenced architecture, consists of various excellent complexes. The elegant **shopping mall** (see p194), flanked by giant sphinxes, is home to arguably the best variety of upmarket shops selling quality goods – you'll find everything from the tastiest of foodstuffs in the legendary **Goodies**, to the most dramatic of home furnishings in **Petals**, to clothes, accessories and gifts galore, and there's plenty to amuse the children at **Encounter Zone**.

The nearby, **Pyramids** is home to Dubai's only independent and much-loved spa, **Cleopatra's**, as well as a bevy of great restaurants. **Planetarium**, one of Dubai's enduringly popular nightclubs, also pulls in the punters.

Creekside Park

Route 81 between Maktoum and Al-Garhoud Bridges, **T** 3367633.
Sat-Wed 0800-2300, Thu, Fri and public holidays 0800-2400. Dhs5.
Map 2, F7, p251

This large, grassy park encompasses 2.5-km of pathways and winding jogging tracks, a mini *falaj* (traditional irrigation system), barbecue pits, fishing piers reaching out to the Creek, beaches and an amphitheatre (used on high days and holidays).

When it's working, the cable car that runs the length of the park is a relaxing way to drink in the scenery from 30 m up (Dhs25 adults,

Dhs10 children). Try the tandem or four-seater bicycles, which are available to rent on an hourly basis (Dhs20-30).

Children's City, *T 3340808, www.childrencity.ae, Sat-Thu 0900-2130, Fri 1500-2130, Dhs15 adults, Dhs10 children 5-15 years, near gates 1 and 2*, is an excellent new educational museum for youngsters, with interactive displays on space exploration, nature, the human body, global culture and more.

WonderLand Theme and Water Park

Off route 81, near Al-Garhoud Bridge, *T 3241222. Water Park: daily 1000-1800 (Wed ladies day). Theme Park: Sat-Wed 1400-2200, Thu-Fri 1000-2300. Combined entry: Dhs75 adults, Dhs65 children under 12s, Dhs20 under 4s. Reduced rates for use of just one park.*
Map 2, H8, p251

Despite hanging on to its status as the only theme and water park in the Middle East, business is hardly booming. Once brightly coloured with vivid blues, pinks and greens, the rides and building façades are now sun-bleached and faded, giving the impression of walking around a model village long since forgotten. Rarely busy during weekdays, this impression is only compounded by the deserted grounds, although things do pick up at weekends and sometimes in the evenings. It's a shame, because the variety of in- and outdoor activities is enormous, ranging from slot machines and arcade games to climbing frames and slides to bumper cars and power karts. There's even an Arabic band on Wednesday, Thursday and Friday nights. The water park section is also home to an excellent array of activities: you can catapult yourself into the pool from a zip line, forget yourself on the lazy river or watch your children manoeuvre the leaking climbing frame in the kids' activity pool. Fantastic for anyone who dislikes crowds and queues.

● *Paintballing is just around the corner from WonderLand. You have to book ahead, T 3241222. It opens daily, but only if there will be enough people to make up two teams.*

Al-Nasr Leisureland

Near the American Hospital, off 10 St, **T** 3371234. *Daily 0700-2200. Dhs10 adults, Dhs5 children (3-9 years).* Map 2, G5, p250

Used more by residents than tourists, this is nevertheless home to one of only two ice-rinks in the city (Dhs10 for a two-hour session). There's also a small bowling alley (Dhs7 per person per game), squash and tennis courts (Dhs10 per hour) and a large outdoor pool where, even if the wave machine hasn't worked for over a year and the children's play area is dry, at least the three modest water slides are still operational (Dhs40 adults, Dhs20 children).

Al-Boom Tourist Village

Near Al-Garhoud Bridge, Umm Hurair, **T** 3243000. Map 2, H9, p251

Best known as an exhibition, conference and wedding reception venue, this is a remarkable name for a place that has next to nothing to do with tourists! That said, it does keep a fleet of single and double-decked dhows that depart every night on a two-hour dinner cruise up and down the Creek. Boarding time is 2000, departing at 2030, but be aware before you book that there's no alcohol served and no belly dancing. Dhs100 adults, Dhs50 children under 10, free to under 5s.

Sheikh Zayed Road

*The main event along this road is the initial stretch running from Trade Centre roundabout to the first intersection. Lined with hotels, malls, office and apartment blocks, the architecture speaks of fabulous wealth and deliberate ostentation. It rises up in a single avenue of stunning high rises, glittering with chrome, glass and modernity. The dignified and architecturally intelligent **Dubai World Trade Centre**, for a long time the city's tallest building and major* *landmark, has now been overshadowed by higher, taller, grander buildings. A bevy of record-breaking new developments are in various stages of planning and construction further south. The eight-lane highway itself (dubbed 'kamikaze corridor' by some) never sleeps and has a reputation as an accident black spot, thanks to the complete lack of driving etiquette displayed by all too many speeding vehicles whipping to and fro between Dubai and Abu Dhabi.*

▶▶ *See Sleeping p109, Eating and drinking p136, Bars and clubs p155*

Sights

Dubai World Trade Centre and other notable buildings
Map 2, grid H1, p250

Sheikh Zayed Road is home to a bevy of notable buildings, many of which reflect the city's love of the limelight and preoccupation with cosmetic beauty. The Dubai Trade Centre, built a relative lifetime ago as far as the city's lightning fast pace of architectural development goes, was a true architectural beauty, both in terms of its ground-breaking scale and its environmental sensitivity. Since then, greater emphasis has been paid to exterior appearances rather than structural functionality, and various trendy buildings of innovative and eye-catching design have replaced the dignified World Trade Centre as the talk of the town, including the **Fairmont Hotel**, **Dusit Dubai** and of course the impressively tall **Emirates Towers**.

● *Observe the way the towers of the Emirates Towers change constantly according to the angle from which you look at them.*

★ The Courtyard
4b St, near Interchange 3, Al-Quoz, www.courtyard-uae.com.
Map 1, C4, p248

Dubai

★ Showstoppers

Completely, wonderfully eccentric, visiting the Courtyard feels like stumbling upon an unexpected oasis within the relative arid and featureless buildings that make up the Al-Quoz industrial area. Designed by Dariush Zandi, creative architect par excellence, the idea was to build something quirky and characterful. This he has achieved, and in bucket-loads; improbable architecture, unusual effects and bold colours typify the Courtyard, which is framed by art and arty shops, and the end product is something very different from the usual Dubai scene, varied though it is.

Gold and Diamond Park and Museum

Near Interchange 4, **T** 3477788. *Sat-Thu 1000-2200, Fri 1600-2200. Free. Map 1, C4, p248*

Stuck rather out on a limb, this big building lies largely deserted despite its array of glittering gold shops. You can walk around it accompanied by the echo of your own footfalls, the benefit of which is that the shops are desperate for custom, so you can often knock significant chunks off the original prices quoted. The museum in the visitors' centre is well worth stopping at, and

! In the 1960s when the first oil money appeared, Sheikh Rashid wanted all the roads dual carriageway. People laughed, what a waste of money it was and who on earth would use all these large roads? But he dictated it would be so...

contains displays pertaining to the history of traditional Arab jewellery. Furthermore, it runs 30-minute guided tours around the manufacturing plant so if you don't succumb to retail temptation, at least you can come away with a decent understanding of how the jewellery is made.

Jumeira and Satwa

*Running 10 km west from the exquisite **Jumeirah Mosque** is the luxurious stretch of an affluent suburb yawning with all the facilities needed to live the good life. Desirable properties, medical practices galore, lovely parks and beautiful people are all trademarks of Jumeira. Directly translated, Jumeira means 'burning embers' – a term which perhaps appropriately describes the bank balances of rash shoppers frequenting the huge raft of malls and beauty salons pepper-ing **Jumeirah Beach Road**. Those simply wanting a relaxed drink with friends will find that café culture is very much alive, well-serviced by the array of pleasant eateries. **Jumeira Beach Corniche** offers a convenient place to top up the tan, while the relative oasis of **Safa Park** is a popular stop for the more active with fairground rides and sports.*

*An easy drive from Jumeira and bursting with tailors' shops is bustling Satwa, where on Thursday and Friday nights **Al-Dhiyafah Road** transforms its relatively modest daytime appeal into a throbbing catwalk for the world's hottest wheels. Here, the young and fabulously wealthy Emirati jetset peacocks around for the benefit of those out enjoying the roadside eateries and shisha joints.*

▸▸ *See Sleeping p112, Eating and drinking p121, Bars and clubs p158*

 Sights

★ **Jumeirah Mosque**
Opposite Palm Strip, Jumeirah Beach Rd. *Map 4, B5, p254*

A much-photographed Dubai landmark, especially when lit up against an evening sky, the beautiful Jumeirah Mosque is an exact copy of a mosque in Cairo which is eight times its size. The Jumeirah Mosque has a capacity of 1,200 people. It's also the only mosque in the UAE to throw open its doors to welcome non-Muslims. Every Thursday and Sunday morning at 1000 the Sheikh Mohammed Centre for Cultural Understanding organizes tours as part of its 'Open Doors, Open Minds' policy designed to bring people of different nationalities together. The tour lasts 1½ hours – just make sure you're at the mosque a few minutes before 1000 respectfully dressed with minimal flesh on show.

Iranian Hospital and Iranian Mosque
Al-Wasl Rd, near Al-Hudaiba Rd. *Not open to the public.* Map 4, C5-6, p254

A far cry from the drab, characterless buildings of the hospitals many of us are used to back home, the Iranian Hospital is just as stunning as the exquisite Iranian Mosque opposite. Both look as though they've been lifted straight out of the pages of a fairy story, and are covered in fantastically elaborate mosaic work of startling blues and gleaming greens that typify Perisan building designs.

Dubai Zoo
Jumeirah Beach Rd, **T** 3496444. *Wed-Mon 1000-1700. Dhs3.* Map 4, F2, p254

What started as the private collection of an animal-oriented resident and metamorphosized into Dubai Zoo as it grew too unmanageable is now due for another face-lift with a proposed move to Mirdif within the next few years. Overdue, as the fairly grim reality of small, limiting cages means that despite the loving attention of the manager and his staff, while you can come away having seen lions, tigers, bears, giraffe and more, you can't come away feeling happy with their lot in life.

● *Behind the zoo is the Green Art Gallery which is filled with Arabic inspired sculptures and paintings, see further p179.*

Safa Park

Al-Wasl Rd and Al-Hadiqa St, **T** 34932111. *Daily 0800-2300 (ladies only Tue). Dhs3. Map 1, C6, p248*

You won't go bored in here. Bumper cars, ferris wheel and electronic games keep the youngsters occupied, while sports enthusiasts can make use of the jogging tracks, gym, bikes for hire (Dhs100 deposit + Dhs20-30 per hour), volleyball courts and tennis facilities or even have a go on the obstacle course. Plenty of grassy areas and barbecue sites confirm it as a good spot for families.

● *A cab ride away from here, up Route 69 (Muscat Road), is Dubai Camel Racecourse which hosts the extraordinary spectacle of camel racing; well worth experiencing, see p205.*

Jumeirah Beach Park

Jumeirah Beach Rd, **T** 3492555, www.dm.gov.ae. *Daily 0800-2300 (ladies day Sat). Dhs5 per person, Dhs20 per vehicle. Map 1, B6, p248*

A very popular spot with its minimal entrance fee, this long, thin stretch of beach, well-shaded in parts, also has grassy areas and barbecue pits. Always busy, despite swimming not being permitted after sunset when the lifeguards go off duty.

Dubai Ladies Club

Next to Jumeirah Beach Park, Jumeirah Beach Rd, **T** 3499922. *Daily 0830-2100. Dhs75 or Dhs100 at weekends. Map 1, B7, p249*

Opened at the tail end of 2003, this is a relaxing place for ladies only to come for a spot of 'time out'. With a beautiful beach frontage, pool, tennis, squash, spa and fitness facilities, and an art and talent centre running a variety of courses (from pottery to piano), it attracts mainly residents, but tourists are more than welcome.

Jumeirah Beach Corniche
Next to *Dubai Marine Beach Resort*, Jumeirah Beach Rd. *Free.*
Map 4, D3, p254

The basic facilities – showers, toilets, loungers, parasols and refreshments – are all that's needed if it's just lying and frying you're after.
● *Continue some way down to arrive at the beach near Wollongong University – a popular hangout for kite-surfers, especially on Fridays.*

Mercato
Jumeirah Beach Rd, **T** 3444161. *Sat-Thu 1000-2200, Fri 1400-2200.*
Map 4, G1, p254 See also p192

This multi-coloured mall looks like more of a confectionary masterpiece than an architectural wonder – although it certainly makes you wonder! Impossible to miss and hard to ignore when within these walls are a host of excellent (and sometimes extraordinary) outlets. Also home to Fun City to keep your offspring happy.

Jumeirah Archaeological Site
16 St, off 27 St, near Jumeirah Beach Park. *Not open to the public.*
Map 1, B6, p248

Dubai Museum is the best place to go to learn about the early settlements around the city, and the curator there may be able to help with access to otherwise restricted areas. Discovered in 1968, excavations at the site have uncovered a series of low stone walls surrounding an old souk, flanked by various dwellings including a large stone house, possibly belonging to a governor. Various other structures have also been unearthed, the purposes of which remain food for debate. This site is one of the most significant in the UAE, dating settlement in Jumeirah to before the first Islamic era (AD600-700), in the days when the area was nothing more than a caravan station on the route between northern Oman and what is now Iraq. Remains found at the site suggest a link with pre-Islamic cultures, subsequently wiped out by Arab tribes with the coming of Islam in seventh century. The original buildings subsequently came to bare the marks of their new Arab owners, until the settlement ceased to exist some time after 10th century.

Creative Art Centre

Between Choithrams and Town Centre mall, off Jumeirah Beach Rd, **T** 3444394, arabian@arts.com. *Sat-Thu 0800-1800. Map 4, H1, p254*

Two villas set back from Jumeirah Beach Road play host to this large art gallery. Run by Lynda Shepherd, herself a watercolourist of some repute, the gallery is alive with Omani antique chests, Arab doors and jewellery. The artwork ranges from originals to limited edition prints and poster art, most of which has an international flavour, although there's always a strong line in Arabic calligraphy. Picasso's camel is a popular souvenir, and this is the only gallery in town that stocks a range of children's art.

Dar Al-Ittehad (Union House) Building

At the western end of Al-Dhiyafah Rd, Satwa. *Not open to the public. Map 4, off A6, p254*

Impossible to miss thanks to the UAE's largest – at least for the time being – flag rising authoritatively just outside, Dar Al-Ittehad has secured its place in history as the venue at which the treaty that created the United Arab Emirates was signed on 2 December 1971. The flag itself measures 40 m x 20 m, and flies on top of a 120-m reinforced column.

The Southwest

The southerly stretch of the west coast leads away from the heart of old Dubai into a totally different world – one of desirable residential complexes, exclusive five-star resorts, a burgeoning collection of chart-topping attractions, and, after just a little more waiting and a lot of baited breath, a raft of all-singing, all-dancing new developments. With Dubai's architectural ambitions knowing no limits, this area really is bulldozing its way into the 21st century to accommodate the ever-increasing residential and tourist populations, not to mention the emirate's thirst for global prestige and acclaim.

Devastated by plague at the turn of the last century, **Umm Suqeim** – *which translates as 'mother of the stricken' – bears no signs of lingering malaise. It boasts the* **Burj Al-Arab, Wild Wadi** *and the package holiday Mecca that is* **Jumeirah Beach Hotel**. *Further south, and home to the exquisite* **Royal Mirage,** *Al-Sufouh is sandwiched between the high profile* **Madinat Jumeirah** *and* **Dubai Marina** *developments, and controls the entrance to the manmade* **Palm Island** *project. Past Al-Sufouh,* **Marsa Dubai** *is also in the grip of serious development that will only raise the game of its existing five-star resorts.*

▸▸ *See Sleeping p113, Eating and drinking p142, Bars and clubs p160*

Sights

★ Majlis Al-Ghorfat Um Al-Sheef

17 St, off Jumeirah Beach Rd, **T** 3946343. *Sat-Thu 0830-1330, 1530-2030, Fri 1330-2030. Dhs1. Map 1, B6, p248*

An absolute gem, the summer residence of the late Sheikh Rashid is a wonderfully unexpected find slap bang in the middle of modern Jumeira. Built in 1955 when the area was a rustic spattering of date palms and fishermen's shacks, this humble

Sheikh Rashid Bin Saeed Al-Maktoum

Father of today's modern city, it was the much-loved Sheikh Rashid whose vision pulled Dubai from relative obscurity and led it to unprecedented prosperity. A humble man of phenomenal intelligence and determination, he maintained a friendly independence from his neighbouring emirates and often flew in the face of Arab political orthodoxy in order to pursue the liberal policies on which he knew his city would thrive. It was his idea to open a new port at Jebel Ali, ignoring opposition from his advisers and ultimately watching it establish itself as a booming free zone. It was he who saw to the dredging of the Creek, allowing for the passage of bigger boats and further boosting trade. He refused to impose trade restrictions, concentrating instead on building up his city-state with the addition of the cutting-edge Dubai Airport; the development of fresh water resources and a growing number of residential districts, schools, hospitals and (importantly) hotels. He welcomed expats with open arms and one of his lasting legacies is the attitude of religious and social tolerance that makes Dubai such a safe and hospitable community. Sheikh Rashid was a key figure in the development of the UAE, spearheading projects that benefitted the poorer emirates, and his hands-on approach took him on twice daily tours of Dubai to see his projects progressing and meet his people, for whom he made a point of always being accessible. Anybody, not matter how humble, was welcome to go to his *majlis* to talk to him, and his people knew and loved him for it.

building of coral stone and gypsum has since been restored, yet retains much of its old charm. The first floor *majlis* (reception) is one of the most delightful examples of its kind, looks much as it would have done in Sheikh Rashid's day, and will have witnessed various delicate negotiations in the run up to a unified country.

Al-Ghorfat Um Al-Sheef used to be a date palm farm, supplying healthy food to its dependents, although the traditional garden within its grounds – incorporating a *falaj* and *barasti* coffee shop (complete with an effective wind tower worth stepping under to appreciate fully the clout of this early form of air conditioning) – has been added by Dubai Municipality, to better educate visitors about the broader register of local culture.

Wild Wadi

Jumeirah Beach Rd, **T** 3484444. *Nov-Feb 1100-1800, Mar-May and Sep-Oct 1100-1900, Jun-Aug 1100-2100. Dhs140 adults, Dhs 120 children (aged 4-12). If you arrive after 1600 in summertime or 1500 wintertime, you'll receive a small discount. Map 1, B3, p248*

Outrageously popular, and with visitor numbers rising year on year, you can't top this for a family day out. Twelve acres of pools, sun-decks, fast-food joints and sophisticated rides are the order of the day. The rides are generally very child-friendly, with the possible exception of the Jumeirah Scierah, which people can pelt down at 80 km per hour before lying for a moment collecting themselves (and sometimes their swimming costumes!) before hopping up and on to the next event. Surf simulators test your surfing prowess, and crowds quickly gather to watch the skill of some and wipeouts of others. The other rides are exceptionally well designed, featuring 'master blasters' that jet-propel you upwards and ensure the whole experience isn't over too quickly. One teeny criticism here might be that not one of the various routes down affords the kind of white-knuckle ride appreciated by hardened adrenaline junkies. Particularly busy in the summer, as one of the few refreshing outside venues, it's best to get there early, before the other 3,499 people tip up! Recommended.

▶ Coming soon...

Burj Dubai, Sheikh Zayed Rd near Interchange 1, www.burjdubai.com. Having already created the tallest building in the world once, it's time to do it again now that the record has been broken. Details about the exact height of the Burj Dubai are a jealously guarded secret, but with the new Taipei 101 building in Taiwan weighing in at 508 m, Emaar Properties has a challenge and a half.

Dubai Festival City, Al-Garhoud, www.dubaifestivalcity.com. The 4-km stretch along the waterfront will soon be home to a top-notch dining, shopping and family entertainment paradise. Dubai Shopping Festival will be based at the international pavilions. Highlights include a marina, winding waterways and an 18-hole Robert Trent Jones golf course. First phase 2006.

Dubai Marina, Marsa Dubai, www.dubai-marina.com. One of the largest waterfront developments of its kind in the world, Dubai Marina will have a luxury residential project designed to accommodate 150,000 people. Here, for the first time in Dubai, foreigners will be able to own their properties outright. Built around an artificial harbour with plenty of open space, eateries, shopping outlets, fitness facilities and 11 km of waterfront walkways. Completion 2008.

Dubailand, Emirates Rd, inland from Al-Barsha, www.dubailand.ae. Having set itself the ambitious target of becoming 'the biggest, most varied, leisure, entertainment and tourism attraction on the planet', it's hardly surprising that there will be six themed 'worlds' comprising over 200 individual projects encompassing sports, recreational activities, theme and water parks, spas, museums, galleries, resorts and hotels, and of course the usual expanse of shopping opportunities. Completion 2006.

Hydropolis Hotel, Marsa Dubai, www.ddia.ae. Here comes the world's first underwater hotel at an estimated cost of half a billion US$. Set 20 m under the sea and boasting all the conveniences of five-star accommodation, this must surely constitute one of the most unique holiday destinations on record. Completion 2006.

Mall of the Emirates, Al-Barsha, www.majidalfuttaim.com. No one's about to let the little matter of Dubai's desert climate get in the way of building the world's largest indoor ski resort! The slope itself will drop 62 m over its 400m-long descent and use real snow, while other attractions will include a hotel, a multi-screen cinema, obligatory shops and eateries. The previously quiet suburb of Al-Barsha won't know what's hit it. Completion 2005.

Palm Islands, Al-Sufouh, www.palmsales.ca. Such is the scale of this project that it's visible from space with the naked eye. The two palms are the largest manmade islands to date, and look set to make further inroads into the lucrative tourism market. Design-wise, they're enormously appropriate for Dubai – neatly creating the maximum beach frontage possible (60 km of shoreline each!) whilst nodding a tribute to the date palms that have sustained the region for years. Completion 2007.

The Dubai Mall, Sheikh Zayed Rd, near Interchange 1, www.emaar.com. This project is likely to breathe new meaning into the whole concept of the mega-mall. Even if facts and figures mean little to you, the idea of a nine million square foot shopping mall (50 soccer pitches) must give the impression as absolutely enormous. The world's largest mall (of course), will be linked to Burj Dubai, the world's largest tower, and the combined structure will be full of shops, restaurants and entertainments. Completion 2005.

The World, adjacent to the Burj Al-Arab. Another fantastically ambitious project, 1.8 billion is being poured into the creation of 250 entirely manmade islands, set 4 km offshore and grouped together to resemble the shape of the world. The plan is to sell off each island so private developers can then turn them into highly individual water-fronting retreats. Completion 2008.

★ Burj Al-Arab

Jumeirah Beach Rd, Umm Suqeim, **T** 3017777. *Map 1, B3, p248*
See also p113

The Burj, standing 320 m tall on its own artificial island 280 m from the shore, is loved by some and detested by others, and cannot help but provoke a strong reaction from all who behold the elegantly contoured sail-shaped exterior and quite astoundingly extravagant interior of this hotel. Dancing fountains, vast aquariums, vividly swirling carpet designs, plenty of gold trimming and a startlingly blue-hued atrium tall enough to accommodate the Dubai World Trade Centre all conspire to make the Burj a feast for the eyes. It has already triggered a great deal of controversy and indignation amongst some of the locals on account of the potentially religious symbol – that of a large cross – it presents to the sea (and from which angle it is therefore rarely photographed). Criticism is also levelled at it for merely taking on the shape of a sail rather than distilling a more imaginative concept from the idea of a sail. Security on the gate is ferocious, but there are various ways of avoiding a cut and run: reserve a table at one of the various eateries; guests of other Jumeirah International properties can book themselves onto a guided tour; or, as long as the hotel isn't over-full, it is sometimes possible to pay Dhs200 (redeemable at any of the food or retail outlets) to gain admittance. Trainers or flip-flops might well scupper your chances of getting in.

Jumeirah Beach Hotel

Jumeirah Beach Rd, Umm Suqeim. *Map 1, B4, p248   See also p113*

This is another resort that needs no introduction. The familiar, broad, wave-shaped hotel stands facing the nearby Burj Al-Arab and flanking Wild Wadi. Its visual appeal, even when trapped as an image within glossy holiday brochures, consistently pulls in a never-ending torrent of sun-worshipping package holidaymakers.

An excellent array of bars and restaurants secure it yet more business from other visitors and residents alike, and, putting your cultural cap aside for the moment, as an overall Dubai experience and a great place to people watch, it's a bit of a must.

Madinat Jumeirah
Near the Burj Al-Arab, Al-Sufouh. *Map 1, B3, p248*

A new face on skyline, this vast development is topped by countless wind towers that second-guess its focus on the region's cultural heritage (despite the fact that wind towers traditionally stood atop buildings of only a couple of storeys!). Completed in 2004, these 42 hectares comprise winding waterways, plenty of delightful bars and restaurants, and plenty of retail outlets to part you from your Dirhams in its traditional style (albeit distinctly airbrushed!) souk. The souk, by the way, sells some understandably popular 'atmospheric photos' of the dreamy Madinat complex, both in colour and in black and white.

★ One&Only Royal Mirage
Off Route 94, roughly parallel to Interchange 5 on Sheikh Zayed Rd, Al-Sufouh. *Map 1, B1, p258 See also p114*

Beautiful Moroccan architecture, sensitive landscaping and some excellent eateries means the Royal Mirage features high on any 'things to do in Dubai' list drawn up by most expats for their visitors. Kasbar, see p162, is the hotel's hugely popular nightclub, and the Rooftop Terrace (see p161) can't be beaten for an evening drinks venue. Recommended.

Museums and galleries

- **Abrash Gallery** Fabulous Iranian carpets, ceramics, paintings and sculptures, p181.
- **Al-Ahmadiya School** First school in Dubai, now a museum on education in the region, p33.
- **Courtyard Café and Gallery** Café within a modern gallery. Modern and intriguing, p50.
- **Creative Art Centre** Large gallery showcasing fine art, antiques and souvenirs, p56.
- **Dubai Museum** Outstanding museum that tells the remarkable story of this former fishing village, p40.
- **Green Art Gallery** Features work by mainly Arab artists, p54.
- **Heritage House** Traditional house displaying interiors from the 19th century, p34.
- **Heritage and Diving Villages** Displays on archaeological treasures, pearling and social history, p45.
- **Hunar Gallery** Eclectic mix of tiles, glass, pewter and other art from around the globe, p179.
- **Intex**, Colours on Canvas, Satwa, **T** 3456272. Contemporary Indian art in various forms.
- **Majlis Al-Ghorfat Um Al Sheef** Peaceful old summer residence of Sheikh Rashid, p57.
- **Majlis Gallery** Traditional Dubaian house showcasing exciting variety of art, p43.
- **Original & Unique Art Gallery**, Sheikh Zayed Road, **T** 3434375. Huge range of European and Russian fine art
- **Profile Gallery**, Jumeirah, **T** 3491147. Lovely little place selling mainly watercolours and sculptures.
- **Sheikh Saeed Al-Maktoum House** Now a museum featuring historical documents and some wonderful photographs of old Dubai, p45.
- **XVA Gallery** Showcases predominantly modern art, p43.

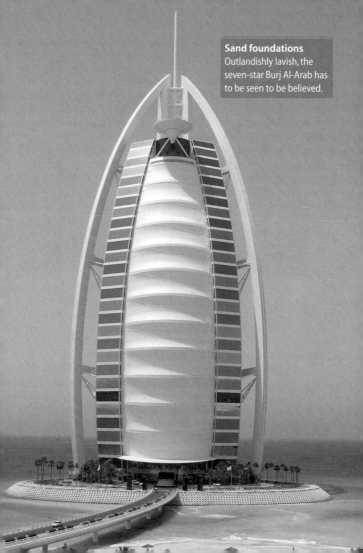

Sand foundations
Outlandishly lavish, the seven-star Burj Al-Arab has to be seen to be believed.

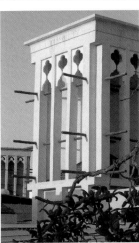

1 *Jumeirah Mosque is a carbon copy of a mosque in Cairo eight times its size. This minature version still manages to pack in 1,200 worshippers.* ▶▶ See page 52.

2 *An oasis of calm, the Majlis Al-Ghorfat Um Al-Sheef was Sheikh Rashid's summer residence and reflects the great man's humility.* ▶▶ See page 57.

3 *The Creek remains an integral part of the city and unlike other areas, time has almost stood still. Dhows continue to load and unload a 1001 types of cargo.* ▶▶ See page 31.

4 *For a taste of the unexpected, the bright colours and quirky architecture of the Courtyard fits the bill.* ▶▶ See page 50.

5 *The ambitious gleeming high-rises of Sheikh Zayed Road reflect much about the personalities of those who live and work in their shadow.* ▶▶ See page 49.

6 *Bastakia is hopelessly romantic, with a good line in historial architecture. These tall wind towers capture the breezes, funnelling them down into the houses below.* ▶▶ See page 42.

Arabian nights
Yesterday's Dubai – Bastakia skyline and minarets of nearby mosques.

Carpet talk
Captured in a cup of tea; the relaxed character of Muzeirah's market.

Jebel Ali, 67

Last bastion of undeveloped coastline and only place in Dubai you can barbecue on the beach, Jebel Ali is a great place to get away from it all in the evenings.

Sharjah and around, 67

Cultural capital of the Arab world, Sharjah's arts scene is flourishing while the choice and price of carpets at the famous 'Blue Souk' can't be bettered.

The East Coast, 75

Still relatively untouched by developers, head east for a glimpse of the UAE's traditional maritime past, old ruins and the best diving and snorkelling around.

Hatta and around, 83

Cool pools and constant balmy weather make this rustic retreat a popular getaway.

Al-Ain and the Buraimi Oasis, 86

Shady oases, winding *wadis* and ancient villages, step back into yesteryear and see the ancient *falaj* (irrigation) systems at work.

Jebel Ali

Known chiefly for its free zone and port, Jebel Ali lies south of the city towards Abu Dhabi. It's a bit of a misnomer, since 'jebel' means 'mountain' and Jebel Ali is little more than a mole-hill! These days it's taking off as a residential area, and the much-feted Palm Island Jebel Ali project has now begun to take shape. For tourists, its appeal lies mainly in its beach, where, if you can shut your eyes to the industrial skyline nearby, you can enjoy the last swathe of undeveloped coastline, running 15 km along the Arabian Gulf. Barasti shelters are dotted over the wide beach offering shade to picnickers and campers, and showers. It remains one of the only places you can light a barbecue on the beach, but remember: there are weekend police patrols that take a stern line if they discover you drinking alcohol in public.

▶▶ See Sleeping p115, Eating and drinking p146

Sharjah and around

Proud of its UNESCO-awarded epithet 'the cultural capital of the Arab world', Sharjah lies just a hop, skip and a jump away from Dubai. Driving here can take as little as 15 minutes or – if you're unlucky enough to get caught up in the horrendous inter-emirate rush hour – a never-ending two hours. With the earliest settlements dating back 5,000 years, Sharjah carved out a niche for itself as a successful fishing, pearling and trading nation, and the city grew up around the creek and lagoon, now beautifully landscaped and carpeted in lush green grass and shady trees. A number of excellent museums and heritage areas stand as testimony to its commitment to promoting art and preserving its heritage, and make a day trip extremely worthwhile. Those with a more materialistic agenda will find plenty to sing and dance about in some of the malls and souks, especially the Central Market (Blue Souk), famed for its cheap carpets and Omani jewellery.

▶▶ See Eating and drinking p146, Getting around p23

⊙ Sights

Al-Hisn Fort

Burj Ave, **T** 065685500. *Tue-Sun 0900-1330, 1700-2000, closed Fri am, women only Wed pm.*

Originally built in 1820, this double-storey fort was largely demolished in 1969 before the possibilities of tourism were even imagined. It was painstakingly restored in 1996 and 1997 and now houses a fascinating collection of photographs, documents and other artefacts, many of which date back to the different world of the 1930's, when the British Trucial Oman Scouts were stationed here. The range of exhibits is pretty good: everything from photos depicting the outbreak of smallpox in 1942, to the late Sheikha's beautifully ornate bed, to the gold sword handed to every ruler of Sharjah. Standing erect outside the fort is the 'Repentance Wood' – an old ship's mast to which pearl divers who refused to dive were once tied and whipped, underlining quite how important the trade was to the community.

Heritage Area

Admission to all the buildings is free.

This whole area has been painstakingly restored to afford visitors the chance to indulge their interest in local history. The traditionally renovated old buildings display architecture and artefacts and displays about domestic life as it was more than 150 years ago.

A 100 years ago **Bait Al-Gharbi**, *T 065357711, Tue-Sun 0900-1300, 1700-2000, closed Fri am, women only Wed pm*, belonged to Sheikh Sultan Bin Saqr Al-Qassimi and today's building is a traditional reconstruction. Built around a courtyard, there are rooms displaying some of the usual favourite exhibits – cooking utensils, jewellery, ceramics, furniture and traditional costumes. The real interest of the house lies in its structure, with its three different types of wind tower and the hollow walls behind some of the ground floor alcoves, which were also designed to funnel cooling air from the outside down into the room below.

Islamic Museum, **T** 065683334, *Tue-Sun 0900-1300, 1700-2000, Fri 1700-2000, women only Wed pm*, is not the place for novices to develop an understanding about the religion, although with its fabulous array of ancient artefacts from Islamic countries it's a fascinating stop. There's a vast coin collection; manuscripts dating from the mid 13th century, 12th-century Afghani armlets, ninth-century Iranian ceramic bowls, 700-year old Syrian pottery and much more. There's also what is said to be the very first map of the world, drawn up 1,200 years ago and amazingly accurate, if you forgive the fact that it's upside down. One of the most exciting displays is perhaps that of the Ka'baa stone in Mecca, which includes an exquisite copy of the original embroidered cloth and an original Holy Ka'baa key bag which once held the very key used for opening and closing the Ka'baa.

At **Bait Al-Naboodah** (Heritage Museum), **T** 065693999, *Tue-Sun 0900-1300, 1700-2000, Fri 1630-2000*, again, the main area of interest in this house is the architecture; the displays show nothing new. Unlike many old houses, Bait Al-Naboodah doesn't have wind towers. The alcoves on the ground floor conceal air vents, which ran the entire length of the walls so that the air circulated and cooled the lower rooms. At the same time, the shaded corridors immediately outside the rooms helped keep the hot air of the courtyard away from the cooler air within. A number of openings were built into the upper rooms to catch the sea breezes, making them comfortable sleeping quarters during the hot summer. The importance of privacy is also apparent from the

! Strict laws on public conduct were introduced in 2001. Visitors, both men and women, should dress in nothing remotely clingy or revealing. See further p26.

high, windowless exterior walls, the L-shaped entrance corridor, and of course the usual heavy teak main door.

Maritime Museum, *Tue-Sun, 0900-1300, 1700-2000, Fri 1630-2000*, is more light-hearted than the other museums, with posters depicting the fish found in UAE waters, wonderful photos of fishermen at work, rooms adorned with old anchors, hooks, lines, weights, tools, rocks and even shells. Some wonderful models of ships, alas, have no accompanying explanatory passages next to them.

Majlis of Ibrahim Mohammed al-Midfa, *Sat-Thu 0830-1300*, is the former *majlis* of Ibrahim Mohammed al-Midfa, a respected advisor to the ruling Al-Qassimi family and founder of the region's first newspaper, *Oman*, in 1927. His *majlis* is famed for having the only round wind tower in the Gulf. Now a small museum, it remains home to some of his personal effects.

Centre for Arabic Calligraphy & Ornamentation, *0900-1300, 1700-2000*, was founded to promote the art of calligraphy. This collection of buildings contains a museum, studios for the master calligraphers and an institute for teaching, which runs two-month courses at a minimal charge.

Ceramics House, *0900-1300, 1600-2000*, opened in 2003, is a bright little courtyard hung with ceramics made by the artists working in the surrounding studios. The best time to visit is after 1700, when the place usually perks up after the midday siesta.

Sharjah Institute of Theatrical Arts, **T** *065681333, 0900-1430*, despite being built of coral, gypsum, mangrove poles and palm leaves, nevertheless house two state-of-the art theatres, which opened in 1999. Call for details of forthcoming events.

★ **Al-Arsah Souk**
0900-1300, 1630-2100.

Sandwiched between the Arts Area and the Corniche is possibly the oldest souk in the emirates, now traditionally renovated complete with a *barasti* roof, heavy wooden doors and hanging lanterns. Inside you'll find a host of shops selling all sorts of souvenirs, an increasing number of which are, lamentably, not entirely local. Date-lovers will find Al-Harmoul an absolute joy, and the coffee shop and restaurant are worth testing.

★ Arts Area
Admission to all the buildings is free.

Another handful of buildings dating back to the late 1700s has been restored to form an area dedicated to the promotion of all manner of arts. The new and searingly modern (but architecturally sympathetic) Sharjah Art Museum presides over this square, around which a happy half day can be spent drinking in the various galleries and stopping for a refreshing drink at the café.

Sharjah Art Museum, T 065688222, *Tue-Sun 0900-1300, 1700-2000, Fri and public hols 1700-2000*, is the largest and finest art museum in the UAE. In 1997, the pictures housed in the old Art Museum (now Sharjah Art Institute) were rescued from the heat, humidity and lighting problems that beset them there, and shifted to this imposing building with state-of-the-art facilities. The 72 galleries spread out over three floors contain oils, watercolours and lithographs from Sheikh Sultan bin Mohammed Al Qasimi's (the current ruler) private collection, along with a host of work by international artists.

● *The equally modern Sharjah Museum of Contemporary Arab Art can be reached from inside the Art Museum keeping the same hours.*

Bait Obeid Al-Shamsi, T 065688811, is another carefully renovated old building, where a series of studios now overlook the central courtyard. Artists come here from all over the world by invitation of the Sharjah Directorate of Arts to use the studios. The best time to appreciate the current flavour of the old house is after 1800, when the place is normally alive and buzzing.

Sharjah Art Institute, **T** 065688800, was once the home of the British Commissioner's agent for the coast of Oman; later – during the 1960's – the first hospital in Sharjah to specialize in Gynaecology; latterly – until 1997 – the old Sharjah Art Museum. This beautiful building is now a teaching centre geared towards promoting art in the Emirates.

Very Special Arts, **T** 065687812, is a workshop and a small gallery with two teachers and between 30 to 40 students, most of whom are disabled. The concept behind the organization is to encourage the integration of disabled artists in society, promoting equal opportunities in the arts field – a huge step for a part of the world not particularly well-geared towards its disabled populus.

● *The Arts Café, attached to Very Special Arts, is a convenient stop for refuelling with real Arabic coffee, snacks and sweets.*

Al-Majarra Souk
Along the creek to the east of the Arts Area.   *0900-1300, 1630-2200.*

Topped by a golden dome and boasting a unique combination of old and modern Islamic architecture, that alone makes a visit worthwhile, it's also home to a variety of shops specializing in perfumes and clothes/textiles favoured by locals.

Around Khalid Lagoon
Dhs60 to be taken around the lagoon to the bridge, a 30-minute trip.

A ride on a dhow offers an excellent opportunity to soak up the hustle and bustle of the town from the relative tranquillity of the water. The corniche area curling around the lagoon has been beautifully landscaped, and you can usually spot a handful of snoozing residents enjoying the lushness of the grass, trees and flowers. As the lagoon winds towards the Gulf, you get the constant activity of the dhows loading and unloading their myriad goods. You can take your own refreshments on board.

Bird and Animal, Plant, Fruit and Vegetable and Fish Souks

On or behind Corniche Rd. *Birds Sat-Thu 0830-1300, 1600-2300; animals Sat-Thu 0700-1900; plants 0900-2200; fruit and vegetable 0730-2230; fish 0630-1230, 1700-2200.*

After the bend in the Creek, this cluster of souks is well worth visiting if you have some spare time. Bursting with all sorts of colours and constant hives of activity, they are a great places to watch the comings and goings, haggling and hunting, of the local community.

The bird and animal souk is divided into two main areas according to the size of the animal for sale; 'bigger than a goat' and 'smaller than a goat'. The larger beasts include camels, cows, goats etc, while the smaller varieties include all sorts of birds from falcons to parrots to budgies, as well as freshwater fish, hamsters, rabbits and the like. The fruit and vegetable stalls are piled high with every fruit under the sun and are best seen in the early mornings when the mountains are at their tallest.

★ Central Market

Kind Faisal Rd, near Sharjah Bridge, 0900-1300, 1600-2200.

Also known as the Blue Souk, thanks to the beautiful blue tile work on its outside walls, this is the most famous souk in Sharjah. Upstairs is where the best deals and most exciting finds are to be had. Bursting with countless little shops selling everything from rugs and carpets galore to brass coffee pots, Omani chests, Indian textiles, silver jewellery, ancient pottery and so the list goes on, the strength of its allure is awesome, attracting bargain hunters from all neighbouring emirates. It's generally considered to house the best selection of oriental carpets in the UAE and is well-stocked with rugs from China, Iran, Pakistan, Persia, Turkey and more. Haggle hard!

● *Southeast is the Gold Centre, on the corner of Al-Wahda and Al-Qassimi roads (1000-1300, 1630-2200), and, as its name suggests, this souk is brimming with gold shops. Shop around for the best prices.*

Sharjah Archaeological Museum

Off the Airport Rd, next to the TV station near Cultural Roundabout in Halwan, **T** 065665466. *Mon-Sat, 0900-1300, 1700-2000, Fri 1700-2000, ladies only Wed pm.*

There's nothing stuffy about this archaeological museum. Its exhibition rooms showcase objects from Sharjah's past, from around 5000 BC to the present day. A raft of hi-tech gadgetry and video footage provides in-depth information on the displays, through which it's a joy to chart the different eras in the history of the Emirates. Children can dig for 'artefacts' in the café's sandboxes.

★ Sharjah Desert Park

28 km out of town between Interchanges 8-9 on Al-Dhaid Rd. *Tue-Sun 0900-1730, Thu 1100-1730, Fri 1400-1730. Dhs 15, children free.*

Exceptionally worthwhile, particularly for families, this remarkable complex plays host to Arabia's Wildlife Centre, Sharjah's Natural History Museum and the Children's Farm.

Arabia's Wildlife Centre, *Interchange 9,* **T** *065311999,* is both a zoo and breeding centre, where many animals whose natural habitat is – and was – the Arabian Peninsula are represented here. Over 100 species live in spacious, natural surroundings (a welcome first for the Gulf), from camel spiders to puff adders, blind Omani cave fish to Egyptian fruit bats, Houbara Bustards to baboons. The centre's pride and joy is the success of its breeding scheme, most particularly for the endangered Arabian leopards: from just two in 1999 the family has expanded to 12. This is a fabulous stop for an informative dip into local animal life.

Sharjah Natural History Museum, Interchange 8, **T** 065311411, is another cracking museum, well-pitched to entertain the youngsters, incorporating everything a top-notch natural history experience should include. And more... it is not everywhere you see a mechanical camel. Experiencing a volcanic eruption, learning about local marine life as though from the bottom of the sea and tracing the changing face of the desert is just part of an exceptional overall experience. The gardens are lovely and well worth investigating.

Children's Farm, opposite the Natural History Museum, **T** 065311127, is home to a wide variety of domestic animals: ducks, donkeys, goats, camels etc. It's a great hit with the kids who can feed the animals, ride ponies and carry off eggs and cheese as trophies.

The East Coast

*A far cry from the glittering towers, modern malls, non-stop drilling and incessant movement of Dubai, the beautiful East Coast is – for the time being at least – delightfully undeveloped. Less than two hours' drive from Dubai through the rugged **Hajar Mountains**, that are dotted with places of interest en route, this tranquil stretch rolls gently out along the Indian Ocean from **Kalba** in the south to **Dibba** in the north. From Dibba, you can often see the fishing dhows, sails unfurled, gliding gracefully off in search of a big haul. Other northerly spots offer the best snorkelling and diving sites in the UAE, and are enduringly popular as overnight stops with camping and barbecue enthusiasts. Further south among the string of sweeping beaches, marine reserves, sleepy little towns and quaint old buildings, **Fujairah** attracts an increasing number of off-roading and watersport aficionados, and **Khor Kalba** is home to the region's oldest mangrove forest and its abundance of incumbent birdlife. When life in Dubai's fast lane gets too much, you can't beat the East Coast for a peaceful retreat.*

▸▸ *See Sleeping p115, Eating and drinking p146, Tours p25*

Sights

Masafi
35 km from Fujairah.

A permanent fixture despite its misleading name, the **Friday Market** is a long stretch of countless rug, pottery, fruit and knick-knack shops lining the Dubai-Fujairah road on the approach to Masafi. Watched over by proprietors who spend their waking hours by turn snoozing, drinking copious cups of sweet coffee and animatedly gesturing to undecided passers-by to come and investigate their wares, this is a great place to assume the bargaining position and get stuck in. The rugs are generally of the cheap, machine-made variety, but you should also be able to find some more exciting, earthy handmade examples from Afghanistan, Turkey and other such places. There's also the 'Antique Shop' whose owner readily admits there's nothing remotely old about any of his wares, but it's a cheap place to buy souvenirs.

Bithna
12 km from Fujairah.

Best known for its fort and archaeological site, you can't miss Bithna's complex just off the main highway. In its hey-day the old fort controlled the strategic Wadi Ham pass through the mountains, and has weathered the years well, remaining largely untouched by renovators. As such, it is perhaps the most authentic – and therefore exciting – example of any fort left standing in the UAE. Sadly though, this may not be the case for much longer, as word on the street suggests that renovators may be moving in before long to continue where they left off after rebuilding the collapsed southwest tower.

The archaeological site nearby, known as the T-Shaped or Long-Chambered Tomb, consists of a collective burial ground, thought to have been looted and re-used several times. The tomb's main period of use was probably the Iron Age (1350-300 BC), although it was built before then and reused more than 1000 years after its initial construction. Although there are many oddly positioned stones scattered over this area, some of which clearly denote graves, don't be misled into believing you've located the Long-Chambered Tomb itself, which is in fact now hidden from view under protective covers. Fujairah Museum, p78, contains an excellent display about the site.

★ Al-Hayl Palace
2 km before Fujairah. Turn off right to follow the brown signs to the palace. Follow the paved road for just over 4 km before turning off left as though to the quarries. Take the second turn-off at the roundabout, and follow the road for 1 km then turn right and drive along the wadi. *After 3.6 km is the quarry. Carry straight on along the newly tarmacked road for a further 3 km and you're there.*

The old palace at Wadi Al-Hayl, previously the summer residence of a branch of Fujairah's ruling Al-Sharqi family, is accessible by a two-wheel drive, even if your rental company won't thank you particularly for it. Impossibly romantic, the palace residence, once an enclosed compound, now stands derelict in this magnificent location, flanked by imposing mountains, and looking down upon the fields hewn out of the valley floor below. The main *majlis*, attached to the tower and now set behind a row of freestanding pillars, still bears all the signs of a finely decorated room, with intricately carved windows and carefully wrought niches livening up the walls. A second *majlis*, with one open wall, lies outside the main compound and would have been a more informal spot for people to wait for an audience with the sheikh. The defensive fort a little way above the compound still bears its original door, and the remains of various other buildings around the compound walls hint at the size of the family's retinue. Look out for the 65 known petroglyphs located within the vicinity of this old palace.

Fujairah
An hour and a half drive from Dubai.

Fujairah is the main event along the East Coast in terms of things to do, but even so, it's hardly a hive of activity. The road from Dubai is dotted with places of interest, while Fujairah itself is a charming if seemingly haphazard mix of old and new. Marine and water-sports enthusiasts will find plenty to busy themselves with, the seas and coral reefs are rich in marine life, and the Marine Club (see Sports, p219) can fulfil pretty much any watersports whim. It's a haven for birdwatchers, too, especially during the spring and autumn migrations, and adventurous types will find plenty to explore in the surrounding mountains and *wadis* should they choose to go off-roading from here.

The **old fort**, said to be around 300 years old, presides over the old town. It has recently undergone severe cosmetic surgery in the name of restoration, but has been left looking suspiciously like a new building. As yet, it remains closed to the public, and stands somewhat at odds with the numerous ancient watchtowers and forts that still rise protectively out of the mountains, not yet harmed by over-restoration.

A visit to the information packed **Fujairah Museum**, **T** 092229085, *Sun-Thu 0830-1330, 1630-1830, Fri 1400-1830, Dhs3*, sets you up with an excellent grounding about the most interesting archaeological features of various other destinations within easy striking distance of Fujairah. Bidiyah's mosque, Bithna's burial sites and Dibba's tomb all feature in displays containing considerably more information than anything you'll find at the sites themselves. There's also the ubiquitous collection of old photos, traditional jewellery, and exhibits on maritime activities. While the archaeological section is excellent, some of the other displays frustrate in that they have only Arabic explanations.

Heritage Village, *Ittihad Rd, 0900-1800, free*, is a small enclosure fenced in by *barasti* walls, and has been constructed to represent a typical coastal desert village. A solitary cow may well be the only sign of life you encounter while rattling about these empty palm shacks. It's surreal, but appealing.

Bullfighting, *Fujairah corniche, near Kalba roundabout, Fri 1630 onwards*, is a sporting tradition unique to Fujairah Emirate, and a far cry from its better-known Spanish equivalent. Spectators gather together in a human arena circling these hefty zebus, who lock their horns in combat until one turns tail in capitulation.

Kalba
Less than 10 km from Fujairah.

Not much further south from Fujairah is the UAE's most southerly village. Gently modernized now, its buildings are not what they were a few short decades ago. That said, there are still a few dilapidated streets fringed with dusty shops and cloaked in the oldy worldy feel that ensures the quaint charm of this old fishing village lives on in present-day Kalba. The white and blue building on the sea shore is the local fruit and veg market, behind which you'll find plenty of fishing boats bobbing about in a sheltered little harbour. Next door is the fish market, which opens its doors early in the morning and then again for the evening trade. Worth a visit on the other side of the roundabout and newly restored by the Heritage Department is the **House of Sheikh Saeed bin Hamad Al-Qassimi**, and Kalba's **Al-Hisn Museum**, *inland on the opposite side of the road, T 092777689, Sat-Thu 0800-1300, 1630-1930, Fri 1630-1930, free*. This defensive fort was built 150 to 200 years ago near the coast for the dual purposes of reconnaissance and defence. Surrounded by a thick wall, the upper levels of the fort have vertical and circular shooting outlets, known as 'mezaghil'. People would have gathered on the platform in front to meet friends and watch the comings and goings on the sea.

Khor Kalba Conservation Reserve
16 km from Fujairah.

Khor Kalba Conservation Reserve, located further south of Kalba in a beautiful tidal estuary, is a timeless place, known chiefly as the most northerly mangrove forest in the world, and the oldest in Arabia. Happily to date, it has somehow remained largely undisturbed by tourism. A birdwatcher's paradise, especially during the spring and autumn migrations, it's bursting with a wide variety of birds including the extremely rare white-collared Kingfisher, which thrives on the tiny crabs living in the muddy mangrove swamps. It is also rich in plant and marine life not found elsewhere in the emirates, and a great way to see it is to hop on board one of Desert Rangers' canoe trips or you can negotiate a hire fee with the local fishermen to borrow a boat and paddle through the mangroves; cheaper, but you don't get the fascinating commentary. Scattered along the beach on the route to Kalba, you can still see the age-old combination of *barasti* houses, fishing boats and nets scattered ready for use. Toyotas – usually more rust than vehicle – are also a common sight at the waterfront, helping the fishermen haul in the day's catch, avidly watched by expectant gulls.

Khor Fakkan
Under 25 km from Fujairah.

The second largest town on this coastal stretch, Khor Fakkan lies in a beautiful, sheltered bay about half way between Kalba and Dibba. The charming old harbour with its jumble of ageing fishing boats and nets now lies cheek by jowl with a new neighbour at the southern end; a thriving port, important because it shaves two days off the old journey to the west coast through the Strait of

Hormuz. Further up the sweep of the beach, the Oceanic Hotel sits on a headland denoting the town's most northerly tip and the best area for shelling. The town is a popular stop for holidays and weekend getaways with an attractive, palm-lined grass corniche and lovely sandy beach peppered with swings for the children. Serious tourism is, however, held in check by Sharjah emirate's alcohol ban.

Shark Island remains a popular diving spot, despite the lack of handy moorings nearby which means that sailors just drop anchor any old where, destroying much of the soft coral. Furthermore, the proliferation of sea urchins denotes the rising level of pollution in these busy waters. There are much better snorkelling and diving alternatives further up the east coast towards Dibba.

★ **Rifaisa Dam** is one of the area's greatest treasures. To reach this beautiful spot tucked away amongst the mountains, turn inland off the main street at the Emarat petrol station and head left at the T-junction. Then turn off onto the graded track on your right between the mosque and the bridge. Follow this track, keeping to the right where the road forks, for 4.7 km until you reach the dam itself. Lack of rain over the last few years has kept the water level much lower than usual, and local legend about there being a lost village at the bottom of the dam has been proven true; its remains can be seen clustered silently along the far side of the water.

Bidiya
8 km north of Khor Fakkan.

Parts of this sweet little fishing village have been dated by archaeologists back to the third millennium BC, fostering the opinion that it is possibly the most ancient settlement within Fujairah.

Bidiya's greatest claim to fame is the small, whitewashed **Al-Bidiya Historic Mosque** made of stone and mud-brick, thought to be the oldest mosque in the UAE. Clearly visible from the road, it's flanked by two elevated watch towers, in which 800-year-old pottery has been unearthed. The mosque is still used for worship today, so non-Muslims can only admire from the outside. Carbon dating suggests construction dates ranging from 1446 to 1668. Its roof, consisting of four pointed domes supported by an internal pillar, indicates a style untypical of contemporary religious architecture in the region. The mosque and watch towers have been carefully renovated, and the views from the slits in the towers take in much of the fertile grounds inland, set off by the multi-tiered mountains behind. There are old black and white photos of the mosque in Fujairah Museum.

Snoopy Island is another popular snorkelling spot, about 6 km north of Bidiya, with plenty of reef fish and the odd shark. However, despite there being a marine reserve around this area, the island's proximity to the shore means that bus loads of tourists have traipsed through with their knives to chip away at the coral for souvenirs, and to date the management of the nearby Sandy Beach Motel hasn't objected.

Dibba
About 60 km from Fujairah.

Another wonderfully beautiful spot at the most northerly point on the UAE's east coast, Dibba lies on the border of the Mussandam. Remarkably, it is divided into three fishing villages, Dibba Al-Hisn belongs to Sharjah, Dibba Muhallab to Fujairah, while Dibba Bayah comes under Omani jurisdiction. There's no hint of this in the town itself, though, as all three merge smoothly into a very informal, friendly whole.

Along the waterfront, there are still a handful of old-style, rustic houses, with wooden beams protruding from the walls below the roofs. There's a distinctly Arab feel to the other buildings here, too, thanks to the very decorative metalwork on the gates in the high walls and the iron bars crisscrossing frosted-glass windows. Unmissable, too, is the fact that the architecture's primary function is clearly to make sense of both environment and the traditional importance placed on privacy. Boats line the waterfront in places, there's a dhow 'graveyard' at the southern end of the bay, and swings and things to keep the children amused. The sea is particularly beautiful, sweeping round in a graceful curve of shimmering blues, set off against the towering Hajar Mountains inland. It's undeveloped, buildings-wise, but they've obviously made a bit of an effort with the corniche. Driving along the street parallel to the beach road, you'll see hundreds of thousands of little fish drying in the sun in age-old tradition. Dhow trips are offered from Dibba along the Mussandam Peninsula, see Tours p25.

Another big attraction is the marine life around the Peninsula and **Mount Dibba**, where snorkellers will invariably see Green and Hawksbill turtles, black tip reef sharks and plenty more besides. Maku Dive Centre, located within Holiday Beach Motel, offers wonderful trips, see p117.

Hatta and around

A land of rolling red sand dunes framed by the barren majesty of the imposing Hajar Mountains, it's a deservedly popular getaway destination at weekends and public holidays. The age-old village of Hatta itself nestles comfortably in the foothills of the mountains, guarded by numerous crumbling watch towers strategically peppering the nearby slopes. Once an important staging post on the trade route between Dubai and Oman, and known also as an important source of tobacco, Hatta's contemporary appeal rests largely in its relatively humidity-free climate, and its convenience as a platform from which to explore the mountains. The nearby rock pools are also a considerable magnet. Hatta is an enclave of Dubai Emirate, although the road here from Dubai (about 100 km) does run through Omani territory. While there are no border posts or check points to manoeuvre, if you're driving a hire car be aware that your insurance is unlikely to cover any mishaps that occur along this stretch.

▸▸ *See Sleeping p115, Sports p203*

Sights

Big Red
On the Dubai-Hatta Rd.

Rising 100 m up to the left of the highway, not 50 km out of Dubai, is Big Red. It's one of the most popular spots for those with four-wheel drive vehicles to come to let their tyres down and bomb over the undulating red sands. Thanks to the dune buggy hire shops (see Sports, p208) on either side of the road you can't miss it. Some of these outfits also offer camel rides as an alternative to dicing with death on the dunes. It's possible to climb to the top of Big Red in about 20 minutes, presuming your efforts aren't foiled by a rogue quad-biker. The area gets very busy, especially at weekends.

Muzeirah Rug and Pottery Market
12 km west of Hatta on the main highway.

The sprawling town of Muzeirah has an abundance of roadside rug and pottery stalls. The pots are great value and range from the very small to the utterly vast. If you're a rug enthusiast, it's worth looking beyond the usual abundance of thin, machine-made rugs, to find some wonderfully earthy, handmade items from Afghanistan and Iran, Turkey and Kashmir. Haggle hard to get some excellent prices, but don't be beguiled into forgetting the matter of excess baggage.

Hatta Heritage Village
Sat-Thu and public holidays 0800-2030, Fri 1430-2030. Free.

Still under construction, this recreation of a traditional mountain village set in its own oasis offers an informative series of displays and videos depicting the traditional life and culture of the area.

All sorts of topics are explored, with numerous buildings each dealing with a particular theme from aspects of social life to weaponry, from village economics to local songs. The complex also houses the oldest fort in Dubai, constructed from mountain stone and mud bricks, with mud also used as mortar. Hatta Towers, built in the 1880s to protect the village from external attack, offers great views of the village and surrounding area. Their doors are 2.5 m above ground level to prevent invaders gaining access.

● *Across the road is Traditional Handicrafts with displays on perfumes and cosmetics, traditional dress, spinning, pottery etc.*

Hatta Pools

20 km south of Hatta. Leaving the Heritage Village on your left, turn left at the T-junction by the mosque. Follow for about 900 m, then turn right and continue down a road full of speed bumps and lined with identical houses. After 6.5 km take the graded track leading off to the right by the stop sign. Continue for 6.5 km, pass signs to Al- Qarbi A'Sharqiyah and Al-Bon. After the Al-Bon turn off, there's soon a sharp drop after which is an immediate left turn. Take it and continue along this bumpy track until you reach a slightly broader area next to a falaj *that serves as a car park. The pools are to the right.*

The pools are an intricately carved network of fissures that run along a canyon-like stretch of valley amid the barren mountains. Multi-layered rocks, weathered and moulded by years of standing fast against the constant press of the waters, rise silently from the shady depths of the pools. Swimming between these narrow crevices and frolicking under the odd mini-waterfall spaced intermittently along its downward path has been a

! There are reputed to be around 50 cemeteries dating back to 3000 BC in the mountains around Hatta.

glorious way to while away free time for some years now. Sadly though, the lack of rain over the last few years means that the pools are currently as low as anyone can remember. Piles of litter left by all too many thoughtless visitors hardly set them off to their best advantage, either. The location, however, remains as dramatic and mysterious as ever, tucked away amongst the Hajar Mountains and practically hidden from view almost until you're stumbling upon the pool crevices themselves. Strictly speaking, you don't need a four-wheel drive vehicle to get here from Hatta, although your hire company would definitely cringe at the pasting you'll be putting their vehicle through. To continue to Al-Ain, however, will require a four-wheel drive.

Dam
Leaving Heritage Village on your left, turn left at the next T-junction and take the first right after the mosque.

Built in the late 1990's with the idea that once the dam is full, Hatta would be hard pressed to run out of water, there hasn't actually been enough rain to fill it. So it stands there, parched and skeletal-white, as dry as the desert, but an interesting diversion nevertheless.

Al-Ain and the Buraimi Oasis

Straddling the border between the UAE and Oman, the Buraimi Oasis lies around 135 km southeast of Dubai. The oasis has two towns side by side, Al-Ain (on the Emirati side) and Buriami (over the border in Oman). Both are awash with winding wadis, *quiet pools, ancient villages, verdant fields and varied wildlife. The area is also famed for its traditional* falaj *(irrigation system), some of which dates as far back as 1000 BC. Its prime location right on the ancient trading route between Oman and the Arabian Gulf holds the key to understanding the area's historical significance.*

Always much enjoyed as a cool retreat from the soaring summer temperatures and crippling humidity of the coastal settlements, zipping here today in under 1½ hours is a much easier undertaking than embarking on the dusty, five-day camel trek it once took from Abu Dhabi, not 40 years ago. The dry summer air also explains why many Emirati sheikhs have their summer residences here.

Museums, archaeological sites, livestock souks and various shady palm plantations mean there's plenty to see and do in Al-Ain itself when not using the town as a base from which to explore the surrounding area. And in the evenings, a great place to unwind is the stretch between the Hilton and the InterContinental, packed with picnickers, people having a drink or smoking shisha.

▸▸ *See Sleeping p115, Eating and drinking p146*

◉ Sights

Eastern Fort and Al-Ain Museum
Sultan bin Zayed St, Al-Ain, **T** 037641595, www.aam.gov.ae.
Sun-Wed 0900-1400, 1530-1730, Thu-Fri 0900-1100, 1530-1730.
Opening hours are wildly erratic so it's worth ringing ahead. 50 fils.

The Eastern Fort, built in 1910, was where HH Sheikh Zayed bin Sultan Al-Nahyan was born, and now, within the compound, is a cracking little museum which opened in the early 1970's. It plays host to some excellent displays about local life and history. The photographs are normally what draws the most attention, depicting life as it was here in the 1960's – a whole world away from the here and now. With a huge section dedicated to the ruins of yesteryear, there's plenty to whet the appetites of budding archaeologists about to head for the nearby Hili Archaeological Gardens, or interested in learning about the first millennium BC tombs found at nearby Qarn Bint Saud. Interesting, too, is the large collection of gifts received by the president from visiting dignitaries.

⬤ *A stone's throw from the coffee pot roundabout and Al-Ain Museum the old prison stands quietly, surveying this desert city and its oasis. Admittance is decidedly hit and miss, but if the padlock isn't blocking access to the turret, it's worth quickly scaling the steps to enjoy the view from the top.*

Al-Ain Oasis
Near the Al-Ain Museum, Al-Ain. *Free.*

Huge and shady, this date plantation is permanently open to visitors. There are numerous farms which divide the whole area into a patchwork of smaller plantations, easily accessible to farm vehicles and pedestrians alike. Two small mosques nestle amongst the palm groves, and the whole thing is really rather enjoyable to stroll around.

Jahili Fort and Park
Near Al-Ain Rotana Hotel, Al-Ain. *0900-2200. Dh1.*

This large restored fort, set within its own walled grounds near the public garden, was originally built in 1898. It remains a good example of traditional architecture – note the main tower, with its multiple battlements. Access is denied to the fort itself, but the gardens are a pleasant place for a wander.

Livestock souk
Off Sultan bin Zayed St, Al-Ain.

Not far from the entrance to the museum is a great place for anyone wanting to sit back and absorb the sight of countless traders from all over the UAE flexing their haggling muscles before

! Al-Ain's claim to fame is that HH Sheikh Zayed bin Sultan Al-Nahyan was born here.

Well thought out

The Al-Ain region boasts the world's oldest known *falaj*, dating back to about 1,000 BC. These water channels were used for irrigation mainly in the Al-Ain region, Afghanistan, Iran, Oman, Pakistan, the CIS States and other countries plagued by long spells of little or no rain. Underground channels were devised to bring water from distant sources to cultivated land, and the ingenuity of the *falaj* constructors and the sophistication of their systems can be judged by the fact that many *aflaj* (plural of *falaj*) are still the main source of irrigation in Al-Ain and other countries today.

carting off their newly acquired cows, sheep or even Persian cats. Great photo opportunities, especially if you tip up before 0900, as the general attitude coincides with the idea that the early bird catches the worm. Or the livestock, in this case.

Camel market
Near the border, off Bani Yas St, Al-Ain. *0700-1100.*

A dying breed of souk, this camel market is the last of its kind in the UAE, and a bastion of the traditional culture and flavour that has informed the lives of Arabs for centuries. A fantastic spot, always busy, but the market itself only operates in the mornings.

Hili Archaeological Gardens
10 km north of Al-Ain on the Dubai Road. *1600-2300, holidays 1000-2300. Dh1.*

Some of the area's oldest and most treasured finds have been unearthed here, indicating the overseas contact this ancient settlement has been enjoying for centuries. Important excavations of tombs have dated the first settlements to the end of the third millennium BC, and the famous Grand Garden Tomb was found to contain the remains of well over 200 people, many ceramic and soft-stone vessels, and featured two 5,000-year-old petroglyphs, one of two cheetahs catching a gazelle, the other of two people and an Arabian oryx. Rather ironically, another ancient structure within the garden, the famous Hili tomb, might in fact never have been used as a tomb at all. Although this is indeed an archaeological site, if it's information you're after, the Al-Ain Museum does a much better job of explaining the significance of the finds here, as on-site you'll find little information to make sense of what you're beholding. However, these public gardens are quite beautiful and well worth strolling around.

Al-Ain Zoo and Aquarium
Off Al-Nahyan Al-Awal Rd, **T** 037828188. *Sun-Fri 0800-1730, Wed women and children only. Dhs 2.*

Spread over 400 hectares, this is the largest zoo in the Gulf. First opened in 1969, it has recently undergone a Dhs87million refurbishment, raising the standard of facilities provided for the animals, and there are further plans afoot to incorporate a safari park. As you'd expect from such a vast expanse, there are plenty of animals, both rare and common, indigenous and shipped in from abroad. There are breezy tented areas to find shade under, and some people have compared the whole zoo experience to something akin to appearing in a Bollywood musical, as you might find yourself refreshingly sprayed with mist!

Jebel Hafit
30 km to the south of Al-Ain.

Rearing majestically up out of the surrounding flats is the saw-toothed, 1160 m-high limestone Jebel Hafit. The winding drive to the top affords some staggering views of the surrounding country-side, taking in the *wadis*, oases and rolling desert sands. At the base of the mountain are some slightly radioactive looking hot springs and a picnic area, enormously popular with locals and always packed at weekends. Basically a rocky mountain has been greenified and thus transformed to look like the Peak District – there's even a boating lake here. It's a very pleasant spot to while away a bit of time before resuming a more active itinerary.

Buraimi

Crossing the UAE border into Buraimi poses no problems, as the official border post is about 50 km east.

Once on the Omani side, it's immediately noticeable that this is the poorer of the two towns. While Al-Ain is the second most important city in the Abu Dhabi emirate, honoured as the birthplace of Sheikh Zayed and has benefitted from the wealth derived from the emirate's oil reserves, Buraimi has been relatively left out in the cold.

Buraimi Souk, on the horse roundabout, bustles with activity, colour and character. It is a wonderfully authentic souk, stocked up to the hilt with meat, vegetables, fruit and household goods. A motley selection of Omani jewellery and *khanjars* are available in the enclosed area, and behind the souk are some rather poignant-looking, crumbling old mud walls.

Nearby the souk is **Al-Khandaq Fort**, *Sat-Wed 0800-1800, Thu-Fri 0800-1300, 1600-1800, free*. Opinion is divided as to how old this fort is, with some sources putting the figure at 400 years old and others setting the date at nearer 1780. Whatever the date, this historical building has now been comprehensively restored and around its four highly decorative towers winds a 7.3-metre moat. It's untypical of other Omani forts in that it boasts both inner and outer defence walls, but typical in that the views from the ramparts are magnificently comprehensive, and well worth a peek. Buraimi's public prayer ground lies just east of the fort. Locals gather in this large, walled compound at the end of Ramadan to pray (note the *mirhab* (niche) in the wall facing Mecca).

'Hanging Gardens' of Jebel Qatar

From Buraimi leaving the Al-Buraimi Hotel on your left, turn left at the next roundabout (signed Mahdah) and continue for 16 km. Turn off the tarmac road onto the rough land on the right just beyond a sturdy line of rock that curls down to the road. The dirt track runs for 4 km before leading down to the left to a solitary tree that denotes the parking area. This is the start of the walk up towards first the cave, and then on to the extraordinary gardens.

This really is a spectacular find, quite unlike anything else you're likely to see in your explorations of the area, and well worth scrambling over the rocks to reach. One of the better routes is to hug the mountain, rather than striding off along the *wadi* bed only to find yourself hemmed in by huge rocks blocking the way.

The area is unique for a number of reasons. Firstly, a bat-riddled cave gapes open in the wall of Jebel Qatar, from which you can command panoramic views for miles around. Secondly, the area has extraordinary shaped rock formations which protrude like spikes along a dragon's back from the otherwise smooth rock face between the cave and the gardens. Lastly, the gardens themselves, though small, are constant wild burst of greenery (though particularly spectacular during the winter). If making the trip in the summer it's particularly important to take sufficient water.

When it comes to accommodation, there could hardly be a more diverse choice than that offered by Dubai's truly enormous selection of hotels. At the top end of the scale you've got household names such as the extravagantly lavish Burj Al-Arab and the wave-shaped Jumeirah Beach Hotel. Huge swathes of the west coast have been developed to accommodate a string of top-quality, beach-fronting, package-holiday pulling properties which jump out of all the glossy brochures intent on selling Dubai. Certain city hotels, usually located in Deira and along Sheikh Zayed Road, also offer fine luxury and service. While there are some excellent lower-star properties, cheaper options can be hit and miss, and the swinging prostitution scene is thinly veiled at some establishments. One relatively inexpensive option is to rent furnished accommodation, usually found in the heart of Deira or Bur Dubai, while at the lowest end of the scale are budget hotels galore, catering mainly for African, Asian and Arab businessmen, and necessarily popular with backpackers. The one and only youth hostel is exceptionally good value, if slightly out on a limb.

Sleeping codes

Price

LL	Over Dhs1600	**C**	Dhs301-450
L	Dhs1201-1600	**D**	Dhs201-300
AL	Dhs901-1200	**E**	Dhs151-200
A	Dhs651-900	**F**	Dhs100-150
B	Dhs451-650	**G**	Under Dhs100

Prices are for a double room in high season. Prices given for hotel apartments are based on a daily rate but are generally rented for a week or more. Single occupancy rooms/one-bed apartments tend to be discounted by 10-30 per cent.

A mammoth marketing campaign undertaken by the Dubai government to promote the emirate abroad, combined with general Western suspicion of the rest of the Middle East, means that Dubai is seen by many as the one stable holiday destination in the area. At the same time, with Arabs finding it harder to travel to America and Europe these days, Dubai is also one of only a few decent Gulf playgrounds and so is cashing in more than ever on the local market. And the net result for the hotel industry? Business is booming at every level: occupancy rates have rocketed to rest somewhere around 95 per cent, and advance booking for every type of accommodation has become highly advisable.

Room rates across the board tend to be lower during summer (May-September). Many of the five-star properties – especially the beach hotels – have traditionally offered excellent seasonal deals to keep numbers up during the swelteringly hot summer months. While this still holds true, the odd property has begun to stick to a consistent rate throughout the year, due to constant demand.

! If the idea of booking a hotel without seeing it first fills you with foreboding, check out http://dubaitourism.ae, where some of the hotel booking pages operate virtual tours.

One further thing worth knowing about the local hotel scene is that the top level hotels aren't merely hotels. Many of the city's favourite restaurants, bars and clubs are located within their walls, and form an integral part of Dubai's buzzing social scene, throwing open their doors to a constant throng of locals, expats and visitors in a grand mix of cultures and nationalities that's typical of so much of Dubaian life and has been through the ages.

Deira

Hotels

L InterContinental Dubai, Baniyas Rd, **T** 2227171, reservations @ihcdubai.co.ae. *Map 2, B5, p250* A veteran of Dubai's hotel scene, this place was the city's first five-star property, and looks smugly down over the Creek. Despite being somewhat tired, it remains popular with business travellers, and (somewhat randomly) has one of the few 24-hour health clubs. Its major claim to fame is its host of award-winning restaurants. Seafood, Persian dishes, Japanese specialties and the new charcoal grill all keep the discerning foodies piling through the doors.

L JW Marriott,**T** 2624444, www.marriott.com. *Map 2, A8, p251* A Dubai institution, and very well promoted by an excellent management team. Beautifully decorated and boasting 'the Middle East's largest skylight'. Its coffee shop runs enormously well-received theme nights at least three times a week, with Thursday's seafood night arguably topping the popularity stakes. A very relaxed option.

L Sheraton Dubai Creek Hotel & Towers, **T** 2281111, sheradxb@emirates.net.ae. *Map 2, B5, p250* A monumental revamp has left a wonderfully homely feel to these elegant rooms.

Fabulous views (for which you pay extra) can be enjoyed from those overlooking the Creek. A smattering of excellent restaurants attracts the hoards while helping the largely business clientele relax at the end of a hard day. It's directly under the flight path, so a good place for plane spotting.

AL **Al-Khaleej Palace Hotel**, **T** 2231000, kpalace@emirates.net. ae. *Map 2, B5, p250* Built in 1988, this long-standing hotel, much favoured by GCC countries, boasts some rooms with the most interesting wall displays; framed collections of historically and culturally interesting local artefacts. Some great views of the Creek and the cargo dhows loading their spoils if you get a room on the appropriate side. Rather pricey for its four stars though.

AL **Hilton Dubai Creek**, **T** 2271111, hiltonck@emirates.net.ae. *Map 2, C6, p250* An elegant, ultra minimalist building gleaming with glass, chrome and wood which people seem either to love or (strangely) hate. Not a style that goes down well with the Arab crowd, this is nevertheless a sleek option for businessmen and sophisticates, with some rooms looking out over the bustling dhow wharfage.

AL **Le Meridien Dubai**, Al-Garhoud, **T** 2824040, lmdxbbsc@emir ates.net.ae. *Map 2, E11, p251* Think not of beautiful views, but of convenience. Not only is it near the airport, it is a short flip away from the Dubai Tennis Stadium's popular restaurants and watering holes. It also has its own array of excellent eateries in Le Meridien Village, so food is perhaps what this hotel is best known for. With a core clientele of businessmen it now caters for a growing number of leisure guests who can now enjoy the newly opened spa, Essential Elements.

AL **Taj Palace Hotel**, corner of 23d St and 36a St, off Al-Rigga Rd, **T** 2232222, tajdubai@emirates.net.ae. *Map 2, B7, p251* A really lovely hotel with unusually large rooms, well-placed for business travellers with dealings in Deira, and a moment's drive from Al-Maktoum Bridge, Bur Dubai and the beaches beyond. Exemplary service, exquisite decor, an excellent Ayurvedic spa, great restaurants (including the awesome Indian, Handi) and perhaps most remarkable of all – drinkers be warned – is the way it bows to Islamic tradition, opting to be Dubai's only five-star hotel without an alcohol license.

A Hallmark Hotel, off Al-Rigga Rd, **T** 2221999, hallmark@emirates .net.ae. *Map 2, B6, p250* Newly opened in 2004, warm colours, spaciousness and Monet prints help create a relaxed feel in the rooms, and the ensuites have nice, deep baths. The pool area is small, but planted with flowers. No alcohol is served on the premises.

A Hyatt Regency, **T** 2091234, dubai.regency@hyatt intl.com. *Map 2, off A3, p250* Another veteran on the hotel scene, this monster has recently been refurbished (and not before time); it looks much sleeker on the inside. Caters mainly for business guests. The rooms boast great views of the Gulf, the city or distant Sharjah.

B Al-Bustan Rotana, Al-Garhoud, **T** 2820000, albustan.hotel@ rotana.com. *Map 2, E11, p251* Along with a convenient airport location, this place plays host to some decent restaurants including the ever-popular Benihana, Rodeo Grill and The Blue Elephant. Younger, smaller and arguably better value than Le Meridien Dubai, it's architecturally more modern, has an array of conference rooms and attracts mainly business guests.

B St George Hotel, Al-Khor St, **T** 2251122, stgeorge@emirates. net.ae. *Map 3, F4, p252* The 'architectural masterpiece' described in the brochure is actually a distinctly shabby looking monstrosity that correctly lowers expectations. The views from some rooms are pretty fantastic and the quarters themselves are fine, despite having seen better days. Clipped-voiced staff exude the illusion of efficiency, but consistently high occupancy rates mean it must be doing something right.

C **Landmark Plaza Hotel**, Al-Maktoum Hospital Rd, overlooking Baniyas Sq, **T** 2275555, lanplaza@emirates.net.ae. *Map 3, off D12, p253* Half-tiled corridors with swirling patterns are reminiscent of old- fashioned swimming baths. There's no lack of decoration here, even the room windows are meringue-shaped, and some look out over the rooftops to the Arabian Gulf. Some ensuites are intriguing, with washing facilities that are not quite baths, yet rather more than showers – ideal dog-washing troughs. Staff are friendly and efficient. A bit of charm can lead to a reduced room rate.

C **Marco Polo Hotel**, **T** 2720000, marcohot@emirates.net.ae. *Map 2, off A6, p250* Another decent, clean option operating a great Mexican restaurant with superb live music. Service and facilities are good, without being particularly memorable. Breakfast is included, as are transfers to and from the airport.

C **Millennium Airport Hotel**, Route 70 off Airport Rd, Al-Gar-houd, **T** 2823464, www.millenniumhotels.com. *Map 2, E11, p251* Standard rooms are big and warmy decked in Spanish hues of red and orange. The Dubai-themed prints on the walls are a nice touch, and the ensuites are surprisingly big. Predominantly UK business guests, with a sudden influx of rugby fans during the Dubai Rugby Sevens, which the hotel sponsors. Unfortunately, 2004 should see the demolition of the cheaper villa accommodation, seeing the end of this budget airport option. Also home to the wonderfully individual English pub, Biggles, bedecked with Second World War flying memorabilia. Its club, Terminal, is THE place to hang out.

C **Quality Inn Horizon**, Al-Rigga Rd by 23 St, **T** 2271919, qualitin@emirates.net.ae. *Map 2, B7, p251* Comfortable, decent-sized, much-mirrored rooms with plenty of storage space and good bathrooms. Popular with Arabs, but the western market also gets a fair look-in. Small roof-top pool.

C Riviera Hotel, Baniyas Rd, **T** 2222131, rivierahotel-dubai.com. *Map 2, A4, p250* Money well spent if you value a view, manage to get a room overlooking the fascinating dhow docks and intend to stay in most of the time, but otherwise overpriced for what you get. Furnishings are pleasant enough; there's a business centre, no leisure facilities but links with the Aviation Club where, for Dhs50, use can be made of their pool, sauna and steam bath.

D Hotel Florida International, Al-Sabkha Rd, opposite the bus station, **T** 2247777, floridai@emirates.net.ae. *Map 3, D10, p253* Well positioned in the heart of Deira, the balconied rooms overlooking the busy bus station are pleasant and afford a surprisingly enjoyable view of the vibrant character of this bustling area. Good value.

D Landmark Hotel, Al-Maktoum Hospital Rd, **T** 2286666, land1@emirates.net.ae. *Map 3, off D12, p253* Sister hotel to the ever-popular Landmark Plaza and Rigga's new Hallmark Hotel. Good-sized, well-maintained rooms with decent bathrooms for a change. Constantly busy with guests from all over the world. Cyber café on the first floor charges Dhs10 per hour. Pool and 'health club' facilities are very basic, but at least they're there.

D Phoenicia, Al-Maktoum Hospital Rd, overlooking Baniyas Sq, **T** 2227191, hotphone@emirates.net.ae. *Map 3, off D12, p253* Blues, oranges and browns are a definite theme throughout this determinedly colourful hotel, with room upholstery taking up the challenge with aplomb. Decent framed pics in the rooms are a blessed relief from the ubiquitous waterfalls. The ensuites are surprisingly basic.

D Vendome Plaza Hotel, Rd 42a not far from Taj Palace Hotel, **T** 2222333, vphotel@emirates.net.ae. *Map 2, B7, p251* The odd rug alleviates the otherwise stark whiteness of these large but space-wasting rooms. Ensuites are hardly classy, but manage well enough. No pool, but a friendly atmosphere makes this a decent choice.

E Al-Khayam Hotel, corner of Sikkat Al-Khail Rd and Souk Deira St, **T** 2264211, khayamh@emirates.net.ae. *Map 3, C8, p253* Small, reasonably clean quarters; the tiled walls lend character to the rooms and positively make the eyes swim in some of the bathrooms. The best positioned rooms overlook the entrance to the Gold Souk, and guests are a real mix of nationalities with a healthy percentage of UAE locals on business trips. Great staff.

E Marhaba Inn Hotel, Street 9A, just off Al-Khor St, **T** 2255133, marhabahotel.com. *Map 3, B7, p253* Pleasant staff, a vigorous cleaner and good-sized, airy (if bare) rooms make this small, well-maintained hotel an absolute joy compared to some of its fellows in the budget range. The views are nothing to write home about, but for the (mainly Indian and Arab) clientele it's a good deal nevertheless, just a stone's throw from the bus station and a short walk to the Gold Souk.

F Al-Arraf Hotel, 25B St, near the intersection with 40 St, **T** 2250700, **F** 2250550. *Map 3, B9, p253* One of cheapest and best options. Though the rooms are basic and there's nothing lavish about the ensuites, they're all pleasant enough and an effort has been made to add a splash of colour, with the ubiquitous waterfall prints strung up in each room, and even some corridor decorations. Balconies overlook the bustling main road, yet the double glazing manages to keep out most of the noise. The extremely friendly staff add to rating of this budget option.

F Deira Palace Hotel, on the corner of Sikkat Al-Khail Rd and Al-Soor St, **T** 2290120, **F** 2255889. *Map 3, C9, p253* A huge, brown, wobbly looking edifice that on closer inspection is not wobbly, merely strangely designed. Clean rooms and friendly (if constantly distracted) staff mean it's usually full, despite having significantly more rooms than most of its rivals.

F Galaxy Plaza Hotel, Baladiya St, near Intersection with Al-Ahmadiya St, **T** 2257444, **F** 2250112. *Map 3, C5, p252* This place has small but decent rooms, typically full of African businessmen enjoying ensuites that are a definite step up from many alternative budget options. Views encompass the satellite-peppered rooftops of surrounding buildings, and, if you manage to advance book in time, it's a decent option.

F Gold Plaza Hotel, Souk Deira St, off Sikkat Al-Khail St, **T** 2250240, **F** 2250259. *Map 3, C8, p253* Enviously positioned just seconds from the Gold Souk and manned by friendly, efficient staff, this is one of the better basic choices. Unusually, the ensuites have baths, not showers, and all rooms have balconies, but not necessarily a view. More westerners are now muscling in on this traditionally African stronghold.

F Hotel La Paz, 6St off Souk Deira St, **T** 2268800, **F** 2269797. *Map 3, D8, p253* Enormous doors lead onto rather small, but well-kept rooms with more character than most in this price category. The walls boast both a clock and a picture instead of the usual expanse of dirty cream paint.

F Marhaba Hotel, next to Gold Land, Al-Daghaya St, **T** 2257766, marhabahotel.com. *Map 3, A8, p253* Sister establishment of the nearby Marhaba Inn, this hotel is equally immaculately kept, with light, breezy-feeling rooms and a receptionist with a better command of English than many in the budget range. Worth a pop.

Hotel apartments

LL **Marriott Executive Apartments**, **T** 2131000, dubaimea@
emirates.net.ae. *Map 2, C7, p251* These American style apartments
are fully furnished with washing machine and kitchen. Facilities
include business centre and health club. Reduced summer rates
start during May. A two-bed apartment costs Dhs11550 for a week
stay. Rates diminish if you stay for a month.

LL **Taj Palace**, **T** 2232222, www.tajpalacedubai.ae. *Map 2, B7,
p251* It's rare for guests to have to pay the full rate (two-bed apartments Dhs18480 for a week) for these beautiful apartments as hefty
seasonal promos run almost constantly. Airport transfers included.

AL **City Centre Residence**, Al-Garhoud, **T** 2941333,
www.citycentre-sofitel.com. *Map 2, D9, p251* These de luxe
apartments are ideal for shopaholics addicted to Dubai's favourite
mall. Included in the price is the daily housekeeping service,
satellite TV and internet use. There's 24-hour room service and
access to the health club, tennis and squash courts etc. A two-bed
apartments costs Dhs8400 for a week.

A **Galleria Apartments**, **T** 2096788, Galleria Shopping Centre,
dubai.regency@hyattintl.com. *Map 2, off A3, p250* Part of the
Hyatt uber-brand, these apartments look out onto the sea and
have daily housekeeping, with access to all the hotel facilities.
A two-bed apartment costs Dhs5500.

A **Rayan Residence**, Doha Centre (behind Etisalat), Al-Maktoum
St, **T** 2240888. *Map 2, B5, p250* Fully furnished and cleaned daily.
No pool, bar or business centre. Single bed has two bathrooms.
Two-bed apartments costs Dhs 4900. The longer you stay, the
more you can negotiate down the price.

B Al-Nakheel Hotel Apartments, **T** 2241555, Nr Al-Ghurair Centre, behind Marks and Spencer, alnakhel@emirates.net.ae. *Map 2, A6, p250* Daily room service and cleaning. Family oriented. Two-bed apartments cost Dhs3500 for a week.

D Al-Muraqabat Plaza, **T** 2690550, Salahuddin Rd, muraqabt@emirates.net.ae. *Map 2, A7, p251* These one-bed apartments are cleaned daily but offer no access to other facilities. Unusually, there are no washing machines, but reception will arrange for you.

Hostels

F-G Dubai Youth Hostel, Al-Nahda Rd, next to Al-Ahli Club, Al-Qusais, **T** 2988151, www.uaeyha.org. *Map 1, D12, p249* Sharing a room here is the cheapest accommodation option in town, with prices for YHI members starting at a mere Dhs45 (Dhs15 cheaper than for non-members). The old wing with its strip lighting, tatty furnishings and lurid green walls looks fairly dilapidated, and the communal loos often make do with no shower curtain or loo seat. That said, the no-frills 2-, 3- and 4-bed dorms are clean and perfectly adequate. The new block, added in 2002, has raised the game; these 50 rooms come complete with ensuite, TV, fridge and air conditioning, making them truly fantastic value. With three-star facilities, they're a considerable step up from every other budget option available. YHI cards can be bought on the premises (Dhs100), and bus numbers 13, 31 and 17 will scoop you up on their way into town.

Bur Dubai

Hotels

A Ascot, Khalid bin Al-Waleed Rd, opposite 26 St, **T** 3520900, info@ascothoteldubai.com. *Map 2, C1, p250* Lovely colour schemes in these well-appointed, Georgian-style rooms, with green carpets and subtle yellow stripey wallpaper (somewhat marred by some rather unexceptional framed prints) and walk-in wardrobes. Popular with all sorts, especially UK and Indian business travellers, the Ascot also houses two exceptional restaurants: Yakitori (Japenese) and Troyka (Russian), and the attached Waxy O'Connors is one of the most popular bars in town, though only opened in 2003.

A **Four Points Sheraton**, Khalid bin Al-Waleed Rd, near Mankhool Rd, **T** 3977444, www.fourpoints.com\burdubai. *Map 2, C2, p250* A popular four-star option with a cosmopolitan mix of guests, most of whom are business travellers. Its Antique Bazaar won the 2004 'What's On' Best Indian Restaurant in Dubai award and the Viceroy dishes up some decent pub grub.

B **Ramada**, Mankool Rd, near Spinneys, **T** 3519999, ramadadubai. com. *Map 2, C2, p250* It's predominantly business travellers staying at this four-star de luxe hotel. A striking stained-glass mural rises the entire height of the lobby, making interesting viewing from the glass lifts. Rooms are what you'd expect and the service is good. There's a small pool which only gets the morning sun.

B **Sea Shell Inn**, Khalid bin Al-Waleed Rd, opposite 16 St, **T** 3934777, seashellinndubai.com. *Map 2, C1, p250* There is a real mix of business and leisure guests in this three-star establishment. Stuffy corridors lead onto decent rooms and no-nonsense bathrooms with the odd, sloppily repaired or replaced tile. Very efficient reception staff. It's worth knowing that rates practically halve from April to August, making it very good value.

B **XVA Gallery**, 15a St, Bastakia, **T** 3535383, xva@xvagallery.com. *Map 3, H8, p253* An unbeatable treat. These newly opened guest quarters offer THE most fabulously authentic accommodation experience in the whole of Dubai. Climb the stairs (past the camel bones!) to reach the three rooms set on the upper story of a traditionally renovated merchant's house in the historic Bastakia quarter. They overlook the lovely central courtyard of the gallery below, and also afford views out onto the narrow alleyways winding silently through the area. Each room has been decorated differently: two along relaxing, sedate lines while the third is a 'kitsch room' containing a hilarious mix of hideous towels and bedspreads in a really lovely, traditional, almost colonial setting. And as if that wasn't enough, the vegetarian Arabic food served is the stuff of dreams. Can not be recommended highly enough.

B-D **Ambassador Hotel**, corner of 11a and 13c Sts, **T** 3939444, ambhotel@emirates.net.ae. *Map 3, H1, p252* The first hotel to be built this side of the Creek (in 1968), the Ambassador once commanded fantastic views and boasted wonderful 1960's furniture. Lamentably, both have now disappeared due to new buildings and recent refurbishments, which mean the rooms, though big, are now largely characterless. The odd black and white enlarged photo from the late 1960's/early 1970's are the last remaining vestiges of the good old days. It's nice though, despite its dilapidated air, and the staff are friendly. There's a relatively large and little-used pool.

C **Admiral Plaza**, Al-Nahdha St, **T** 3935333, admplaza@emirates. net.ae. *Map 2, B1, p250* There is nothing exceptional about these perfectly serviceable rooms, although the choice of pictures is at least traditional, with the odd *khanjar* and dhow gracing the walls. Bathrooms are surprisingly small, but still have adequate space for potions and lotions. Try to avoid cleaning time, air freshner rules.

C **Palm Beach Rotana**, Khalid bin Al-Waleed Rd, near 10a St, **T** 3932222, palmbhtl@emirates.net.ae. *Map 2, off C1, p250* Oodles of storage space in the rooms. Some of the ensuites have mirrored walls by the baths, and the tiling makes the bathrooms feel more upmarket than the rooms themselves, which are largely characterless. A very family-oriented hotel and friendly staff.

C Regal Plaza Hotel, junction of Khalid bin Al-Waleed Rd and Mankhool Rd, **T** 3556633, regaldxb@emirates.net.ae. *Map 2, C2, p250* Despite its location on a busy crossroads, the noise is well blocked out. Rather smart rooms with decent furniture for a three-star hotel. The first-floor pool is small and overlooked from every angle by higher rising buildings, and gets only the morning sun. The first floor Goodfellas sports bar has well-trodden wood flooring, gangster posters covering the walls, plenty of TV screens and a constant flow of human traffic.

C-D Astoria Hotel, **T** 3534300, astoria@astamb.com. *Map 3, off H2, p252* Sister hotel of the Ambassador, rooms here vary enormously in look and feel, are well kitted out with the usual furniture and offer ensuites with plenty of surface space. It's well-run and attracts a variety of guests, largely from the Indian, Pakistani and Asian shipping communities. On the first floor, Pancho Villa's is one of Bur Dubai's best known restaurants, best visited for lunch to avoid the sometimes predatory atmosphere of the evenings.

D Dubai Nova Hotel, Al-Fahidi St, near Al-Hisn St, **T** 3559000, thotel@emirates.net.ae. *Map 3, off H5, p252* Very clean, large, tile-floored rooms, some with balconies, the whiteness punctuated by a variety of colourful paintings or huge cracks. Let down by some extremely grotty looking ensuites, so it's a bit of a lottery. Balconied rooms look down onto the washing of the flats opposite.

D Time Palace Hotel, 11b St off 34 St, **T** 3532111, timehotl@ emirates.net.ae. *Map 3, H3, p252* Decent enough rooms with cool, tiled floors. Some great views of the mosque opposite, and even a glimpse of the Creek, if you get a room on the appropriate side.

Walls could do with a lick of paint, but they're okay, as are the (basic) bathrooms. The lift takes forever.

E Dallas Hotel, 26 St, opposite the Admiral Plaza, **T** 3511223, siavash2@emirates.net.ae. *Map 2, B1, p250* Decent-sized, well-lit rooms with hard-wearing carpets and quite the tackiest flowered, butterflied and sunsetted pictures imagineable on the walls. Tiny ensuites, most of which have showers, so shout if you want a bath.

E Hyde Park Hotel, 16St, by 26bSt, **T** 3939373, hydepark@emirates.net.ae. *Map 2, off B1, p250* One of the very cheapest hotels this side of the Creek and exceptionally good value, the rooms are basic but perfectly adequate, and those at the front have balconies encased in interesting, flower-patterned wrought iron mesh. Room service is incredibly slow. No visitors allowed upstairs.

E Vasantam, 27c St, off 26 St, **T** 3938006, **F** 3938005. *Map 3, off H1, p252* Popular with business and family travellers from India and the UAE. Large, fairly airy rooms with safe, desk and chairs. Dim lighting at night, and basic bathrooms with some wildly slap-dash tiling and grouting holding some of the baths in place. Just.

Hotel apartments

AL Rolla Residence, **T** 3592000, from Al-Khaleej Centre turn right. *Map 2, D1, p250* This rather upmarket alternative, centrally located, has a sauna, gym and rooftop pool that looks out over Sheikh Zayed Road's skyscrapers in the distance and is high enough not to be badly overlooked itself. The rooms are adorned with the odd local print and the carpets are pretty loud. A good choice.

A Golden Sands 3, Al-Mankhool Rd, behind Standard Chartered Bank, **T** 3555553, goldensands@emirates.net.ae. *Map 2, D1, p250* Pool, sauna, gym, squash courts. Cleaned daily. Two-bed, Dhs 495.

A Winchester Grand, 10b St, off Mankhool Rd, behind Ramada Hotel, **T** 3550222, wingrand@emirates.net.ae. *Map 2, C2, p250* Apartments are cleaned daily and you have access to the pool, sauna and jacuzzi. Room rates are easily negotiated down. The weekly for a two-bed is Dhs6300.

B Oasis Court Hotel Apartments, Bank St, near National Bank of Fujairah, **T** 3976666. *Map 2, C1, p250* Fully furnished apartments with access to a gym, sauna and swimming pool. Dhs4000 per week for a two-bed.

C Al-Faris Hotel, Apartments 2, Al-Rolla Rd, **T** 3935847, afarisre@emirates.net.ae. *Map 2, C1, p250* Fully furnished, with access to a gym, these rooms are cleaned twice a week. Dhs2450 for a week stay.

C Pearl Residence, 18b St overlooking 7 St, behind BurJuman Centre, **T** 3558111. *Map 2, D2, p250* Well situated a short flip away from downtown Bur Dubai, these fully furnished, one-bed apartments have large rooms with some very determined colour schemes. A small pool gets the afternoon sun. Breakfast (in the lobby area) is included in the price. Breakfast, in the lobby area, is included in the price (Dhs2800 for a week).

Sheikh Zayed Road

Hotels

L Emirates Towers, **T** 3300000, eth@emirates-towers-hotel.com. *Map 4, H10, p254* There's a distinctly masculine, corporate feel to this whole place, far more so than at other business hotels. This, combined with its excellent service, means it's not hard to see why it was voted 'Favourite Overseas Business Hotel' in the Conde Nast

Best

Places to stay

- XVA Gallery, p105
- Ritz-Carlton, p114
- Royal Mirage, p114
- Oasis Beach Hotel, p115
- Al-Maha Desert Resort, p119

Traveller Awards 2003. It is also one of the tallest hotels in the world, has a bevy of popular restaurants doing a roaring trade at ground level, and a glass-lift ride that is worth a booking in itself.

L Shangri-La, **T** 3438888, sldb@shangri-la.com. *Map 1, C8, p248* Built in 2003 this place still feels like a relative newcomer to Dubai. Its mostly Asian staff are gentle and friendly, if sometimes rather inefficient. The bright and breezy atrium features so many curved balconies it makes you think it must have Glyndbourne-esque acoustics. This rounded furniture theme is picked up again in the rooms, which also boast rather interesting padded bits on the walls. The bathrooms are all modernity, with ridiculously wide baths, ferocious taps and basins that look like white mixing bowls.

AL Crowne Plaza, **T** 3311111, cpdxb@cpdxb.co.ae. *Map 4, G9, p255* Very 1980s and desperate for a refurb, but understandably unwilling to close its doors to the public when business is booming. Despite being rather dated, the hotel is not at all unpleasant, with its richly decorated rooms. Convenience must be its main selling point, and on a number of levels: at the Creek end of Sheikh Zayed Road, it's not far from anywhere; it boasts some excellent restaurants and bars, not to mention one of the city's preferred nightclubs, Zinc; and it's attached to a surprisingly good little shopping mall, Holiday Centre, which is home to the incomparable Abrash (carpet) Gallery, amongst others.

AL Dusit Dubai, T 3433333, info@dusitdubai.com. *Map 1, C8, p249* Such unique architecture sadly plays host to a relatively dark and characterless interior with little of the vibe that could have made it spectacular. The service is equally unremarkable. The sombre rooms are decked out in dark greens and browns, with blinds at the windows completing the no-nonsense, no-distractions atmosphere. A surprising and rather lovely touch is the way the ensuites are separated from the main room by openable shutters, creating a much-needed intimate feel to an otherwise fairly cold environment. The loos look a little 'public' in their glassed off cubicles, but the overall bathroom effect is pretty funky.

A Fairmont Hotel, T 3325555, fbconcierge.dubai@fairmont.com. *Map 4, E10, p255* An exceptionally fine hotel, the Fairmont caters for a largely corporate clientele to whom it offers a comprehensive range of business facilities. That said, those with more time on their hands are also well-catered for, and can enjoy day-round sun at either the sunrise or sunset pools as well as a pampering session at the spa. Rooms are beautifully elegant, and the beds are ridiculously comfortable. Service is exemplary, and with its collection of quality bars and restaurants (try the Friday Moet brunch at Spectrum On One), it's hard to find fault with the altogether polished service consistently dished out here. Recommended.

A Novotel World Trade Centre, T 3320000, reservation@accorwtc.ae. *Map 4, G12, p255* Another business-oriented hotel with light, bright, rather characterless rooms with white walls and grey carpets. The wardrobes are pretty extraordinary – lights go on when the doors are closed, shining through the white Perspex to compliment the room's decor, but automatically turn off when you open them to get at your clothes! Some rooms have rather nice views showing the desert sand that's never too far away even if usually well masked by the location of most other hotels. Decent bathrooms (complete with speakers!).

D Ibis World Trade Centre, T 3324444, novotel.ibis@accor
wtc.ae. *Map 4, F11, p255* By far the cheapest hotel in this area,
it's really excellent value, with Accor high standards for the most
reasonable prices in the area (so far). The French-influenced rooms
have a rather austere feel, with dark green and brown furniture,
clearly designed for busy businessmen intent on using their rooms
only to collapse into bed at the end of a long day. Excellent location,
but beware that securing accommodation here when an exhibition
is on will need serious advance booking.

Jumeira and Satwa

Hotels

LL Jumeirah Beach Club, T 3445333, info@jumeirahbeach
club.com. *Map 1, B7, p249* Although in the middle of busy Jumeira,
these intimate villas have a relatively secluded, Southeast Asian
feel to them, set amongst exquisitely maintained tropical gardens,
with a private beach at their disposal. A lovely retreat, offering
great service and bags of atmosphere.

L Dubai Marine Beach Resort & Spa, T 3461111, sales@dxb
marine.com. *Map 4, B4, p254* Better known as 'Dubai Marine',
these slightly tired villa-style rooms are prettily nestled in tropical
gardens, promoting an earthy and rather wonderful sense of
escapism, as though you're miles away from the melee of Dubai.
Better suited to fitness addicts rather then beach bums, the spa
and health centre are well-equipped while the beaches are packed
with loungers and worshippers and better can be found elsewhere.
Another main attraction is the ever-lively bars and restaurants.

AL Rydges Plaza Hotel, T 3982222, rydges@emirates.net.ae.
Map 4, B9, p255 This is a great four-star hotel with a fabulous

location nicely sandwiched between the beaches and bustle of Jumeira and Satwa on one side, and the more culturally rich Creek area on the other. It's notable for being totally unpretentious (perhaps because of its Australian roots) and has a truly excellent array of bars and restaurants. Recommended.

The Southwest

Hotels

LL Burj Al-Arab, **T** 3017777, reservations@burj-al-arab.com. *Map 1, B3, p248 See also p62* The world's only 'seven star' hotel and quite extraordinarily lavish, the Burj would be laughed out of town in some places, but somehow works rather well in Dubai. Its signature sail shape and outlandish opulence make some of the world's more traditional five-star properties look as though they're flirting with bankruptcy. An army of staff fully caters for every whim of every guest, and every floor has its own reception desk and butler service. Think superlative extremism and then be ready for reality to exceed expectation. A whopping Dhs5000 per night.

LL Jumeirah Beach Hotel, **T** 3480000, info@thejumeirahbeach hotel.com. *Map 1, B4, p248 See also p62* With its signature wave-shape, this is one of Dubai's best-known hotels, featuring in all the glossy brochures. Its awesome array of restaurants, cafés and bars do a roaring trade, and shoppers won't be disappointed either, thanks to its countless retail outlets. It's a package-holiday Mecca, crammed full with sarong-clad, red-bodied tourists complete with screaming children, all enjoying the excellent facilities and service consistently dished out. Mayhem!

LL Mina A'Salam, Al-Sufouh Rd, Al-Sufouh, **T** 3668888, reserva tion@madinatjumeirah.com. *Map 1, B3, p248* This is another fantasy resort, traditionally Arabic in architecture and yet somehow only a shade removed from Disney. Rooms feature sepia photos of Dubai in the good old days, heavy wooden furniture and lavish bathrooms. Combine that with private balconies and beautiful sea views, you've got a package-holidaymaker's dream. It's part of a monumental development project, Madinat Jumeirah, due for completion in 2004 which will complete the giant theme park feel and include a huge spa and health centre, souk, cultural village and waterways galore.

LL **Ritz-Carlton**, Al-Sufouh Rd, Marsa Dubai, **T** 3994000, rcdubai@emirates.net.ae. *Map 1, off B1, p248* Beautifully elegant, it's the exceptional service that makes this place stand head and shoulders above its rivals. Despite being small there's a relatively huge private beach area, which never feels as crowded as many of the other properties, especially as the main pool winds river-like through the grounds, so people are spread out along it. Oh, and the afternoon teas here are excellent! Recommended.

LL **Royal Mirage**, Al-Sufouh Rd, Al-Sufouh, **T** 3999999, royal mirage@royalmiragedubai.com. *Map 1, B1, p248* More a fantasy than a hotel, this magnificent resort is the epitome of traditional Moroccan architecture at its palatial best. Often cited as Dubai's nearest rival to the Burj, this is unfair to the Mirage. Its elegance is more restrained and the whole experience quite different. Its pictu-resque canals and beautiful terraces arguably put it in a class apart. Service can be a little inconsistent, but you can't help loving it.

L **Le Meridien Mina Seyahi Resort**, Al-Sufouh Rd, Al-Sufouh, **T** 3993333, reservations@lemeridien-minaseyahi.com. *Map 1, B1, p248* Young and funky, this resort has a chilled out vibe both inside and out. Closely affiliated to Dubai International Marine Club (DIMC), this is THE watersports hotel offering everything from boat charters to fishing trips to hobie cat sailing and plenty more. Views from the rooms are therefore never dull, looking out over constant activity from F1 powerboats to traditional dhows. It's also the only hotel with a football pitch, boasts one of the longest private beaches (where you're practically guaranteed a sun lounger), and of the five swimming pools (two for children) the infinity pool commands fantastic views over the sea. Oh, and the ever-popular Barasti Bar is a great place to sit with a sundowner at the end of the day. Recommended.

L **Metropolitan Resort & Beach Hotel**, Al-Sufouh Rd, Marsa Dubai, **T** 3995000, a.saliba@metbeach-dubai.com. *Map 1, off B1, p248* With nothing particularly distinguishing about architecture, service or facilities here, it's nevertheless a very relaxed, low-rise hotel with no pretensions and plenty of Russians. The bad news is the imminent addition of a further 450 rooms in May 2005 with the completion of a nearby tower block. Since the grounds are already packed, who knows what effect this'll have on the available beach space, but it can't be good.

L **Oasis Beach Hotel**, Al-Sufouh Rd, Marsa Dubai, **T** 3994444, obh@jaihotels.com. *Map 1, off B1, p248* A gem. Comfortable and warm, this hotel is less pretentious and very much more relaxed than most of its fellow beach properties. Despite invitations to join the five-star brigade, it clings determinedly to its four stars to offer excellent value, and is the only hotel operating on a half-board policy. Recommended.

Around Dubai

Jebel Ali

LL **Jebel Ali Golf Resort & Spa**, **T** 048836000, jagrs@jaihotels. com. This is a really lovely hotel. Out of the hustle and bustle of the main city, it's bang on its own extensive beach, offering an excellent variety of activities and facilities including horse riding and shooting. It is well known for its enormously popular nine-hole golf course (home to the annual Challenge Match). Situated amongst 128 acres of beautifully landscaped gardens and their incumbent wildlife, it boasts a stunning view of the Arabian Gulf and is possibly one of the most relaxing places to stay in the whole of Dubai.

The East Coast

L **Le Meridien Al-Aqah Beach Resort**, Bidiya, **T** 092449000, www.lemeridien-alaqah.com. This is the only seriously modern-looking building currently standing on the East Coast and all 218 rooms face the sea. It's everything you'd expect of a luxury hotel in a beautiful location, and even the bathrooms come complete with rubber ducks! The Penguin Club is there to keep the children happy, while adults can enjoy sumptuous seafood at the Baywatch Restaurant, sit back and relax at the hotel's cinema, puff on shishas at the Beach Bar, or investigate the various packages offered by the Dive Centre.

A **Siji Hotel**, Fujairah, **T** 092232000, www.aldiarhotels.com. September is not the time to stay here if you're battling the blues about middle-age spread, since most of your fellow guests will be here for the Fujairah Classic International Body Building Championships. That aside, the lovely, elegant rooms with stripy yellow Georgian wallpaper and warm carpeting make this an attractive option for a night or two away from Dubai. Restaurant-wise, Asmak is good, with tasty Iranian fare served in a relaxing, marine-themed environment. Recommended.

B **Ritz Plaza**, Hamad bin Abdullah Rd, Fujairah, **T** 092222202, ritzplza@emirates.net.ae. There's no pool here, but the rooms are a decent size and adorned with modern Mediterranean prints complimenting the relaxed decor. A favourite with 'shady ladies'!

C **Holiday Beach Motel**, 8 km south of Dibba, **T** 092445540, **F** 092445580. The major attraction of this resort is the Maku Dive Centre, which accounts for most of the resort's mid-week customers. Run by a fabulous Swiss couple, Kurt and Margrit, they know the marine reserve here like the backs of their hands, and offer the most environmentally friendly snorkelling and diving options around. This and the proximity of Mount Dibba, where snorkellers will invariably see Green and Hawksbill turtles, black tip reef sharks and plenty more besides, makes it rather easier to overlook the shortcomings of the resort itself. Gunship-gray paintwork and dingy lighting do nothing to set the chalets off to their best advantage, but at least the relative scarcity of guests means you can usually shop around for the rooms with brighter paintwork and better views. Another bonus is that at high tide you can often see the turtles feeding on the rocks under the water just off the beach. Overpriced, especially when the rates rise during public holidays, although using the dive centre entitles you to a healthy reduction.

● *Maku Dive Centre, **T** 092445747, maku@emirates.net.ae, is the main attraction here.*

C **Sandy Beach Motel**, north of Bidiya, near the little village of Aqa'a, **T** 092445555, www.sandybm.com. Attractively landscaped gardens, a pool prettily fringed with trees and flowers, and a golden beach overlooking the nearby Snoopy Island, this is an understandably popular resort. While some hotel rooms benefit from floor to ceiling windows overlooking the beach, some of the chalets suffer from pink rooms and lighting that is way too dim. Overpriced, and the food isn't much to write home about, but it's still one of the better options if you want to flex your barbecuing muscles.

● *Sandy Beach Diving Centre, T 092445050, sbdiving@emirates. net.ae, operates from the grounds of the motel.*

C Oceanic Hotel, Khor Fakkan, **T** 092385111, www.oceanichotel. com. There's a pleasant, nautical feel to this four-star property, in keeping with the nature of its location. With six different views to be had from the various rooms, it's worth angling for one taking in the long sweep of the beach, or the jagged mountains. Al-Gargour Rooftop Restaurant is worth a visit for its fabulous 360 degree views. Snorkelling trips to Shark Island can be arranged, as can fishing jaunts, and it's a good platform from which to set out, primed with advice from the management, for a day of *wadi* bashing.

Divers Down, T 092370299, ddown@emirates.net.ae, is the attached dive centre.

D Breeze Motel, Kalba, **T** 092778877, breezemotel@hotmail. com. This is the only accommodation in town. Rarely busy, it's basic but very white, clean and rather sweet, with those ubiquitous market blankets swirling over the beds, and gold-nobbed clothes stands instead of wardrobes. There is a restaurant and a pool, but you'd better let them know if you want water in it!

D Fujairah Beach Motel, on the roundabout just before EPCO petrol station, Fujairah, **T** 092228111. Despite its name it has no beach frontage, though the location isn't bad. Decent sized rooms with cool, tiled flooring and very white walls alleviated by the odd mirror or print. A big pool is set in a rather bleak concrete yard and the whole place feels rather tired.

G Khor Fakkan Youth Hostel, on the roundabout by the Oceanic Hotel, Khor Fakkan, **T** 092370886, www.uaeyha.org.ae. Six clean if basic rooms, with two pairs of bunk beds and a minimum of wardrobe space in each. Don't expect any local knowledge from the proprietor, and know that the kitchen is woefully under-equipped by way of utensils. Booking ahead is advised for public holidays, when it does get busy.

Hatta and around

A **Hatta Fort Hotel**, **T** 048523211, hattafort@relaischateaux.com. Set in the foothills of the imposing Hajar Mountains, this is the only place to stay in Hatta, so it's lucky that it's such a gem. Built in 1981 and with no renovations since then, it has worn in extremely well, and the friendliness of the staff and high quality of service is immediately obvious. The 47 chalets are very comfortable and look out over rolling green gardens and the town beyond. The hotel often runs special offers that make a stay here exceptionally good value. Facilities are many and varied including clay pigeon shooting (the first range in the UAE); archery; mountain biking; mini golf and more. The restaurants serve up tasty fare while Ruben can whistle up some exceptional beverages behind the cocktail bar. Recommended.

Al-Ain

LL **Al-Maha Desert Resort**, 65 km southeast of Dubai along the Dubai-Al-Ain highway, **T** 033034222, www.al-maha.com. It doesn't get much better than this. Al-Maha is the last word in luxury – each suite has its own pool! – and sets new heights for quality of service – there's a three-to-one guest-to-coordinator ratio. Included in the price are two on-site activities per day, with the choice including a fascinating falconry display, camel trekking, horse riding, guided nature walks, wildlife safaris and more. There is one restaurant and one bar, catering exclusively to in-house guests, with all food included in the price of accommodation though drinks cost extra. But what really makes this place shine is its total dedication to conservation. And real conservation at that, rather than some half-hatched plans born of good intentions but marred by ignorance: there are small windows designed not to conduct heat, all water is recycling sooner or later, private vehicles are strictly prohibited to help ensure the 25 sq km of reserve and its wildlife is left as untrammelled and undisturbed as possible (which is gradually reverting to its original balanced condition). As of July 2004, only four tour companies (Arabian Adventures, Lama Tours, Travco and Alpha Tours) will be allowed within the confines of the reserve, thereby reducing the number of visitors by half from 300,000 to an altogether healthier 150,000. There is a hefty price tag for all of this. The privilege of staying in the most expensive hotel in Dubai comes in at Dhs5880 per night.

A **Al-Ain Rotana Hotel**, Mohammed bin Khalifa St, **T** 0375 15111, alain.hotel@rotana.net.ae. A plush hotel catering more for the Arab end of the market. South Seas themed Trader Vics is good for a meal out and a drink at the bar. The pool is circular and more for lolling in than swimming, but there's a reasonable gym for fitness fanatics.

A **Hilton Al-Ain**, Khalid bin Sultan Rd, **T** 037686666, alhilton@ emirates.net.ae. The oldest of the Al-Ain options, it's also the most tired, but plans are afoot to refurbish. The sports bar is a pleasant place to sit outside, overlooking the landscaped gardens.

B **Al-Ain InterContinental**, Khalid bin Sultan Rd, **T** 037686686, alain@interconti.com. Their new marketing mantra is the best kept secret in the Gulf and it really is a nice destination – very green chalet gardens and a pleasant relaxed atmosphere to lounge in makes for a nice break from Dubai.

The array of restaurants and cafés mirrors the melting pot of different cultures and nationalities that make up Dubai. Countless eateries allow for pretty much every taste and all budgets. Most of the more popular restaurants are in hotels, and these are usually the only establishments with alcohol licenses, so if an evening with not so much as a brandy snap is your idea of Purgatory, then it's wise to pick your venue with some degree of caution. That said, there are plenty of exceptional independent restaurants well worth sampling.

Cheapest are the Indian and Pakistani joints which churn out tasty fare. Costs can creep up significantly for more specialized international cuisine, although eating out in Dubai is normally excellent value. The one major exception is alcohol – which ramps up the price of your bill significantly. Many places throw open their doors at about 1800, although business tends to pick up nearer 2100.

Surprisingly, traditional recipes from Dubai itself remain almost completely unrepresented, with the newly opened Local House being the only truly authentic Emirati restaurant unearthed to date.

Eating codes

Price

♥♥♥	Over Dhs150
♥♥	Dhs50-150
♥	Under Dhs50

Prices refer to a three-course meal without drinks including taxes and service charge.

The Creek

Restaurants

It's generally true to say that you pay more for the atmosphere and experience than the food itself on one of the lunch and dinner cruises. However, as an overall Dubai experience, snaking along the Creek that has formed the cornerstone of Dubai's very existence for centuries shouldn't be missed. The more traditional option than those listed below is the wooden dhow, where dining under the open top deck is a wonderful way to spend a balmy evening – as long as you've remembered to bring a jacket.

♥♥♥ **Bateaux Dubai**, boarding near the British Embassy, Al Seef Rd, Bur Dubai, **T** 3371919, www.bateauxdubai.com. *1315- 1500 and 2000-2300. Map 2, C5, p250* Though not traditional, this is one of the better cruise options. A glittering glass and metal construction with capacity for around 350 people sees the Creek dining experience step up a gear. Offering lunch, sunset and dinner trips with a good variety of great Eastern and Western cuisine, it's no holes barred on the Al-Minsaf, which comes complete with fireworks and laser show.

♥♥ **Danat Dubai Cruises**, boarding near the British Embassy, Al Seef Rd, Bur Dubai, **T** 3511117, www.danatdubaicruises.com.

1245-1500, 2000-2300. Map 2, C5, p250 A couple of noteworthy cruise options are offered by this one outfit. The large catamaran provides a most untraditional and determinedly showy dining experience. Its superior speed means that instead of the usual Creek circuit you'll find yourself heading out to sea whilst watching the chefs at work. You can either let your tasty fare go down or work it off on the dance floor. Some have described the experience as being akin to that suffered on a cross-channel ferry!

Deira

Restaurants

¶¶¶ **Benihana**, Al-Bustan Rotana, Al-Garhoud, **T** 2820000. *Sat-Thu 1200-1445, daily 1700-2330. Map 2, E11, p251* One of the internationally popular chain of American-Japanese restaurants specializing in teppanyaki. The chefs are renowned for the show they put on as they rustle up tasty dishes at the station built into each table. There's also an attached sushi bar, with buffets every Saturday and Tuesday nights – all you can eat for Dhs99.

¶¶¶ **Blue Elephant**, Al-Bustan Rotana, Al-Garhoud, **T** 7054660, www.rotana.com. *1200-1500 and 1900-2330. Map 2, E11, p251* Opinion is divided as to the merits of this venue. Some maintain that its reputation tops even it's wildly popular namesake on London's Fulham Road, while others find the Thai fare faintly disappointing. Whichever side of the fence you fall on, it's essential to book ahead for a table here, especially for the Royal Thai buffets on Saturday and Tuesday nights. The setting is idyllic, complete with waterfall and fish-filled lagoon; the staff are most attentive and the air-conditioning most effective (take a jumper!). If it's Far Eastern fare you're after and money doesn't matter, give it a go.

¶¶¶ **Café Chic**, Le Meridien Dubai, Al-Garhoud, **T** 2824040. *Sat-Thu 1230-1445, daily 2000-2345. Map 2, E11, p251* This relatively small, French restaurant is a gem: lovely atmosphere, stylish decor, exemplary service, extremely good food and excellent variety – every dish that you try is different, and beautifully presented.

¶¶¶ **Fish Market**, InterContinental Dubai, Deira, **T** 2057333. *1300-1500 and 2000-2330. Map 2, B5, p250* A bit of an old favourite which is built around the concept of buying fish at a market stall (albeit a seriously ritzy one). Choose from the vast array of freshly caught fare, and tell the waiting chefs exactly how you want it cooked. The result is guaranteed heaven. While the decor is purposely simple, the views are fine. Prices range from high to astronomical; the wine list may bring tears to your eyes!

¶¶¶ **The Glasshouse**, Hilton Dubai Creek, **T** 2271111. *1230-1530, 1900-2400. Map 2, C6, p250* One of Gordon Ramsay's two enterprises here (Verre being the other), the food at this ultra modern hotel, as you'd expect, doesn't disappoint (though the service can be patchy). Particularly noteworthy are the interesting deals on beverages, such as the booze buffet: as long as you haven't finished eating, you can replenish your glass as many times as you like.

¶¶¶ **JW's Steakhouse**, JW Marriott, Deira, **T** 2624444. *1230-1500, 1900-2330. Map 2, A8, p251* A great and justifiable favourite with carnivores, this relatively small venue is a cosy, New York style steakhouse with a distinctly authentic and masculine air about it – high-backed leather chairs and enormous menus. Steak is obviously the main event, and my goodness, they're mouth-watering, but the menu also caters for a range of tastes, and the service can't be faulted. Recommended.

¶¶¶ **Kiku's**, Le Meridien Village, Al-Garhoud, **T** 2824040. *1230-1500, 1900-2330. Map 2, E11, p251* Good food, served in authentic Japanese surroundings with a variety of seating options including booths, tatami rooms, the sushi counter and teppanyaki station. Chef TeruYoshi Ito rustles up imaginative dishes with supremely fresh ingredients. If you know Japanese food, you can order pretty much anything here. Particularly recommended are the sesame soba noodle salad; the aigamo tataki and the green tea ice cream. When busy, service can be very slow.

¶¶¶ **Rodeo Grill**, Al-Bustan Rotana, Al-Garhoud, **T** 7054620. *Sat-Thu 1200-1500, daily 1900-2400. Map 2, E11, p251* The signature dish here is bison, but the 'Cut and Weigh' option is also popular, whereby if you guess the weight of your chosen prime beef within three grams you get it free! The sweet-toothed will be equally as content as the carnivore. The chocolate soufflé is quite superb, taking 25 minutes to whip up to perfection. With friendly staff and a decent setting, you can't go wrong. Dinner reservations are vital.

¶¶¶ **Seafood Market**, Le Meridien Village, Al-Garhoud, **T** 7022492. *1230-1500, 1930-2330. Map 2, E11, p251* One of the best places in town for fresh seafood, cooked the way you want it. On entering there's a fish tank embedded in the floor to walk over and a rock pool. Quality ranks high on the agenda here, with ice-packed counters overflowing with a wide variety of seafood such as New Zealand oysters, Boston, Indonesian and Omani lobsters, snow crabs from Australia as well as an impressive array of fresh fish from the local market, plundered twice daily. Helpful staff.

¶¶¶ **Verre**, Hilton Dubai Creek, **T** 2271111. *1900-2400. Map 2, C6, p250* Call off the search! The food and service at Gordon Ramsay's restaurant are unmatchable, making this a firm favourite. Decor is undeniably sophisticated and cutting-edge, so loved by some but leaving others cold. It's the booze that really does damage to the pocket, but the extensive wine list proves too much of a temptation for some. A great place for a special occasion.

★ **Best**

Mouth-watering food

- •Café Chic, p125
- •Verre, p126
- •Vu's Restaurant, p136
- •La Baie, p143
- •Celebrities, p143

🍴 **Boardwalk**, Creek Golf & Yacht Club, Al-Garhoud, **T** 2956000. *0800-2400. Map 2, F9, p251* Bags of atmosphere and the most stunning view of the Creek make this place a great favourite for an al fresco dining experience. The food can be average, although things have vastly improved recently and they do a very good line in fish 'n' chips (not cheap at Dhs46). Service is remarkably fast, but it's without doubt the ambience that draws the people back.

🍴 **The Cellar**, Aviation Club, Al-Garhoud, **T** 2829333. *1200-1600, 1900-2300. Map 2, F10, p251* There's a little of everything on this international menu, catering for mainly business lunches and family feasts. The food, while never sublime, is always of a high standard. The Cellar, split into two and with an ecclesiastical theme, is turning more into a wine bar with a recently extended wine list. Once a month it hosts a fantastic wine evening, offering a four-course meal with five wines. A sponsor or vintner normally gives a talk, so at Dhs150 it's one of the best value dinners in town for wine-buffs. A critizm might be that the atmosphere is a little dark.

🍴 **Handi**, Taj Palace Hotel, off Al-Rigga Rd, **T** 2232222. *1200-1500, 1900-2330. Map 2, B7, p251* Widely believed to offer the best Indian food in Dubai, Handi is hard to fault. It is inviting, the service is attentive and the food exceptionally good at surprisingly low prices. Alcohol does not feature on the menu, but a range of mocktails offer a refreshing alternative.

¶¶ **La Moda**, InterContinental Dubai, **T** 2057333. *1300-1500, 2000-0230*. *Map 2, B5, p250* The concept here is to provide the InterContinental standard of food at a slightly lower prices, and although price-wise they don't always succeed, the standard food is very good. There's a resident house band, usually African, playing popular, easy listening tunes, and the waiters all sport boiler suits, so look like F1 groupies! Its Japanese architecture means it has a somewhat surreal Japanese-Italian feel, and it's very popular, especially after 2100. The wine list is extensive and reasonable.

¶¶ **More!**, behind Lifco, Al-Garhoud, **T** 2830224. *0800-2200*. *Map 2, F11, p251* Based on the style of a large warehouse, More!'s atmosphere is very modern, yet wonderfully informal, with magazines on the tables and photoshoots often held at the back. The food is fusion – a mixture of Indian with European and North African – although despite there being daily specials it all begins to taste the same after a while, the cooking style not varying.

¶¶ **Sakura**, Taj Palace Hotel, off Al-Rigga Rd, **T** 2232222. *1200-1500, 1900-2330*. *Map 2, B7, p251* A wonderfully tranquil setting plays host to arguably the finest Japanese dining experience in Dubai. If you're after an alcohol-free evening of sushi, sashimi or teppanyaki, Sakura has a fabulous choice at very reasonable prices.

¶¶ **Shabestan**, InterContinental Dubai, **T** 2057333. *1300-1500 and 2000-2300*. *Map 2, B5, p250* Widely held to offer the best Persian food and hospitality in town, the largely Iranian clientele gives Shabestan a huge vote of confidence. With excellent cuisine all-round, it's the breads that stand out, they're wonderful. The entrance is warmly adorned with Persian carpets, and as you go in there's a fascinating array of Iranian pots and arty bits.

¶¶ **Sukhothai**, Le Meridien Village, Al-Garhoud, **T** 7022307. *1230-1445, 1930-2345*. *Map 2, E11, p251* For truly glorious food in an authentic, classically Thai setting, this is the place to come. Every evening from 2000-2345 you'll find yourself munching to the sounds of the kim (traditional Thai stringed instrument). For a lovely, peaceful, southeast Asian experience, you can't do much better than this. And if you like some of the individual artefacts, there's also a menu for the items you can buy. Thai Red Curry fanatics can rejoice in sending their taste buds into an absolute frenzy over this particular recipe – it is, quite simply, exquisite. And the Tom Yum has kicked other recipes of its kind into touch to run off with a well-deserved Prime Ministerial accolade. Highly recommended.

¶¶ **Topkapi**, Taj Palace Hotel, off Al-Rigga Rd, **T** 2232222. *1200-1600, 1900-2330. Map 2, B7, p251* Relatively unknown but well worth discovering, Topkapi offers top-notch Turkish and Arabic fare for a relative song. The lentil soup is done to perfection and the casseroled white beans with prawns also come highly recommended. Sit back and relax on one of the comfortable couches along the wall while listening to the oud player and congratulating yourself on your choice of venue. As with all Taj Palace restaurants, no alcohol is served here.

¶¶-¶ **Hatam Restaurant**, Baniyas Rd. *0730-0100. Map 3, E12, p253* It's easy to see why this buzzing little place is so popular. Excellent Iranian and Persian dishes in large portions and exceptionally well- priced. Most of the main dishes are Dhs20, while seafood options push the price up to nearer the Dhs70 mark.

¶ **Sarovar Restaurant**, 45 St, just off Sikkat Al-Khail, Gold Souk, **T** 2250020. *Map 3, C7, p253* A great place specializing in purely vegetarian North and South Indian dishes for under Dhs5, snacks, bhaji, puri, cheap sandwiches and Punjabi dishes. If you really like it you can get 30-day lunch coupons for Dhs140!

🍴 **Tehran Restaurant**, 18 St near 5 St, behind Carlton Tower, **T** 2292434. *1030-2400*. *Map 3, off E12, p253* Small, manically busy and wonderfully friendly, this place is brimming with colourful Iranian textiles and happy customers. The bread, baked in front of you, is delicious. Great kebabs cost between Dhs18-25.

Cafés

Al-Abra, next to Sabkha abra station, opposite the tip of Al-Sabkha Rd. *0630-0030*. *Map 3, F11, p253* More of a snackery than a café, expect to pay no more than Dhs15 for fried fish, shrimp or curry dishes. The shawarmas (from 1800 onwards) are mouth-watering, and just the thing for a speedy evening energy injection.

Café Mozart, 18 St, Deira, **T** 2216565. *0800-2300*. *Map 3, E12, p253* Tucked away in an alley between some of the towers over-looking the Creek, this quaint, slightly faded Viennese coffeehouse has a faithful following thanks to the selection of simply delicious mini pastries and biscuits.

Popeye, Baniyas Rd, **T** 2225557. *0800-0300*. *Map 3, off E12, p253* Most incongruously named when their speciality is caviar not spinach. Russian caviar sandwiches to be precise (Dhs25). Good, fresh fare including Russian favourites like Okroshka, Holodec and 'Kotleta from home'. Plenty of sandwiches and grilled meats, and a good line in humous starters.

Bur Dubai

Restaurants

🍴 **Thai Terrace**, Trade Centre Rd, opposite Spinneys, Karama, **T** 3969356. *Sat-Thu 1130-1430, 1930-2330, Fri 1900-2330*. *Map 2,*

D3, p250 Decor is very plain, simple and low key, so on walking in you can be forgiven for thinking the prices seem a bit steep, but the food is worth every dirham and then some. A real mix of people and nationalities flock here for quite possibly the best Thai food in the city. Around Dhs70 should cover the cost of two dishes.

Yakitori, Ascot, **T** 3520900. *1230-1400, 1830-2400.* *Map 2, C1, p250* A quick glance at the number of Japanese clients immediately confirms the quality and authenticity of the food. The menu is extensive, the food a treat, and a particular magnet for sushi-lovers, as the Japanese chef whistles up unusual and exquisite sauces for each type of fish.

Al-Khayaam Restaurant, Al-Baharna (25c) St, behind Al-Fahidi St, **T** 3519589. *0730-1330, 1830-0030.* *Map 2, B2, p250* The buffet lunch, daily except Friday, is cracking value at Dhs5, and the Indian music isn't quite as loud upstairs as down. All Indian dishes can be bought for Dhs10 or less, with only the Chinese options bumping up the price to Dhs15. Basic, but not bad.

Bhavna Deluxe Restaurant, 25c St, **T** 3530707. *Sat-Thu 0700-2330, Fri 0700-1130, 1330-2330.* *Map 2, B2, p250* A scruffy but popular, family-friendly vegetarian restaurant, also catering for vegans, where the window arrangement looking like a school canteen. Lunch buffet (1100-1500) and dinner buffet (1700-2330) cost only Dhs8 (Dhs10 for takeaway). The Chat Masala offerings are worth it if you're after a tasty snack.

Fatafeet, Al-Seef Rd, near the British Embassy, **T** 3979222, *1030-2400.* *Map 2, C5, p250* Superbly positioned overlooking the Creek, Fatafeet is also a truly outstanding ambassador for Egyptian fare. You won't find falafel, kebabs, humous and meze much better than this, and the pizzas and pastas are also good, as are the chicken shawamas. Evenings are particularly popular, with the sunset over the water and buildings on the opposite bank attracting an appreciative, shisha-puffing crowd settling down to enjoy the end of the day. Few places come so highly recommended.

♥ **Kwality**, opposite the Ascot, Khalid bin Al-Waleed Rd, **T** 3936563. *1300-1500, 2000-2345. Map 2, C1, p250* It might not look much and suffer from one of the most appalling names in the business, but if you can overcome these initial horrors to venture inside and order, it quickly becomes apparent why this place is such an enduring hit. Enormous portions of excellent Indian food from an extensive menu, delivered with 'kwality' service means it's wise to book ahead at weekends and holidays.

♥ **Local House**, Al-Fahidi St, Bastakia, **T** 3539997. *Sat-Thu 1000-2200, Fri 1300-2200. Map 3, off H8, p253* Opened in 2004, this, amazingly, is the city's only specifically Dubaian restaurant. Seating options include both traditional and contemporary alternatives – you can sit cross-legged in one of the *majlis*-like rooms or outside at tables in the old courtyard. Some dishes are simply fantastic (try the spicy chicken), while others fairly unexciting, but as an all-round authentic culinary experience, you just can't top it.

♥ **Saravna Bhavan**, Karama, almost opposite Lu Lu's, through Karama Park, **T** 3345252. *Sat-Thu 0730-1500, 1730-2300, Fri 0730-1130, 1330-1500, 1730-2300. Map 2, E4, p250* You can feed an army here for a pittance, and the food is always exceptional. This is the place to get some of the best masala dosa outside India. Even South Indians swear by it and compare it favourably to home.

Cafés

Basta Art Café, Al-Fahidi Rd, near Al-Musallah Roundabout, **T** 3535071. *Sat-Thu 1000-2000. Map 3, off H8, p253* This breezy courtyard café and shop offers a peaceful escape from the hustle of Bur Dubai's streets. On the edge of the quarter, this traditionally renovated setting (complete with its corner *majlis*) is a popular venue, concentrating on the healthier side of eating. Delicious juices, scrumptious salads, excellent soups, sandwiches, wraps and jacket potatoes are par for the course. Particularly recommended is their lemon-mint cocktail, a traditional old Dubaian drink.

XVA Gallery, 15a St, Bastakia, **T** 3535383. *Sat-Thu 0930- 2000. Map 3, H8, p253 See also p43* The vegetarian Arabic food prepared here is the stuff of dreams.

Oud Metha

Restaurants

₩₩₩ **Indochine**, Grand Hyatt Dubai, Umm Hurair, **T** 3172400. *1900-2330, Wed -Thu 1900-0100. Map 2, H8, p251* Authenticity is a word that rings with delightful clarity through every dish on this particular menu. The use of herbs, so prevalent in Vietnamese and Cambodian cooking, is both obvious and utterly delicious. The beef soup (in the set menu) won't disappoint; one could happily die for the steamed dumplings while the fresh rice paper rolls are equally capable of carting you off to heaven!

₩₩₩ **Peppercrab**, Grand Hyatt Dubai, Umm Hurair, **T** 3172222. *1900-1400. Map 2, H8, p251* Good food is a constant from a menu that's a mixture of mainly oriental-style seafood and other stir-fry items – try the rock lobster for a treat. The modern bamboo decor and candlelit terrace make it a relaxed, almost colonial venue, and waiters are friendly and knowledgeable, if the service is sometimes a little patchy. Rather pricey (largely because its seafood), it is nevertheless an understandably busy restaurant, popular with Arabs as well as westerners.

★ Tables with a view

Best

- Boardwalk, p127
- Dhow cruises, p123
- Vu's Restaurant, p136
- Beach Bar & Grill, p144
- Zheng He's, p146

Sphinx, Pyramids, Umm Hurair, www.pyramidsdubai.com, **T** 3244100. *1230-1500 and 1930-2330*. *Map 2, H6, p250* Even the most discerning foodies come out of this delightful contemporary European restaurant with few criticisms of these the melt-in-the-mouth dishes. The meat options are amongst the best in town and the quality of food is matched by the level of service and romantic ambience. The look is very turn of the century Grand Tour in Cairo.

Asha's, Wafi City, Umm Hurair, **T** 3240000. *1230-1500 and 1930-0030*. *Map 2, H6, p250* Named after the legendary singer Asha Bhosle, this is a pretty cool venue. The atmosphere and decor is a real pull: modern with mango coloured walls, funky black and white photos, contemporary fusion paintings, subtle lighting and cascading blue beads. The terrace is beautiful, too. Food-wise, it's a bit hit and miss; the modern Indian fusion dishes can be a little wild, so it's may be safer to stick to the more traditional fare. The wine list is not cheap, but there are interesting cocktails.

Carter's, Pyramids, Umm Hurair, www.pyramids dubai.com, **T** 3244100. *1200-0100 (later on weekends)*. *Map 2, H6, p250* See also p152 Extremely popular with the more casual element of the Western expats as a meet, eat and dance joint.

Khazana, near the American Hospital and Lamcy Plaza, **T** 3360061. *1230-1430, 1900-2330*. *Map 2, G5, p250* Famous chef

Sanjeev Kapoor's restaurant, this is a sure bet for authentic Indian fare with regional specialities. A treat to find somewhere this good when there are plenty of mediocre alternatives.

¶¶ **Medzo**, Wafi City, Umm Hurair, **T** 3240000, www.pyramids dubai.com. *1230-1500 and 1930-2330*. *Map 2, H6, p250* Medzo doubles as a relaxing lunchtime retreat from the shopping melee, and a chic, al fresco evening venue, with the breezy terrace just begging for the steady chink of wine glasses. Imaginative modern Mediterranean fare is the order of the day, beautifully presented and utterly delicious. Flipping across to Carter's, see p152, to soak up their live music is a good way to round the evening off.

¶¶ **Vintage**, Pyramids, Umm Hurair, www.pyramidsdubai.com, **T** 3240000. *1900-0200*. *Map 2, H6, p250* One of the more expensive wine bars, Vintage manages to attract a wide variety of clientele from the determinedly classy to the cheerfully casual. An exhaustive wine list may have something to do with this, although it could also be the chilled atmosphere, the mean line in nibbles or the ever popular fondue nights every Monday and Friday.

Café

Elements, Wafi City, Umm Hurair, **T** 3244252, www.elements-café. com. *1000-0100*. *Map 2, H6, p250* Industrial chic, with exposed pipes running along the ceiling, and a good stretch of terrace on which to sip their energizing juice mocktails. All sorts of food is served to tempt a modern palate – fusion cuisine with excellent organic salads and a good line in meat and fish dishes. Prices are at the heavier end of the café-scene, but these generous portions and searingly fresh ingredients are worth it. A trendy spot.

Sheikh Zayed Road

Restaurants

Le Classique, Emirates Golf Club, next to Hard Rock Café, **T** 3802222. *1200-1500,1930-2400. Map 1, C1, p248* This classy restaurant is one of the best in terms of food, with a wide menu which is mainly, but not exclusively, French. It boasts a very good wine list, but you have to shell out inordinately for the pleasure of sampling it. The strict dress code requires men to wear jacket and tie.

Al-Tannour, Crowne Plaza, **T** 3311111. *2030-0300. Map 4, G9, p255* At the cheaper end of the expensive bracket, this large restaurant is another popular option. The rather contrived decor can be overlooked in favour of the authentic Lebanese meals with live entertainment. The meze selection on the menu is staggering, and seriously good. Expect the night to be a late one, as the band starts around 2230, and the belly dancers shimmy on at midnight.

Spectrum On One, Fairmont Hotel, **T** 3118101. *1830-0030. Map 4, E10, p255* It's a bit pricey, but with eight different kitchens from all around the world, you'd be hard pressed to find a more comprehensive menu offering such consistently good food. The chefs run everything like clockwork, liaising over headsets with their peers at other stations to ensure each table's order is ready at the same time. Rather than be seated, a nice touch is that diners can have a wander around before picking your own spot. A busy, buzzy place, especially after 2100. Friday Moet brunch is good too.

Vu's Restaurant, Emirates Towers, **T** 3198771. *1230-1500, 1930-2400. Map 4, H10, p255* If you're looking for class, then look no further. With about the best service in town, a stunning view and sublime food, this is dining out in Dubai at its sophisticated best. Try the ravioli with amaretto for an unusual and exquisite taste. Yellow fin tuna comes highly recommended.

🍴 **Al-Nafoorah**, Emirates Towers Shopping Boulevard, **T** 3198760. *1230-1500, 2000-2330. Map 4, H10, p255* A real Lebanese goodie with a warm and welcoming interior and friendly service complemented by excellent authentic Lebanese food from an extensive menu. Al-Nafoorah's popularity is immediately obvious in its heaving tables. Try not to fill up too quickly on the delicious meze.

🍴 **Hoi An**, Shangri-La, **T** 3438888, www.shangri-la.com. *1930-0100. Map 1, C8, p249* Hoi An comes in for some mixed reports. Undoubtedly, its wonderfully authentic setting brings the colours and vibrancy of its namesake to Dubai, the food however – a combination of traditional Vietnamese dishes with a French twist – while leaving some people raving has left others quite cold.

🍴 **Marakech**, Shangri-La, **T** 343 8888. *1300-1500 and 2000-2400. Map 1, C8, p249* A classic and very regal Moroccan venue, Marakech has the canopied marble archway, Moroccan-made filigree doors, rustic lanterns and even a fountain to lend this romantic setting its authentic twang. The chef, Khadija Manar, trained at the world-famous Palais Royale in Rabat, has been shipped in to oversee the creation of fantastic dishes. It's

Eating and drinking

worth going for the beaten tagine pots alone, and the tagine pruneax, Moroccan mezze and knafa are out of this world. A great choice.

¶¶ **Mosaico**, Emirates Towers, **T** 3198754. *Open 24 hours. Map 4, H10, p255* Boasting the largest mosaic in the Middle East, with both inside and outside (by the pool) seating, this place serves up wonderful Italian food. Try the arrabiata for a spicy treat or the perfectly presented pizzas. If you're finding it hard to choose, go for three types of pasta on the one dish. Salads are also excellent.

¶¶ **Noodle House**, Emirates Towers Shopping Boulevard, **T** 3300000. *1200-2330. Map 4, H10, p255* Operating along similar lines as the UK's much beloved Wagamama's, only in the rather more upmarket setting of the unashamedly glitzy Emirates Towers, this is reputedly one of Sheikh Mohammed's favourite venues for an impromptu meal. Food is speedily served up at long tables where you'll find yourself flanked by strangers on every side.

¶¶¶ **Teatro**, Towers Rotana, **T** 3438000. *1130-1500, 1800-0200. Map 4, off H7, p255* A chic, fashionable place, dramatic in a theatrical sense. When the elevator doors open you step right into the restaurant. Movie greats dominate the walls while striking pillars of beads hang low from the ceiling, dividing the room into distinct areas. Depending on where you sit, you get a different (though consistently modern) experience. The food is fusion, and good, rustled up by a very creative chef, so there's something for everyone. A bit of a must.

¶ **Shakespeare & Co**, Kendah House, **T** 3311757. *0700-0130. Map 4, H8, p255* Fabulous. Just fabulous. Tasty main courses costing under Dhs50 are dished up in a wonderfully chilled setting characterized by big sofas, draughts, books and papers galore. The coffees, hot chocolates and juices slip down a treat too. There's also a popular terrace. Recommended.

Cafés

Café Barbera, Holiday Inn, Crowne Plaza, **T** 3310813. *0700-1200, Wed-Thu 0700-0100. Map 4, G9, p255* An unlikely venue with unassuming decor and a faintly old-fashioned feel, this place serves up steaming cups of truly exceptional coffee. You'd be hard-pressed to find better Italian coffee, and the coffee options on the menu alone are enough to rouse your caffeine cravings, both in terms of drinks and desserts.

Cosmo, UP Tower. *Map 1, C8, p249* A trendy but welcoming venue which serves as a stylish coffee shop by day with excellent lunchtime fare including good pizzas, shakes and a phenomenal salad bar, to a popular shisha hangout for locals and Lebanese by night. A great place to people watch, but not that cheap for a café.

Olive House, next to Starbucks, Sheikh Zayed Rd, **T** 3433110. *0900-2400. Map 4, H9, p255* Small and trendy, this is an easy place for lunch with its interesting manouking (fresh bread pizzas) and unusual dips. The salads are good and it's a great alternative to Starbucks if you want more than just coffee and muffins.

Jumeira and Satwa

Restaurants

🍴 **Coconut Groove**, Rydges Plaza Hotel, Satwa, overlooking the roundabout at the east end of Al-Dhiyafah Rd, **T** 3983800. *1200-1500 and 1900-2430. Map 4, B9, p255* Plush red seats set amongst some very dark wooden 'coconut trees' combine to create a very

Indian ambience. The authenticity is stepped up a notch with a menu packed with seriously good southern Indian and Sri Lankan food. They're slowly expanding to include more northern dishes. Popular with southern Indians in particular, a good line in baltis is also attracting the Brits, and the Friday buffet caters for the weekend crowd. It's more a group venue than a couple's joint.

🍴 **Four Seasons**, Rydges Plaza Hotel, **T** 3982222. *1200-1500, 1900-2400. Map 4, B9, p255* A recent rethink has improved the layout and food here immeasurably. With considerably fewer tables there is now plenty of space between them and not so much neck-craning is needed to appreciate the views from this ninth floor venue. The setting sun behind Jumeirah Mosque makes for a great spectacle, and the appalling driving on the roads below usually means there'll be at least one accident throughout your meal!

🍴 **Il Rustico**, Rydges Plaza Hotel, **T** 3982222. *1200-1500, 1800-2400. Map 4, B9, p255* A good cheapish option. Wood is imported from Italy to ensure the wood-fired pizza oven churns out a continuously excellent range of authentic tasting pizzas. Otherwise, it's worth opting for the fish dishes on the extensive specials menu. The calamari starter, slightly spicy is always good, never greasy, and they have a reasonable 1.5 litre bottle of Stellenbosch red, Versus, which is cheap as chips and great to knock back with pizza.

🍴 **Reem Al Bawadi**, Jumeirah Beach Rd, next to HSBC Bank, **T** 3947444. *1200-0200, Fri buffet 1300-1700. Map 1, B6, p248* This is an absolute cracker. Not only is it one of the very few places in town where you'll see Arab families out enjoying each others' company rather than sitting with their male friends or colleagues, but the Lebanese food is exceptional. You can't go wrong with the cold mezze and mixed grill, and the Tikka with yoghurt is a well-deserved show-stopper. Temperatures are kept fairly cool, so as long as you've brought along a jacket of sorts you'll be able to sit back and soak up the atmosphere, listening to traditional music and gazing through an increasingly smoke-sweetened cloud at your fellow diners enjoying their evening shisha. Recommended.

🍴 **Al-Mallah Cafeteria**, Al-Dhiyafah Rd, Satwa, **T** 3984962. *0700-0300. Map 4, B8, p255* Cheap and cheerful, with tantalizing smells issuing from the kitchens pretty much all day, you might have to fight for a table as the evening rush gets underway and people sit to relax over their meals and drink in the Al-Dhiyafah street-scene.

🍴 **Bu Qtair Cafeteria**, follow 41a St off Jumeirah Beach Rd, and turn right when you come to the corniche. *Map 1, B4, p248* You'll see a few dhows on your right next to which is a ramshackle portacabin with a generator hammering away nearby and a motley collection of plastic tables scattered on the sand outside around which people will be tucking into whatever has just been freshly caught. The chances are there won't be another westerner in sight. Go inside and point at whatever takes your fancy, and it will be fried and plonked down in front of you with little ceremony and even less cutlery. Fantastic, but they're developing the area, so be quick.

🍴 **Chinese Kitchen**, near Union Coop, Jumeira, **T** 3943864. *Sat-Thu 1200-1500, 1800-2400, Fri 1330-1500, 1800-2400. Map 1, B6, p248* A cracking little place. Truly excellent sauces, colourful surroundings and friendly staff make for a top night out at a very reasonable price. This is arguably the best value Chinese joint in town, with the menu featuring a good array of traditional favourites.

🍴 **Pars Iranian Kitchen**, Al-Dhiyafah Rd, Satwa, **T** 3984000. *Sat-Thu 1000-0100, Fri 1800-0100. Map 4, B8, p255* The exceptional food is on a 'pars' with the very atmospheric surroundings. You can sit outside on raised, carpeted and cushioned platforms, watching the world go by – and the world on Thursday and Friday nights is always particularly interesting along Al-Dhiyafah Road.

For those who find decision-making difficult when confronted with a lengthy menu, Pars Mixed Grill is excellent – they bring you the little barbecue on which rests the various different types of grill.

Ravi's, near Al-Satwa roundabout, **T** 3315353. *0500-0300. Map 4, C9, p255* Such a basic venue might not at first seem tempting, but the habitually crowded tables are a dead giveaway that this 24-hour place is a real gem. Serving up enormous helpings of delicious Pakistani dishes with the odd Chinese option thrown in for good measure, Ravi's chefs couldn't be friendlier, the waiters more obliging or the food any better value. A legend amongst locals.

Cafés

Lime Tree Café, Jumeirah Beach Rd, next to THE One, **T** 3498498. *0730-2000. Map 4, C4, p254* This popular green haven is a great hit with the expat crowd, dishing out delightful, ever-changing deli-style foods including quiches, wraps, fritatas and salads as well as some rather addictive gingerbread cookies. The upstairs terrace, looking out over Jumeira, is a great favourite with the regulars, but you have to be quick to bag a seat. Rotten coffee though.

The Southwest

Restaurants

Al-Mahara, Burj Al-Arab, Umm Suqeim, **T** 3017777. *1230- 1500 and 1900-2400. Map 1, B3, p248* 007 would feel right at home guiding a beautiful girl into this elegant restaurant, navigating the signature aquarium (complete with sharks and eels) and being unobtrusively cocooned from the rest of the world by an army of formal staff. As you'd expect, the largely seafood menu is exciting, sublimely cooked, exquisitely presented and utterly delicious. Such delights have their price. If caviar is your preferred starter and wine a must, then you could be looking at over Dhs1000 per person.

🍴 **BiCE**, Hilton Jumeirah Beach, Marsa Dubai, **T** 3991111. *1200-1500, 1900-2400. Map 1, off B1, p248* Superb. This modern Italian features very minimalist decor, and its creative menu is well regarded amongst foodies. Prices are pretty steep on some dishes, but not all. This place ranks high on Dubai's list of gems.

🍴 **Celebrities**, One&Only Palace, Al-Sufouh, **T** 3999999. *0800-1030, 1900-2330. Map 1, B1, p248* A very old school place: heavy white table cloths, silver cutlery, subdued lighting and a lovely setting. Its anti-room/bar is beautiful. It's the kind of restaurant you'd imagine finding at the Dorchester – all old fashioned service and dishes like beef Wellington on the menu. The food certainly won't disappoint as it's one of the few serious restaurants in Dubai when it comes to truly excellent food.

🍴 **Eauzone**, One&Only Arabian Court, Al-Sufouh, **T** 3999999. *1930-2400. Map 1, B1, p248* A really smashing place, in terms both of atmosphere and food. Cuisine is Thai, and largely seafood oriented, although for a meaty delight try the chicken on lemongrass skewers – phenomenal! And since it's right on the beach, you can't really top the venue, especially if you manage to get one of the only three tables on the verandah.

🍴 **La Baie**, Ritz-Carlton, Masa Dubai, **T** 3994000. *Mon-Sat 1900-2300. Map 1, off B1, p248* The view from the terrace is almost tropical, while inside it's modern. La Baie prides itself on being old school French, and it succeeds in spades with silver platters, heavy silver cutlery, ornate crystal glasses and jacket and tie dress code. The food is delightfully imaginative and seriously good. One of the few properly top-notch eateries here, it is also cripplingly expensive.

� **Al-Khayal**, Jumeirah Beach Hotel, **T** 4068181. *Thu-Fri 1230-1430, daily 2000-2400.* *Map 1, B4, p248* Dripping in gold and very Lebanese, Al-Khayal boasts excellent food and a great view of the Burj, especially if you can grab a window table. It comes into its own as the evening draws on, and you can expect huge (and rather pricey) portions to accompany your view.

� **Anar**, Madinat Jumeirah, **T** 3686505. *1300-1530, 1930-2330.* *Map 1, B6, p248* Memorable, both in terms of food and setting, for all the right reasons. While the tables spill out of the restaurant onto the bank of the canal, a meal here feels like a true Persian experience; the bread is exceptional, hot from the oven, and the cuisine is based around the grill. Try the signature dish: lamb shank, slow-baked for many hours in various vegetables and Iranian spices and served with green rice (mixed with dill and broad beans) or the chicken buried in barberry rice. Reservations only.

� **Beach Bar & Grill**, One&Only Palace, Al-Safouh, **T** 3999999. *1900-2330.* *Map 1, B1, p248* *See also p114* This place could well be the bees knees – if only the staff would stop telling you it's fully booked when the fact is that if you just pitch up you'll often find plenty of empty tables. During the winter the terrace is a great place to sit and wash down some of the superb seafood on offer (try the oysters – exceptionally good and very reasonably priced). It's a good lunch option, when you can fully appreciate the spectacular view before you. The service could be better.

� **Carnevale**, Jumeirah Beach Hotel, Umm Suqeim, **T** 4068181. *1230-1430, 1900-2330.* *Map 1, B4, p248* A popular, intimate Italian restaurant, where the spotlight's turned on the seafood dishes and the wine – it's a bit of a well-kept secret that if you just ask for the wine of the month and you'll usually get something decent for good value. Definitely worth a try.

¶¶ **Fusion**, Le Royal Meridien, Marsa Dubai, **T** 3995555.
1900-2400. Map 1, off B4, p248 If you like your food searingly hot,
then make your way here. Dishes come extremely spicy, even
when you say medium. Thai, Malay and Indonesian fusion dishes
are beautifully prepared, and the minimalist southeast Asian decor
blends tradition with contemporary most effectively. Great service
and nice atmosphere help make this a place to try.

¶¶ **La Parilla**, Jumeirah Beach Hotel, **T** 3480000. *1300-1500,
2000-2300. Map 1, B4, p248* Its tango dancers make this place
stand out as the only western restaurant with entertainment while
you're eating. It's a great spectacle, with two shows every night,
and that's not all it has to recommend itself; the service is good,
but, being an Argentinean, better yet are the steaks, so
meat-eaters will find La Parilla a safe bet for a great night out.

¶¶ **Maria Bonita**, near Spinneys, Umm Suqeim, **T** 3955576. *1230-
2330. Map 1, C6, p248* Set up by a Mexican pilot fed up with Tex-
Mex and keen to introduce the real thing to Dubai, this is the only
authentic Mexican here. Cheap and cheerful, this restaurant is a real
treat, where you can actually get proper *masa harina tortillas*. In fact,
all the ingredients are flown in from Mexico and prepared according
to traditional recipes. The spicy salsa is a must with the limitless,
freshly fried tostaditos. Veggies are well catered-for too. So good is it,
that you won't miss the lack of an alcohol license.

¶¶ **Tagine**, One&Only Palace, Al-Sufouh, **T** 3999999. *Tue-Sun
1900-2330. Map 1, B1, p248* The first authentic Moroccan in town,
Tagine has been justifiably popular for quite a while. There's more
competition now, but it hasn't thinned the flow of traffic. A singer
and oud-player provide the background music, and the waiters are
also a bit of a spectacle when pouring coffee from improbable
heights. Service is good, and the atmosphere very Moroccan.

¶¶ **Zheng He's**, Mina A'Salam, Umm Suqeim, **T** 3668888. *1200-1500, 1900-2330*. *Map 1, B3, p248* Zheng's exquisite terrace overlooks the peaceful canals of the luxurious Madinat Jumeirah, but while the view never fails to please the eyes, the expert chefs have to work rather harder to satisfy the palate (and not always with guaranteed success). Service, however, will not disappoint, and as a 'Dubai experience', Zheng He's comes highly recommended.

Cafés

The ONE café, Jumeirah Beach Road, next to Jumeirah Mosque, **T** 3456687. *Sat-Thu 0900-2130, Fri 1400-2130*. *Map 4, B5, p254* Trendy place for coffee, tea, juice and snacks, also offering a decent line in salads. Criticism has been levelled at it for trying to do too much for such a small kitchen, food-wise, and with some justification. While it's fun because you're in the trendiest home interiors shop in town, the Afternoon Tea wouldn't leave a gaping hole if removed from the menu.

Sho Cho's, Dubai Marine Resort & Spa, **T** 3461111. *1900-0300*. *Map 4, B4, p254* Seriously good Japanese option known for its sushi and screamingly trendy to boot, this is where you'll find the bold and the beautiful on any given night of the week. Venue-wise it's hard to top, with its outside bar and sea views and it's a fabulous choice for a fancy cocktail while leaning nonchalantly against the bar.

Around Dubai

Sharjah and around

¶ **Sanobar Restaurant**, near Sheikh Sultan Al-Awal Rd, **T** 065283501. *Sat-Thu 1200-2400, Fri 1300-2400*. Seriously good seafood dishes cost a mere pittance compared to what you'd expect to fork out for similar fare in Dubai. There's a very relaxed character to the place, almost like a much-loved local.

The East Coast

⑂ **Al-Meshwar**, flanked by KFC and Pizza Hut on Hamad bin Abdullah Rd, Fujairah, **T** 092231113. *0800-0100*. A favourite here, this Lebanese restaurant has been built to resemble an old ruin. Without quite hitting the mark in the antiquity stakes, it's nevertheless a relaxed affair, offering good food at tables spread out around a central fountain – a feature which helps draw eyes away from the unexciting view out of the windows.

⑂ **Irani Pars Restaurant**, on the roundabout nearest the port, Khor Fakkan, **T** 092387787. *1000-2300*. Shrouded in 10 years worth of creeper, this is one of the better eateries in town, dishing up good, Arabic food in a variety of fried, grilled and kebabed meat and fish dishes. Upstairs offers the best views of the sea.

⑂ **Sadaf Persian Restaurant**, on the corniche by the Hilton roundabout, Fujairah, **T** 2223343. *1200-2400*. This air-conditioned haven is split in two, with a family section tucked away behind a fake rock wall. The venue is pleasant, as is the food – kebabs are ever-popular, and for desert the faloudeh goes down a treat.

⑂ **Taj Khorfakkan**, behind the souk, Khor Fakkan, **T** 092225995. *0700-2330*. This is a nice, fairly new restaurant with traditional Indian decor, serving Indian along with Arabic and western dishes. Very reasonably priced, tasty fare.

⑂ **Taj Mahal Restaurant**, diagonally opposite Union National Bank, Hamad bin Abdullah Rd, Fujairah, **T** 092225225. *Sat-Thu 1200-1545, 1900-2400, Fri 1300-1530, 1900-2400*. Colourful textiles complement the warm, rustic hues, creating a fine environment in which to sit back and enjoy good service and excellent Indian fare.

Al-Ain

♦ **Arabesque**, InterContinental, **T** 037686686. *0630-1100, 1230-1530, 1930-2300*. A vast improvement on its predecessor Cafe Med, Arabesque has a shisha garden attached so you can eat in then go out and loll around smoking strawberry shisha or whathaveyou under the trees by the fountains. Attentive staff help make the place, and the food's pretty good, too – try the lamb soup with saffron.

♦ **Horse and Jockey**, InterContinental, **T** 037686686. *1230- 1530, 1800-0130*. Serves no-nonsense pub grub including great bangers and mash. The open air terrace is a good option if you don't fancy the smoky British pub interior.

♦ **Luces**, InterContinental, **T** 037686686. *1930-0100*. Italian restaurant with its trendy (for Al-Ain!) modern decor showcasing a citrus orange and scrubbed steel look. As well as the dining area there's a nice bar, and you can wander next door to Shooters for a game of pool if the mood takes you. Food is tasty and well-presented.

♦ **The Wok**, InterContinental, **T** 037686686. *Sat-Thu 1230-1500, 1930-2300*. Overlooking the pool, this is an intimate, dimly lit place which lately had a new, very feng shui makeover, making its decor quite refreshing. Good food, too.

♦ **Hiltonia**, Hilton, **T** 037686666. *1000-2300*. This sports bar/ restaurant boasts a faster, better service than the poolside eaterie at the InterContinental. A pleasant outdoor area near the faux Japanese river and bridge, as well as the added attraction of the big slide and boat in the kids pool make it a good family option.

The great thing about Dubai is that the social scene effortlessly incorporates pretty much everybody and age is no barrier – it's very much a twenties to sixties landscape. There's a good concentration of bars and clubs in the beach hotels and on Sheikh Zayed Road, although there are plenty more sprinkled all over the city, so you're never far from a decent night out. Bur Dubai and parts of Deira tend to be more rustic, rough and ready, whereas the hotel hotspots have a certain touristy flavour, and the Sheikh Zayed Road venues tend to pull in the expats.

Chart music is enduringly popular, but live bands and theme nights mean there's a decent mix. The best piece of advice to abide by is pick your night; the trick is to be in the right place on the best night for your preferences. Talk to the hotel concierges if you're stuck, or check out the listings magazines, see p228. Another thing to be aware of is that the night scene is very much later than you'd expect – things don't really get going until at least 2300, so Dubai is a great haunt for night owls.

Deira

Bars

Champions, JW Marriott, **T** 2624444. *1200-0200, Fri 1800-0200. Map 2, C7, p251* A bloke's place: pubby and sporty, with plenty of sporting memorabilia adorning the walls. The atmosphere is nice and relaxed, food is good, and lunchtime specials are excellent value. Thursday ladies nights are popular.

Jules Bar, Le Meridien Dubai, Al-Garhoud, **T** 2824040. *1100-0300. Map 2, E11, p251* Well-known and much feted amongst those whose party hats are still firmly in place, this American-themed bar consistently attracts a large and very mixed crowd. While it's certainly not the food they come for, you'd be hard pressed to find a more fun-loving, permissive crowd enjoying what's guaranteed to be a great night out.

The Pub, InterContinental Dubai, **T** 2057333. *1300-1500 and 2000-2330. Map 2, B5, p250* Popular with expats yearning for home, this is one of the closest things you can get to a traditional British pub in Dubai, complete with dartboard. It's no cosy country pub, though, it's more like one found near Victoria Station, London.

QD's, Dubai Creek Golf & Yacht Club, Al-Garhoud, **T** 2956000. *1800-0200, closed in summer. Map 2, F9, p251* Seriously lovely in the winter, this idyllic setting by the Creek is the perfect place for chatting over wines, beers, cocktails, sheesha, snacks or pizza. But you can forget it as the onset of summer sees the temperatures soar, making this outside venue unbearable. There's a Caribbean feel, with waiters sporting Hawaiian shirts, and a Calypso band.

Clubs

The Premiere, Hyatt Regency, **T** 2091333. *2200-0300. Map 1, B11, p249* The good old days for this venue were a very long time ago. Untouched by decorators for almost as long as anyone can remember, it has become a late night hang-out for a decidedly predatory crowd, prowling about the room to chart toppers.

Terminal, Millennium Airport Hotel, Al-Garhoud, **T** 2821844. *2200-0300. Map 2, E11, p251* This dark, grungy, dingy place is THE new club venue. There's little consistency to its constant array of theme nights, so there tends to be a different scene each night. Despite ridiculously expensive drinks, Terminal pulls them in.

Bur Dubai

Clubs

Rock Bottoms, Regent Palace Hotel, **T** 3963888. *0700-0300. Map 2, D3, p250* This is a Dubai institution, wildly popular and known for its fantastic (chart-based) music and live bands, though people do say the name sums it up! It's the one place in town that is guaranteed to be heaving after 0100 when elsewhere all is quiet. Does a good shawarma to address those late-night hunger pangs and addresses other pangs with its reputation as a pick-up joint.

Oud Metha

Bars

Carter's, Pyramids, Umm Hurair, **T** 3244100. *Daily 1200-0100, Thu and Sun 1200-0300. Map 2, H6, p250* Enduringly popular, this is a trendy joint cum wine bar, where the (very good) band is perched above the bar playing the latest chart hits daily except Sunday – it's amazing the staff aren't deaf. The modern decor and big, comfortable seating, along with a terrace and tasty Friday brunch, make it a cool and relaxed hang-out, particularly buzzing on Sunday and Tuesday ladies nights (from 2200-2400).

Ginseng, Wafi City, Umm Hurair, **T** 3248200. *Daily 1900-0200, Thu and Fri 1900-0300. Map 2, H6, p250* Small and very trendy, it's worth dressing up for a night here. The guest DJs are usually very good. Cocktails are two for one before 2200 on Tuesdays, Happy hour (Wednesdays to Mondays from 1900-2100) cocktails cost Dhs19, and every Saturday there's dim sum and wine for Dhs99.

Rooftop Gardens, enter through Carter's, Wafi City, Umm Hurair, **T** 3244100. *Oct-May, Fri and Sun 2000-0200. Map 2, H6, p250* Offering an unbeatably chilled out night during the cooler months, Friday night is 'Peanut Butter and Jam night', where resident DJs and live acts perform to an appreciative audience draped over enormous bean-bags (with their barbecued food and booze). Sunday movie nights have a similar laid-back appeal with popcorn, pizza and hotdogs complementing the drive-in feel. Recommended.

Seville's, Wafi City, Umm Hurair, **T** 3247300, 1200-0200. *Thu and Fri 1200-0300. Map 2, H6, p250* A very nice tapas bar with a great ambience and good tunes, though the service leaves a lot to be desired. The upstairs roof terrace is lovely in winter, very popular and the perfect place to sip their expertly concocted margaritas. Ladies nights, Tuesdays 2100-2400, Fridays 1800-2000, are ever popular, and Happy hour reigns daily from 1800-2000 except Fridays, 1500-1800.

Vintage, Pyramids, Umm Hurair, **T** 3240000. *Fri-Wed1800-0100, Thu 1600-0200. Map 2, H6, p250* Fabulous, especially for fondue-

★ **Cracking cocktails**

 B e s t

lovers. This cheese and wine bar is quite small and cosy, sprinkled with sofas and coffee tables, high tables and bar stools. With such a range of wines, champagne and cheeses on offer, there's no room for main courses on the menu, but you can order in from other restaurants. The Monday and Friday promos are a dream – Dhs125 for cheese fondue and a bottle of wine per couple.

Clubs

Jimmy Dix, Movenpick Hotel Bur Dubai, Oud Metha, **T** 3368800. *1200-0300. Map 2, G5, p250* Richly decorated interiors and subdued lighting make this place a sort of classier version of Rock Bottoms, with equally good, crowd-pulling R&B music and a live band that starts at 2200 Sunday to Friday. Dishing up tasty Tex Mex fare makes it a good evening venue if you want to bop without stopping. After 0100 it's just heaving. The best nights are Tuesdays, Wednesdays and Thursdays. Happy hour runs daily from 1200-2200 with 30 per cent off all drinks. Ladies night on Tuesdays and Sundays.

The Lodge, Al-Nasr Leisureland, Oud Metha, **T** 3379470. *0900-0330. Map 2, G5, p250* The most famous drinking hole in Dubai, and an institution since its birth in the 1970s, was closed in the late 1990s for breaking the Ramadan curfew but has now reopened much to everyone's delight. It's huge and attracts a

Bars and clubs

predominantly western crowd focused on out-and-out clubbing rather than eating. It is absolutely heaving on Thursdays.

MIX, Grand Hyatt Dubai, Umm Hurair, **T** 3172570. *2100-0300. Map 2, H8, p251* This is a truly enormous venue, so can be completely bizarre on a quiet night. Stretching out over three levels, with an island bar, bags of dancing and sitting space and even a cigar bar, there's also a sound-proofed live music room. Popular with the wealthier Indian and Lebanese contingent, it also attracts a wide mix of people happy to see this new addition to the clubbing arena. Music tends to be R&B, house and Arabic.

Planetarium, Wafi City, Umm Hurair, **T** 3240072. *2300-0300, closed Sat and Mon. Map 2, H6, p250* It may well look in need of a little cosmetic surgery, but thanks to its continuous string of fantastic international DJs, club acts and its almost daily theme nights, it remains a top spot. Sundays and Fridays are R&B nights, Tuesdays and Wednesdays ladies nights, and it's usually house music on Thursdays. A strict door means you'll still need to dust down your smarter clubbing apparel to get in, and single guys may have a problem getting in if not already in mixed company.

Sheikh Zayed Road

Bars

The Agency, Emirates Towers, **T** 3198785. *Sat-Thu 1230-0100, Fri 1500-0100. Map 4, H10, p255* A fantastic wine bar with a very relaxed atmosphere despite its fairly strictly upheld smart-casual dress code. They stock one of the biggest ranges of wine in the UAE; 50 different kinds are sold by the glass and you can try a tray of four country-specific 'flights' if you're undecided on what to choose. The snacks and nibbles are great, with favourites including chorizo and warm potato salad, chicken liver pâté and cheese fondue.

Cigar Bar, Fairmont Hotel, **T** 3325555. *1800- 0200. Map 4, E10, p255* All dark browns, discreet lighting and wonderfully comfortable leather chairs, this is a peaceful retreat for rookies and expert cigar aficionados alike; the expert staff can sniff out the perfect cigar for anyone from one of the biggest and most exclusive selections in Dubai. Cognacs (including Louis XIII at Dhs700 a shot), cocktails and scotch are the accompaniment favourites. Non-smokers can enjoy the soulful music and serene atmosphere just as much due to the air conditioning which keeps the air miraculously fresh.

Harry Ghatto's, Emirates Towers, **T** 3198796. *1930-0300. Map 4, H10, p255* The number one karaoke spot in town, it's small, noisy and usually packed after 2200. Best to dine out first, as the food is decidedly mediocre but you can't beat the atmosphere if it's a mic and an audience you're after. Excellent staff, limited number of tracks; an amusing night out.

Long's Bar, Towers Rotana, **T** 3438000. *1200-1600 1900-0200. Map 4, off H7, p255* Cheers meets Raffles in Singapore. With possibly the longest bar in the Middle East, this underground venue with a dance area and DJs is younger and trendier than most and enormously popular, especially on Tuesday and Wednesday nights (ladies nights) and during Ramadan.

Piano Bar, Crowne Plaza, **T** 3311111. *1800-0200. Map 4, G9, p255* Here the air is permeated with the faint hint of expensive cigars and subtle notes of blues and jazz. Dark and dressed in deep blue, this is a seriously nice place which attracts an older European and high-class Arab crowd that knows its cigars, scotches and cognacs. Clifford, a barman here for 10 years, adds to the intimate ambience.

Scarlett's, Emirates Towers, **T** 3198768. *1230-0300. Map 4, H10, p255* One of the most consistently popular bars/clubs in town, appealing to a broad range of ages from 20 to 60 years, this is a down-to- earth oasis in the middle of Emirates Towers' high-nosed designer shops. Great for either a lively meal or a full-on boogie. Tuesdays (ladies night) are particularly pumping.

Trader Vic's, Crowne Plaza, **T** 3311111. *1230-1500, 1800-0200. Map 4, G9, p255* This place is known for its fantastic cocktails, the choice of which is as great as the damage you're likely to inflict on yourself by overdosing on such masterpieces. It's wonderfully warm and lively, serving up good food from a limited menu. If you sit too near the band, your ears will ring all night. Happy hour, with half-price cocktails, runs from 1800-2000.

Vu's Bar, Emirates Towers, **T** 3198783. *1230-1500, 1930-2400. Map 4, H10, p255* Dark, stylish and smart, the views from this heady height depend entirely on where you sit and can be obscured by steel supports, so try to grab a table by the window. The drinks are pricey and the dress code is smart.

Clubs

Amnesia, Hard Rock Café, **T** 3992222. *2200-0300. Map 1, C1, p248* Still retaining the aquatic theme from its Atlantis days, not to mention its thumping Franco-Arab tunes, it's a popular haunt for young Arabs to people-watch, hoping to throw off their single status, if only for a night.

Tangerine, Fairmont Hotel, **T** 3325555. *2000-0300. Map 4, E10, p255* With torch-lit rich reds and sofas tucked into curtained alcoves, this is atmospheric venue is seriously cool. Prices are fairly stiff, but the cocktails are excellent and while there's no live music, they run about three promoter nights a week to keep the scene fresh. It's been likened to a mini Kasbar and is arguably one of the better club options.

Zinc, Crowne Plaza, **T** 3311111. *1900-0300.* *Map 4, G9, p255* Metallic and hip, with long queues and a guaranteed crowd (including lots of cabin crew!). The door policy is very strict – no trainers or flip-flops – and the music is pretty much R&B, seventies and chart dance tracks.

Jumeira and Satwa

Bars

Aussie Legends, Rydges Plaza Hotel, Satwa, **T** 3982222. *Daily 1500- 0300, Thu 1200-0300.* *Map 4, B9, p255* A really funky option, with excellent bar food and an all-round fantastic atmosphere, especially on their Monday quiz nights, or during Thursday's Happy hour, which stretches from 1300-1900. It's an old favourite in Dubai, especially with the Aussie expat crowd.

Boston Bar, Jumeirah Rotana, Satwa, **T** 3455888. *1200-0200.* *Map 4, A7, p255* Not unlike Cheers with its island bar, it used to be THE place to hang out until it's sister, Long's Bar, opened and rather stole the show, leaving Boston a little old and jaded now. Still, its friendly service and the pull of Dubai's longest Happy hour (1200-2000!) means it's still great value and worth testing. Tuesday and Thursday nights are ladies nights.

Boudoir, Dubai Marine Beach, Jumeira, **T** 3455995. *1930- 0300.* *Map 4, B4, p254* Very sexy and totally Moulin Rouge with every-thing red, velvety and positively screaming 'stroke me'. The bouncers are pretty snotty, but once you're past them it's a great (if wildly expensive) cocktail lounge, particularly busy on Tuesday

Best

Dance dives

- Carter's, p152
- Jimmy Dix, p154
- The Lodge, p154
- Planetarium, p155
- Scarlett's, p157

and Friday nights (free champagne for the ladies). The gals do well on Wednesday and Thursday nights, too, with free cocktails and vodka.

Sunset Bar, Jumeirah Beach Club, **T** 3445333. *1900-2200. Map 1, B7, p249* Extremely popular, this is another great place from which to watch the day draw to a close. Set on a particularly lovely private beach, boasting great sea views, comfortable seating (quickly snapped up), mellow music and a decent line in shisha, if this is where you plonk yourself down, you're unlikely to stir for quite some time.

Clubs

The Alamo, Dubai Marine Beach & Spa, Jumeirah Beach Rd, Jumeira, **T** 3493455. *1200-0300. Map 4, B4, p254* Enduringly popular, though nobody can quite tell you why. English footie players come here, Rod Stewart has played a few numbers... It's always busy, but there's nothing special in terms of ambience, price or anything. Music covers the full range from the 1960s onwards, and there's a DJ/live band Sundays to Thursdays. A great place for women; ladies nights are Sundays, Tuesdays and Thursdays, and on Wednesdays from 2100-0200 they get free champagne.

The Southwest

Bars

Barasti Bar, Le Meridien Seyahi, Al-Sufouh, **T** 3993333. *0900-0200.*
Map 1, B1, p248 Definitely one of the nicest places for winter sundowners. It has been enlarged since the days it was patronized by
fishermen, and there's a scratch band that play Simon & Garfunkle
and the like, lending the place a wonderfully mellow air. A simple
menu offers good food and although the service isn't great things
should improve thanks to an excellent new manager. Happy hour,
with 30 per cent off all beverages, lasts from 1700-1900 daily
except Fridays.

Bhari Bar, Mina A'Salam, Umm Suqeim, **T** 3668888. *1200-0200.*
Map 1, B3, p248 The high ceilings, antique Moroccan lamps,
seriously cool tableware (especially the glasses) and a big
wooden bar, makes for a stylish venue. It's a good spot for
sundowners while looking out onto the Burj and the lagoon
which looks nicer and less artificial from dusk onwards. Prices
have unfortunately jumped in recent months, so it's not quite as
good value as previously.

The Left Bank, Madinat Jumeirah, **T** 3686171. *1200-0200.*
Map 1, B3, p248 A great venue for drinks and sitting outside, this
place is busy pulling in the trendy young crowd – as long as they're
not fussy about quality service or eating well. It's not a place to
linger for food (except chips); you could quite easily use the
chicken as a doorstop and even the waiters have been heard to
admit to an aching guest that his jaw wasn't the first to chew itself
into the certainty that food here often bears a striking resemblance
to old footwear. It's usually packed, though, so worth a pop.

Library & Cigar Bar, Ritz-Carlton, Marsa Dubai, **T** 3994000. *1700-0130. Map 1, off B1, p248* A moneyed, middle-aged venue with dark wood-browns and soft lighting. Chinos and Ralph Lauren polo shirts type of place rather than jeans and T-shirts.

Lobby Lounge, Ritz-Carlton, Marsa Dubai, **T** 3994000. *Fri-Wed 0900-0130, Thu 0900-0200. Map 1, off B1, p248* A largely lofty room with pristine sofas set in such a way as to bring the words, 'polite', 'appropriate', 'Earl Grey' to mind. The all-round exemplary Ritz-Carlton service and wonderful views mean the English teas come recommended. The range of teas is huge, the scones and clotted cream sincerely addictive and the prices surprisingly reasonable.

Marina Roof Deck, Jumeirah Beach Hotel, Umm Suqeim, **T** 348 8181. *Sep-May 1200-2345, Jun-Aug 1700-2345. Map 1, B4, p248* Located out on a limb, the views from this joint are what makes it special, and with no happy hour and only very mediocre cocktails, it's perhaps just as well it boasts such a unique location.

Nakhuda Bar, Mina A'Salam, Umm Suqeim, **T** 3668888. *1200-1500, 1900-0200. Map 1, B3, p248* Big and breezy with heavy wooden tables, a high vaulted roof and lots of wooden barrels completing the underground cellar look, the main selling points of this place are its rustic, harbour-side setting and an extensive wine list. The combination is a heady cocktail of benefits that are hard to resist and harder yet to criticize.

Rooftop Lounge & Terrace, One&Only Arabian Court, Al-Sufouh, **T** 3999999. *1900-0100. Map 1, B1, p248* It simply does not get much more idyllic than this. An impossibly romantic setting straight out of Arabian Nights makes for an unbeatable venue at which to relax with friends or enjoy an intimate tête-à-tête. Sink into the gloriously comfortable cushions that frame the terrace, or sip a cocktail rather more elegantly at one of the tables while enjoying the balmy air and fantastical views. A great favourite with all (despite the patchy service), Thursday nights are particularly busy, so it's worth booking ahead to ensure you get a seat. Highly recommended.

Uptown, Jumeirah Beach Hotel, Umm Suqeim, **T** 4068181. *1800-0200. M1, B4, p248* Well situated on the 24th floor it has panoramic views, black and white photos of jazz legends adorning the walls, plenty of mock- and cocktails and dishes out mainly jazzy music. Happy hour is from 1800-1900 with a 50 per cent discount on regular beverages. It's very busy after 2200. Dress code is smart/casual, and you have to be over 21 years to get in.

Clubs

Kasbar, One&Only Palace, Al-Sufouh, **T** 3999999. *Mon-Sat 2100-0300. Map 1, B1, p248* Stunning decor picks up the Arabian theme, with warm candles lighting the area. The main dance floor is surrounded by tables and there's an upstairs balcony from which to cast your eyes over this unusually romantic scene. Downstairs there's a wonderful lounge area that's a great place to relax. A good mix of people pile in due to its beach location, which picks up much of the tourist trade, and the music, which is a mix of popular dance hits, techno Arabic, R&B, trance and rave.

For a city that competes so competently in various arenas of the world stage, and most particularly in the pursuit of pleasure, Dubai's cultural credentials are surprisingly limited when it comes to comedy, dance, music and theatre. For a long time now, arts culture buffs have relied on touring companies and the occasional amateur production to keep them going. The creation of the Dubai Community Theatre is regarded by many as something to pin their hopes on, and should give the contemporary arts scene a serious kick start from 2006.

For the timebeing, you'll have to keep your eyes peeled for forthcoming events: www.dubaicityguide.com/goingout/concerts.asp, normally lists an up to date schedule of the bigger musical and theatrical events on the horizon. Also visit www.timeoutdubai.com/events which enables you to search by various categories including bands, classical, comedy, concert, dance, DJ nights, theatre and more. For recommended listings magazines, see p228. See also Festivals and events, p171, for more entertainment options.

Cinema

With no cinematic history of its own, Dubai's involvement in the film industry restricts itself to a healthy love of the cinema. The number of screens has rocketed in the last few years, so film lovers have a wide range of venues showing a variety of English-speaking, Indian and Arabic films to choose from. New films are released every Wednesday, and while sometimes they're only a few weeks behind the release dates in the West, at other times you might be waiting for up to a year to see the latest blockbuster. Remember to take your jumper, as the cinemas tend to be ferociously air-conditioned. A full list of cinemas, films and viewing times can be found at www.dubaicityguide.com/going out/cinema.asp, and the local papers will also tell you all you want to know on that score.

Century Cinemas, Mercato, Jumeirah Beach Rd, **T** 3499773. *Map 4, G1, p254* A favourite with expats, these seven screens are conveniently located on the first floor of Mercato and are all modern convenience. Prices are relatively high, at Dhs30 a pop.

CineStar, Deira City Centre, Al-Garhoud, **T** 2949000. *Map 2, D9, p251* With 11 screens, this is a serious cinematic venue located along City Centre's entertainment and eateries strip. It shows all the popular Hollywood blockbusters as well as a few of the more arty European films and the odd Hindi release. Pricey at Dhs30.

Grand Cinecity, Al-Ghurair City, **T** 2289898. *Map 2, A6, p250* Another mall-based multi-screen, boosting Deira's cinematic game, you can catch English and Hindi flicks here.

Grand Cineplex, Umm Hurair, near Wafi City, **T** 3242000. *Map 2, off H8, p251* Dubai's biggest multiscreen caters for the demands of this cinema-loving nation, and is well located near Wafi Mall to round off an exhausting day's shopping with an action-packed evening blockbuster in either Arabic, English or Hindi.

Grand Metroplex, Sheikh Zayed Rd, **T** 3438383. *Map 1, C6, p248*
Right by Safa Park and therefore attracting many families, this eight-screen monster does a good line in Arabic and English films, with the odd Hindi option from time to time. It'll cost you Dhs30 per film.

Rex Drive-In, Madinat Badr, **T** 2886447. *Map 1, G12, p249* At Dhs15 a film, this is a popular option for those happy watching Hindi movies.

Comedy

There's no such thing as a regular comedy scene in Dubai, although there are one-off events, and touring groups (including big names like Jongleurs) stop by relatively frequently. Advertising for such events is often a fairly last-minute affair, so only by keeping your eyes peeled and devouring the local media will you give yourself the best chance of unearthing what's on when. It tends to be the expat crowd that organizes comedy nights, so comics with a typically western sense of humour, often dripping with the sarcasm, make up the majority of visiting stand-ups.

The Aviation Club, Al-Garhoud, **T** 2824122. *Map 2, F10, p251*
It may also pay to give these chaps a ring if you're looking for comic entertainment, as they've hosted plenty of excellent comedy evenings in the past and are set to continue along similar lines in the future.

The Laughter Factory, **T** 3551862, www.factoryproduct.com.
Runs various comedy (and other entertainment) events at different

locations around town.

A step back in time

For centuries, dances formed an integral part of feast days or other events. Separate all-male and all-female dances would perform celebrating different aspects of life and society. Inspiration for the steps and movements traditionally stemmed from the sea, desert and mountainous environment, although all manner of other influences had also been washed in by the shipload to this sea-faring nation. The *ayyalah* is a typical and well-known Bedouin war dance, celebrating bravery and strength. Anywhere between 20 and 200 men take up their sticks or swords to stand facing each other in two rows, arms linked and swaying to the simple beat of a single drum, taking it in turns to sing of courageous deeds in battle.

Arts and entertainment

Dance

Arabia has a long tradition of dance, although you wouldn't know it from a superficial glance at Dubai's dance scene, which is – like so many of the area's cultural credentials – decidedly hidden. Most people, if asked about dance in Dubai, would launch off into a description about what different theme nights the varied club scene offers, instead of dwelling on how for centuries, feast days and celebrations have been the occasions at which dances formed an integral part of the proceedings. Dubai Museum contains video footage and descriptions of these traditional dances, but the opportunities for seeing live displays are fairly rare. The Dubai Shopping Festival and Dubai Summer Surprises (see Festivals and events, p174) will probably be your best bet. During these major annual events, any one of the museums or heritage sites should be able to provide you with the list of cultural entertainments scheduled, and you might just be lucky enough to take in a display. On a more contemporary note, there are plenty of hotels, restaurants and bars running nights dedicated to flamenco, salsa, ceroc and such like. Below are just a couple of the main crowd-pullers, but *What's On* and *Time Out* are your best bet for finding out what's happening during your stay.

Ceroc Dubai, **T** 0504283061, www.cerocdubai.com. This outfit organizes ceroc nights at various locations around town, starting off with an hour's tuition before you can let rip during the freestyle session immediately afterwards.

Salsa Dubai, **T** 0508487188, www.salsanight.com. A similar set up for salsa enthusiasts, with several sessions at different venues each week.

Salsa Time, Coco Cabana Beach Bar, Oasis Beach Hotel, **T** 3994444. *Wed 2000 onwards. Dhs35.* *Map 1, off B1, p248* Salsa and taught in a fun, relaxed environment.

Savage Garden, **T** 3460111, Capitol Hotel, Satwa. *Map 4, A8, p255* Offers classes in salsa on Tuesdays, merengue on Mondays and Thursdays and bachata on Wednesdays and Sundays. Dance classes for Dhs35 per hour. Beginners classes run from 1900-2000, and advanced tuition follows on from 2000-2100. Advance booking essential.

Music

As with the dance scene, Dubai's musical credentials can be quite clearly divided into the old and the new. For the background on the 'old' see the box, Pet Sounds, and perhaps visit Dubai Museum which boasts the city's most comprehensive display on musical instruments. The modern face of music in Dubai is rather more accessible, if not exactly thriving by international standards.

Instruments favoured in days gone by and at traditional musical celebrations are common to other countries across the Gulf. In good Bedouin tradition, when an animal died it was put to good use, and the *shekhlelah* is a sort of 'skirt' made of goats' hooves that jangle as the wearer moves in time to the other instruments. The harp-like and considerably more sophisticated *tamboura* has five strings made of horse or goat gut, stretched between a wooden frame. Camel skin covers the base, while the plectrum is made of sheep's horn.

There are plenty of ad hoc concerts hosted throughout the year, featuring international artists (Bryan Adams is an annual favourite, and Elton John, Tom Jones, Ronan Keating and Jamiroquai have all been amongst the big names to put in an appearance in recent years). The cooler winter months and higher profile sporting events including the Dubai World Cup, the Rugby Sevens, the Tennis Open and the Dubai Desert Classic always coincide with a flurry of concert dates, all of which will be advertised in the local press and radio. Dubai International Congress Centre **T** 3314200, Le Meridien **T** 2824040 and Crowne Plaza Hotel **T** 3311111, host the most concerts and classical music events. Certain bars and clubs operate a very active policy of encouraging visiting DJs and bands, and every month should find a handful of feted industry players descending on Dubai to delight the crowds. Look at www.dubaicityguide.com/goingout/bands.asp which lists bands and DJs playing; scroll down the long list of venues looking for a date in the 'validity' box – a sure sign of fresh talent. Front-runners generally include Irish Village and Rock Bottoms, while Fridays at Wafi City's 'Peanut Butter and Jam' nights can't be beaten for a chill-out venue featuring various live acts throughout the evening.

Arts and entertainment

Theatre

Lamentably, Dubai's theatre scene is full of, as yet, unfulfilled potential. There are no professional theatre companies in the Middle East, and the logistics of staging productions are plagued by lack of suitable venues and the resultant high cost of converting buildings into something more appropriate. The net result is a serious dampener that stultifies what could otherwise be a very healthy scene. The good news, though, is that the Dubai Community Theatre Project (www.dubaitheatre.org) is well under way and, once finished, should lift the curtain on Dubai's theatrical, musical and dance scene. By the end of 2005, it'll be a huge theatre building on the roof of the Mall of the Emirates in Al-Barsha, seating up to 500 people. The projections are that when it's open, 60 per cent of its usage will be by professional performers, so its superior facilities may also help encourage cultural tourism to Dubai.

As things stand, theatre lovers have to keep their ears to the ground to ensure they hear of any touring companies. The Crowne Plaza plays host to all the Streetwise Fringe productions that come over from England about once a month or so. Their website, www.streetwisefringe.com, provides details of all forthcoming shows. There's also the British Airways Playhouse theatre company, details about which are on the Streetwise website. Between them, these two companies put on about 10 productions annually, the vast majority of which are by foreign companies. BA Playhouse productions tend to be upmarket, West End type hits, while the Streetwise scene is more fringe – featuring more unknown writers, scripts or cast. For more information about what's on, contact Philippe on **T** 0506526920 or admin@streetwisefringe.com.

Dubai Country Club, Al Awir Rd, off Route 44, **T** 3331155. *Map 1, E8, p251* This is where the local amateur group, Dubai Drama Group, **T** 3986878, stages its regular, quarterly productions, details of which are on its website, www.dubaidramagroup.org.

Dubai's calendar of events is dominated on the one hand by the two major tourist fixtures, Dubai Shopping Festival (DSF) and Dubai Summer Surprises (DSS), and on the other by the various high-profile sporting events that have become part of the fabric of Dubai's social and tourism scenes. Other important highlights around which a raft of entertainments is organized include Ramadan and the two Eids.

DSF is a riotous month-long shopping and tourism extravaganza that showcases the culture, heritage, achievements and vision of Dubai in an explosion of tourism-driven activities. DSS is geared primarily towards children in a 10-week continuum of exciting educational events. Countless fans descend on Dubai for the various sporting fixtures, leaving the bars and clubs teeming and the streets packed (and the country's gold reserves somewhat depleted). Ramadan sees the proliferation of festive tents popping up all over the city to accommodate a shisha-puffing, mezze-tasting crowd as soon as the daytime fast is broken, while the papers will normally cite a range of entertainments scheduled over Eid Al-Fitr and Eid Al-Adha.

January

Dubai Shopping Festival (mid-January till mid-February) DSF is a month-long bonanza of discounts and special offers that pulls in retail addicts from all corners of the globe. Ferocious marketing and sophisticated attractions pulled in over three million visitors in 2004 whose combined spend topped a staggering Dhs5.8 billion (US$1.6 billion). Shops bedecked in lights and bunting offer spectacular price reductions, and participating outlets normally run draws with cash and car prizes. There are nightly fireworks displays over the Creek, heritage events, music, dancing and theatre at various locations, a carpet oasis bursting with different types and sizes of rugs and a huge, international funfair. The daily lotteries offer ridiculously extravagant prizes, from winning your weight in gold to a couple of lexus cars, so take your four-leafed clovers!

Eid Al Adha (roughly 10 January 2006; 1 January 2007) The Feast of Sacrifice is the most import ant feast of the Muslim calendar. It is the last day of the annual pilgrimage to Mecca and commemorates Ibraham's (Abraham) willingness to obey God by sacrificing his son. The feast re-enacts Ibrahim's obedience by sacrificing a cow or ram. The family eats about a third of the meal and donates the rest to the poor. It lasts for three days.

February

Dubai Tennis Open (last week of February and in to March) Well-attended and enthusiastically supported since its inception in 1993, this open is now an established fixture on the international tennis circuit, attracting a host of top seeds. World Tennis Assoc-

! With dates entirely dependent on the Islamic Lunar calendar,
• Muslim festivals are a bit of a moveable feast, starting roughly 10 days earlier each year.

iation's (WTA) tour fixture runs back to back with the Association of Tennis Professionals (ATP) to ensure a fortnight of top tennis. Held at the Aviation Club, Al-Garhoud, for information call **T** 2828971, or box office **T** 2829166, or see www.dubaitennischampionships.com.

March

Dubai Desert Classic (early March)   Hosted at either Emirates Golf Club or the Dubai Creek Golf & Yacht Club, this US$2 million championship attracts many of the world's top players including the likes of Tiger Woods and Ernie Els. It was incorporated into the European PGA Tour in 1989. For further details, **T** 2956440, www.dubaidesertclassic.com.

Dubai World Cup (last Saturday)   One of the highlights of the social calendar, the Dubai World Cup is held on Saturday, ensuring maximum media coverage (scheduled to coincide with the western world's weekend rather than Dubai's). Billed as the richest horse racing event in the world, it's certainly well-attended by the bold and the beautiful; the biggest names in horse racing, armies of journalists and, of course, topped off with striking array of hats. Prize money tops US$15 million, and as a buzzing, unforgettable Dubai experience, it's not one to miss. Held at Nad Al-Sheba. For further details, **T** 3322277, www.nadalshebaclub.com.

June

Dubai Summer Surprises (mid-June to the end of August) The 'little' to DSF's 'large', DSS is designed to rack up visitor figures during those searingly hot summer months. With the summer discounts offered on room rates, DSS is great for families in particular, with hotels, malls and other areas putting on a wide range of events centred around cultural, historical, technological and food-based themes. For further details, www.mydsf.com.

September (-May)

Dhow Racing (from September to May)   Traditional dhow sailing races occur on a regular, almost weekly, basis during the season, as well as on some high days and holidays. A spectacular sight, these vessels range in length from about 20 to 60 ins and are powered either by up to 100 oarsmen or the wind. Most events can be watched or partially watched at DIMC. For further details, **T** 3994111, www.dimc-uae.com.

Lailat Al Mi'raj (roughly 4 September 2005; 25 August 2006)   This festival celebrates the Prophet's ascension into Heaven.

October

Ramadan (roughly 5 October - 4 November 2005; 25 September to 24 October 2006)   Ramadan is the holy month in the Islamic lunar calendar commemorating the revelation of the Koran. During Ramadan, Muslims abstain from food, drink, cigarettes and other sensual pleasures between dawn and dusk, with the objective of learning discipline, self-restraint and generosity. The daytime fast is broken with the *iftah* feast after sunset, and this tends to be the signal for enthusiastic partying to kick off. Special festive Ramadan tents are erected around town and in most five-star hotels – they're great places to sit back and get social with a diverse and typically convivial crowd.

UAE Desert Challenge (first two weeks)   High profile and high octane, this is arguably the biggest motor sport event in the UAE. The car, truck and motor-cross categories attract the cream of the world's best rally drivers and bike riders. The race itself is held largely in the desert, starting outside Abu Dhabi and finishing in Dubai. The local press provides plenty of information on the event. For further details, **T** 2669922, www.uaedesertchallenge.com.

UIM Class One World Offshore powerboat championships
(mid month) The world powerboat racing championships attract
keen interest within the emirates. Abu Dhabi and Fujairah host
various high profile events, and Dubai International Marine Club
(DIMC) is home to Dubai's annual championships, pulling in an
appreciative, picnicking crowd to watch these monster boats and
their gargantuan engines roar about their business. For further
details, **T** 3994111, www.dimc-uae.com.

November

Eid Al Fitr (roughly 6 November 2005; 27 October 2006) This
festival celebrates the breaking of the fast at the end of Ramadan
and lasts for three days.

December

National Day (2 December) A three-day holiday celebrates the
founding, in 1971, of the UAE. The streets are bedecked in (even
more) lights, and cultural events are held at various locations
around the city. Talk to the Economic Department in Dubai, Deira
side, near Etisalat – first floor.

Dubai Rugby Sevens (beginning of the month) This wildly
popular event explains the sudden influx of around 30,000 rugby
players and fans every December. Sun, beer and more than 250
matches over three days make for an unbeatable atmosphere,
kicking off with a (free entry) day of social, club and veteran games
before the IRB Sevens takes centre stage on the second and third
days. Held at Dubai Exiles Rugby Club (**T** 3331198, www.dubairug
by7s.com), tickets are available at the gate and various locations
around town, and, at around Dhs150, cover both days and the final
concert. With between 12-14 hours of solid rugby a day, matches
start just after 0800 and continue until around 2200.

Dubai is a veritable Aladdin's Cave of retail opportunities. The age-old souks, ultra-modern shopping centres and promise of tax-free prices are enough to quicken the pulse of countless would-be buyers the world over. Those left with the prospect of footing the bill/financing a rogue wife's spending spree may well find their stomachs knotted and their palms clammy at the comprehensive way Dubai sets new boundaries to the whole concept of 'retail therapy'. But the breaks are usually applied by all but the most blasé of spenders when it dawns that not everything in this 'Shopping Capital of the Middle East' is a bargain. Certain specialty items including carpets, electronics, gold and textiles can be bought relatively cheaply, but these are still luxury items that pack a bit of a financial punch. The best bargains are to be found and haggled over in the souks, as many imported goods in the malls cost no less than elsewhere in the world. The true glory of the shopping scene out here is the sheer variety of choice, as seen in the staggering array of shops, stalls and malls all hell-bent on relieving you of your Dirhams.

Art

Basta Art Café, Al-Fahidi St, Bastakia, **T** 3535071. *Sat-Thu 1000-2000*. *Map 3, off H8, p253* Interesting collectibles can be found in the small gift shop attached to this breezy café.

Creations Arts, 1st floor, Holiday Centre, Sheikh Zayed Rd, **T** 3311047. *Sat-Thu 1000-1400, 1600-2200*. *Map 4, G9, p255* This small shop is bursting with modern Indian art, the odd wooden handicraft and some works by local artists. It's stuff you wouldn't really see in the west and worth a browse.

Creative Art Centre, between Town Centre (mall) and Choithrams, Jumeirah Beach Rd, **T** 3444394, Arabian@arts.com. *Sat-Thu 0800-1800*. *Map 4, off H1, p254 See also p56* An enormous range of Arabian prints, antiques and gifts, spread out over two villas.

Green Art Gallery, Villa 23, 51 St, behind Dubai Zoo, Jumeira, **T** 3449888, www.gagallery.com. *Sat-Thu 0930-1330, 1630-2030*. *Map 4, F2, p254* This gallery exhibits and sells work (mostly paintings) from international artists, often with a strong bias for those influenced by Arabia and its culture.

Hunar Art Gallery, Villa 6, 40 St, Rashidya, **T** 2862224, hunarart@emirates.net.ae. *Sat-Thu 0900-1300, 1600-2000*. *Map 1, E11, p249* Sells a good range of traditional and contemporary paintings by international artists, as well as showcasing Belgian glass and pewter pieces and exquisite Japanese tiles.

Majlis Gallery, Al-Fahidi St, Bastakia, Bur Dubai, **T** 3536233, majlisga@emirates.net.ae. *Sat-Thu 0930-2000*. *Map 3, H8, p253 See also p43* The first art gallery in Dubai, with a wonderfully atmospheric setting, has an enormous range of traditional and contemporary art, pottery, glass and much more.

Bookshops

The number of bookshops is steadily increasing, as is the variety of available stock. Chains offering perhaps the widest selections include Book Corner, Books Plus and Magrudy's. Don't be surprised to find black ink determinedly obscuring any even faintly risqué image; traditionally conservative, Arab censorship remains a force to be reckoned with even in Dubai's permissive society.

Book Corner has branches at: Al-Ghurair City, Al-Rigga Rd, Deira, **T** 2282835, *1000-2300, Map 2, A6, p250*; Deira City Centre, Al-Garhoud, **T** 2953266, *1000-2300, Map 2, D9, p251*; Dune Centre, Al-Dhiyafah St, **T** 3242442, *0930-2300, Map 4, A8, p254*.

Books Plus has branches at: Oasis Centre, Sheikh Zayed Rd, **T** 3394080, *1000-2200, Map 1, C6, p248*; Lamcy Plaza, Oud Metha, **T** 3366362, *Sat-Tue 1000-2200, Wed-Fri 1000-2230, Map 2, G4, p254*; Spinneys, Umm Suqeim, **T** 3940276, *1000-2200, Map 1, C5, p248*.

Magrudy's has branches at: BurJuman Centre, Bur Dubai, **T** 3593332, *1000-2200, Map 2, D3, p250*; Deira City Centre, Garhoud, **T** 2957744, *1000-2400, Map 2, D9, p251*; Magrudy Shopping Mall, Jumeirah Beach Rd, **T** 3444193, *0900-2000, Fri 1630-2030, Map 4, C4, p254*.

House of Prose, Jumeirah Plaza, near Jumeirah Mosque, **T** 3449021. *Sat-Thu 0900-2000, Fri 1730-2000. Map 4, D3, p254* A wonderful second-hand bookshop.

Camera equipment

Al-Fahidi Street and the surrounding area in Bur Dubai is bursting with shops taking a flexible stance on the price of all sorts of camera equipment.

Deira City Centre, Al-Garhoud, **T** 2954545. *1000-2200, Fri 1400-2200*. *Map 2, D9, p251* The basement level of this huge mall hosts various electronic shops where you may find some good deals.

Grand Stores has branches at: BurJuman Centre, Trade Centre Rd, Bur Dubai, **T** 3523641, *Map 2, D3, p250*; Emirates Towers, Sheikh Zayed Rd, **T** 2823700, *1000-2200, Fri 1600-2200, Map 4, H10, p255* They sell Dubai's widest selection of Fuji, Mamiya and Nikon.

Salam Studios & Stores, Wafi Mall, Umm Hurair, **T** 3245252. *1000-2200 except Fri*. *Map 2, H6, p250* Best place in town to go for specialized Bronica, Leica, Minolta, Noblex and Pentax gadgetry.

Carpets

The cheapest way to acquire a carpet is to look out for the various men loitering sometimes in the car parks and streets around the busiest parts of town. Of course, with such a here-today-gone-tomorrow trading ground, it's best to know a little about rugs before rushing into it, but if you know your turf, missing out the middle man can see you handsomely rewarded financially.

Abrash Gallery, 1st floor, Holiday Centre, Sheikh Zayed Rd, **T** 3317748. *Sat-Thu 1000-1315, 1630-2130, Fri 1630-2130*. *Map 4, G9, p255* A fabulous little shop, specializing in stunning Miri rugs. This is the Dubai arm of a family enterprise that has revived some of the traditional tribal carpet-weaving techniques of Iran. With a few exciting exceptions, carpets sold here are modern, but made entirely according to traditional methods. Pricey but glorious!

Afghan Carpets, Oasis Centre, Sheikh Zayed Rd, **T** 3395786. *1000-2200, Fri 1600-2200*. *Map 1, C6, p248* Despite its name, there's a variety of carpets here from around the world's major carpet-making destinations.

Carpet Oasis, Airport Exhibition Centre, Airport Rd. *Map 1, F11, p249* This source is available only during the Dubai Shopping Festival (mid-January to mid-February). A treasure trove of carpets, with traders shipped in from all over the world, offering exceptional value on a most comprehensive range of floor coverings.

Carpetland, near Lamcy Plaza, Oud Metha, **T** 3377677. *Sat-Thu 0930-1330, 1630-2030. Map 2, G4, p254* This outfit offers a variety of commercial and residential carpets, and also a less familiar selection of rugs: machine-made from Egypt and handmade from China and France to name but a few.

Central Market, better known as Sharjah's Blue Souk, off King Faisal Rd, near Khalid Lagoon, Sharjah. *Sat-Thu 1000-1330, 1630-2200, Fri 1600-2200. See also p73* This is another prime carpet-buying venue. The first floor is jammed with countless rug and carpet vendors from whom, after a healthy bout of haggling, you can walk away with some extremely reasonably priced treasures.

Deira Tower, Beniyas Sq, Deira. *Map 2, A4, p250* This square has wall-to-wall carpet shops with traders hailing mostly from Iran, Pakistan, Turkey and Afghanistan.

Persian Carpet House, www.persiancarpethouse.ae, has branches at: Deira City Centre, **T** 2950263, *1000-2200, Map 2, D9, p251*; Holiday Centre, **T** 3318878, *Sat-Thu 0900-2300, Fri 1400-2300, Map 4, G9, p255*; Emirates Tower, Sheikh Zayed Rd, **T** 3303277, *Sat- Thu 1000-2300, Fri 1400-2300, Map 4, H10, p255* This is a great place to ferret for carpets. With over 20 shops and a roaring trade around the UAE they're not so concerned about making huge profits on each rug, so haggle hard and you can walk off with a bargain.

Pride of Kashmir, Al-Qorz, Interchange 4, Sheikh Zayed Rd, **T** 3405343, www.prideofkashmir.com. *Map 1, C3, p248* This is possibly the place to find the best Kashmiri rugs and carpets in Dubai. They also sell items from other parts of India, including a decent line in furniture, with wood sourced from Vietnam and Indonesia. They have additional outlets in Deira City Centre, Deira, **T** 2950655, and Mercato, Jumeirah Beach Rd, **T** 3420270.

Red Sea Exhibition, Beach Centre, Jumeirah Beach Rd, **T** 3443949. *Sat-Thu 0900-1300, 1600-2200. Map 4, E3, p254* A good range of handmade carpets from all over the shop: India, Pakistan, Persia, Turkey and elsewhere.

Cigars

La Casa del Habano, Emirates Towers, **T**3303308. *Sat-Thu 1000-2200, Fri 1700-2200. Map 4, H10, p255* Not cheap, but they really know their stuff, with around 35 Cuban brands and 600 different types of cigar.

Clothes

See Malls below for the low-down on the ever-expanding designer and mainstream shopping scene. This is where most of the clothes shops tend to be, though you may have luck along the dwindling number of upmarket outlets on Deira's Al-Maktoum Street.

Al-Noor Charity Shop, opposite Dubai Municipality, facing DNATA, Karama, **T** 3979989. *Sun-Wed 1000-1300, Mon, Wed, Thu 1700-2000. Map 2, G3, p250* You'll sometimes find some nearly-new designer goods selling cheaply here.

Dubai Centre for Special Needs charity shop, in front of Choitram by the fish market, Karama, **T** 3378246. *Sat-Thu 0900-1300, 1600-2000. Map 2, G3, p250* This is another charity shop worth sifting through for second-hand designer goods.

Karama Shopping Centre, Karama. *0830-1400, 1600-2200,*
Map 2, G3, p250 This is an excellent place to look for good, cheap
clothes (including plenty of 'designer' labels), although it can take
a bit of rummaging through the tat to unearth the better items.

Computers and electronics

Al-Ain Centre, near Ramada Hotel on Mankhool Rd, Bur Dubai,
T 3516914. *Sat-Thu 0930-1430, 1630-2230. Map 2, C2, p250* The
first floor is packed with computer shops sitting cheek by jowl,
devoted to computers and related hardware, and a bit of software.

Al-Khaleej Centre, near the Al-Ain Centre, Bur Dubai, **T** 3555550.
Sat-Thu 1000-2200, Fri 1700-2200. Map 2, C2, p250 Attempts at
bargaining are sometimes successful.

Carrefour, in both Deira City Centre, *Map 2, D9, p251*, and Bur
Dubai, *Map 2, B1, p250*. This superstore operates a massive
electronics department where you can pick things up relatively
cheaply. Be warned though, the staff don't really know their stuff
and after service is unlikely to be good.

Jumbo Electronics, opposite Ramada Hotel, Mankhool Rd, Bur
Dubai, **T** 3523555. *Sat-Thu 1000-1300, 1630-2200, Fri 1600-2200.*
Map 2, C2, p250 It's good, but has a fairly limited range,
specializing in Sony and Supra.

Khalid bin Al-Waleed Rd, Bur Dubai. *Map 2, C1, p250*
Often dubbed 'computer street' thanks to the myriad stores selling
computer gadgetry, this road stretches towards Al-Shindagha.
It's a great place to buy software.

Plug-ins, Deira City Centre, **T** 2950404. *Sat-Thu 1000-2200, Fri*
1400-2200. Map 2, D9, p251 A decent range and great service.

> ### Strike gold
>
> If you stumble across the odd pot of honey packaged in rather uninspiring second-hand Vimto bottles and costing a whopping Dhs600 or so, your eyes aren't deceiving you. Collected by hand from Oman's more remote mountains and deserts, it's special stuff, even if the taste isn't much different from ordinary breakfast table honey from the supermarkets.

Food

There are plenty of fancy foods to stock up on while in Dubai from Belgian chocolates to Amaretti biscuits to more Middle Eastern delicacies such as dates. If your Iranian caviar stocks are low, Dubai is a marvellous place to rectify the matter. At prices not significantly greater than those in Iran itself, you can find caviar in local supermarkets, the airport and some five-star hotel retail outlets.

Al-Dhafra Dates, Al-Khaleej Centre, **T** 3591999, *1000-2200, Fri 1600-2200. Map 2, C2, p250* A relative new-comer to Dubai, and not widely known, partially because they're shoveled away in this location. Do a wide selection of dates – those stuffed with cashew, dipped in white chocolate and sprinkled in pistachios are heavenly!

Bateel has branches at: Deira City Centre, **T** 2957536, *1000-2200, Map 2, D9, p251*; Palm Strip, Jumeirah Beach Rd, **T** 3422345, *1000-2200, Fri 1700-2200; Map 4, B4, p254*; BurJuman Centre, **T** 3552853, *1000-2200, Fri 1600-2200; Map 2, D3, p250* Does a cracking line in gourmet dates of every description. They even sell sparkling date juice (which is infinitely more palatable with a hefty dose of vodka).

The Caviar House, Jumeirah Beach Hotel, **T** 3486259. *Sat-Thu 1000-1400, 1700-2200, Fri 1500-2200. Map 1, B4, p248* You'll find five different types of caviar here from Sevruga at Dhs150 per 50g to Royal Beluga at Dhs300 per 50g.

Dolce Antico, Mercato, Jumeirah Beach Rd, **T** 3440028. *1000-2200, Fri 1700-2200. Map 4, G1, p254* This choc shop is a relative newcomer to Dubai, opening in 2003 and selling all Italian produce, with favourites being Tartufo Bianco Dolce, nougat and Amaretti biscuits.

Godiva has branches at: Wafi Mall, **T** 3241755, *Sat-Thu 0930-2200, Fri 1700-2200, Map 2, H6, p250*; Jumeirah Centre, **T** 3493800, *Sat-Thu 0930-2130, Fri 1630-2130, Map 4, C4, p254* This Belgian chocolatier needs no introductions, neither do the snooty staff.

Goodies, Wafi Mall, Umm Hurair, **T** 3244433. *0900-2400. Map 2, H6, p250* Merely walking in is enough to set noses twitching and saliva glands streaming. This glorious place is jammed with ice creams, olives, fruits (both fresh and dried), Arabic foods, baclawa, nougats, chocolates and plenty more. Highly recommended.

Jeff De Bruges, Palm Strip, Jumeirah Beach Rd, **T** 3453365. *1000-2200, Fri 1630-2200. Map 4, B4, p254* Newly opened in 2004, this French company competes with Godiva's with its wide range of Belgian chocolates.

Lebanese Sweet Palace, Al-Dhiyafa Rd, Satwa, **T** 3984869. *Sat-Thu 1000-1400, 1630-2200, Fri 1630-2200. Map 4, B9, p255* This place claims to be one of the oldest shops in Dubai, and with baclawa this good, it's easy to see why it's still going strong.

Patchi has branches at: Al-Dhiyafah Rd, Satwa, **T** 3986038, *0900-2200, Fri 1700-2100, Map 4, A8, p255*; Wafi Mall, Oud Metha, **T** 3244030, *1000-2200, Fri 1700-2200, Map 2, H6, p250*; and Mercato, Jumeirah Beach Rd, **T** 3491188, *1000-2200, Fri*

1700-2200, *Map 4, G1, p254* This Lebanese company was established out here in 1980, and runs circles around the other choclatiers in town. Dangerously good.

Carrefour has branches at: Deira City Centre, Al-Garhoud, *Map 2, D9, p251*, and Bur Dubai by the bus station, *Map 2, B1, p250* This superstore do bigger tubs of dates that are less ritzy but perfectly decent, and your money goes infinitely further. In fact any super-market will stock a variety of good, if bog standard dates.

Jewellery

BurJuman Centre, Trade Centre Rd. *1000-2200, Fri 1600-2200. Map 2, D3, p250* This mall contains a number of outlets heaving with jewellery including **Damas Jewellery**, **T** 3525566; **Fossil**, **T** 3519794; **Mansoor Jewellery**, **T** 3552110; **Philippe Charriol**, **T** 3511112; **Prima Gold**, **T** 3551988; **Rivoli**, **T** 3512279, and **Tiffany & Co**, **T** 3590101.

Deira City Centre, Al-Garhoud. *1000-2200, Fri 1400-2200*. *Map 2, D9, p251* This mall contains still more shops including: **Al-Fardan Jewellers**, **T** 2954238; **Breitling Watches**, **T** 2954109; **Damas Jewellery**, **T** 2953848; **Fossil**, **T** 2950108; **Golden Ring**, **T** 2950373; **Guess**, **T** 2952577; **Paris Gallery**, **T** 3955550; **Prima Gold**, **T** 2950497; **Raymond Weil**, **T** 2953254; **Rossini**, **T** 2954977; **Silver Art**, **T** 2952414; **The Watch House**, **T** 2950108.

The Gem Crafter, www.thegemcrafter.com. New to the Dubai jewellery scene, this is a classy international outfit. If it's bespoke items you're after, Karen Becker (**T** 4769448, Karen_Beckeruk@ yahoo.co.uk) will work with you to design hand-crafted, one-of-a-kind jewellery. Specializing in precious and semi-precious stones this is a particularly good option for great value, good quality diamonds. If your timing is fortuitous you may even be able to arrange for Karen to lead you through the tourist- trap price-perils of the Gold Souk.

Gold & Diamond Park, Sheikh Zayed Rd, **T** 3477788. *1000-2200, Fri 1600-2200. Map 1, C4, p248* Sells all manner of gold, diamonds, pearls, watches etc. Rather a sterile place to rattle around – it's location out on a limb means it's usually pretty empty and that they're keen to get what trade they can, so you can haggle.

Gold Souk, Deira. *0930-1300, 1600-2200. Map 3, C7, p253 See also p35* Famed the world over for its glittering array of very reasonably priced golden goodies. One of the reasons they can be so competitive is that, unlike the rest of the gold and jewellery shops scattered over Dubai, it's the government that covers the cost for the rent of these Gold Souk premises.

Lingerie

The lingerie-loving locals ensure that most malls groan under the weight of shops selling everything from bog-standard pants and bras to fabulously expensive designer scraps of frills and lace.

BurJuman Centre, Trade Centre Rd. *1000-2200, Fri 1600-2200. Map 2, D3, p250* This mall carries the greatest number of designer outlets, including: **La Perla**, **T** 3551251; **La Senza**, **T** 3520222; **My Time**, **T** 3520222 and **Outfit**, **T** 2954545. You won't go amiss if you're looting for lingerie at Deira City Centre in Deira, Mercato on Jumeirah Beach Rd, or Wafi Mall in Oud Metha, either.

Malls

The sheer number of malls in Dubai is so considerable that it might be worth a browse on www.dubaishoppingmalls.com to find out which malls will best serve your needs. Below is a carefully edited list of favourites.

Al-Ain Centre, near Ramada Hotel, **T** 3516914. *Sat-Thu 0930-1430, daily 1630-2230. Map 2, C2, p250* Specializes in computers and computer products, and has a variety of eateries downstairs if you want to log off for a while. Not a bad place to come for computer games and internet access. Dead Sea Gifts sells an interesting array of ceramics and handicrafts from Palestine.

Al-Ghurair City, Al-Rigga Rd, **T** 2225222, www.alghuraircentre. com. *1000-2200, Fri 1400-2200. Map 2, A6, p250* Dubai's first mall, now revamped, offers a fairly hotch-potch selection of shopping outlets (including Body Shop, Espirit, Benetton, Milano, FCUK, Guess, Nine West, Early Learning Centre, Damas Textiles and an Ann Summers (with none of the more 'individual' pieces of stock available in England), eateries and cinema. There's a vast Fun Corner to keep the children happy, too.

Al-Khaleej Centre, opposite Ramada Hotel, **T** 3558590. *Sat-Thu 1000-2200, Fri 1700-2200. Map 2, C2, p250* Another mall with a decent line in computers upstairs, it also boasts a few unique shops including a cracking date shop, www.penscorner.com and Lifestyle Nutrition. Doodles (under MacDonalds) keeps the under 10s happy with all manner of child-oriented entertainments.

Al-Rais Centre, opposite Ramada Hotel, Mankhool Rd, **T** 3527755. *1000-2200, Fri 1700-2200. Map 2, C2, p250* This mall sees little traffic, and hosts a pack of largely unexceptional shops

! Dubai, with over 20 million square feet of retail space, has one
• of the highest per capita availabilities of retail space in the
world – four times as much as the USA which boasts the
world's largest and most advanced retail market.

apart from Braille House Trading, **T** 3526291, Braille@emirates.net.
ae, selling educational toys. There's also Lata's novelty and gift
shop, with its motley range of bits and bobs from around the world.

Beach Centre, near Dubai Zoo, Jumeirah Beach Rd, **T** 3449045.
Sat-Thu 1000-1300, daily 1600-2300. Map 4, E3, p254 A large
building of blue glass with a sociable atmosphere inside denoting
its popularity with Jumeira residents meeting to chat over coffees.
Over 50 outlets address a range of retail markets, although there's
not the variety of some of the other malls.

BurJuman Centre, Trade Centre Rd, **T** 3520222. *1000-2200, Fri
1600-2200. Map 2, D3, p250* One of the most popular malls. Good
for clothes, with a proliferation of designer names like DKNY, Louis
Vuitton and Polo Ralph Lauren jostling for space with the Mangos,
Nexts and Zaras of this world. It's well stocked with perfumes,
cosmetics and jewellery, too, with Crabtree & Evelyn, Lush, Paris
Gallery and Tiffany & Co keeping their end up. Children are well
catered for at Fun City and Fun World, and the food court is fine.

Deira City Centre, Al-Garhoud, **T** 2954545. *1000-2200, Fri 1400-
2200. Map 2, D9, p251* The biggest and arguably best mall in town
is a great favourite with locals and tourists alike thanks to its excellent array of outlets offering everything from clothes (Burberry, Calvin
Klein, Diesel, Dolce & Gabbana, Mango, River Island and plenty more)
to books, electronic goods to genuine Arabian antiques (in Arabian
Treasures), the list goes on; and Magic Planet means there's plenty to
keep the children occupied. The weekend rush can be formidable.

Emirates Towers, Sheikh Zayed Rd, **T** 3198999. *1000-2200, Fri
1600-2200. Map 4, H10, p255* Dubai's answer to Harrods, this seriously upmarket mall is home to a variety of exclusive boutiques and
jewellery shops including Bvlgari, Cartier, Damas Jewellery, Gucci,

Rodeo Drive, Rivoli, Safari Gems. The numerous eateries attract everyone from immaculate sophisticates to a more relaxed crowd looking for a fun night out at either The Noodle House or Scarlett's.

Galleria, Hyatt Regency, **T** 2096000. *Daily 1600-2200 except Fri 1000-1300. Map 1, B11, p249* This fairly small mall is peppered with relatively upmarket shops and really draws the crowds in summer as it contains one of Dubai's two ice rinks.

Gold & Diamond Park, Sheikh Zayed Rd, **T** 3477788. *1000-2200, Fri 1600-2200. Map 1, C4, p248* Jammed with outlets selling gold, diamonds, pearls, watches – the works.

Holiday Centre, attached to the Crowne Plaza, Sheikh Zayed Rd, **T** 3317755. *Sat-Thu 1000-1300, 1600-2200, Fri 1600-2200. Map 4, G9, p255* Small and rarely particularly busy, there are some real gems hidden away in here including the Abrash Gallery with its exquisite carpets, the more feasibly priced Persian Carpet House, Creations Art, Thierry Mugler, Rodeo Drive and TGI Fridays.

Jumeirah Centre, near Jumeirah Mosque, **T** 3499702. *0900-2100, Fri 1700-2100. Map 4, C4, p254* Another popular stop with Jumeirah residents, this very relaxed mall is split into an open-air courtyard, and an enclosed shopping section. There's a good range of bespoke shops: Sunny Days is great for Arabic gifts and romantic sepia photos of old Dubai, and Essensuals Aromatherapy Centre, T3448776, is an all-round top-notch outfit, particularly if you suffer from sinus headaches or allergies.

Jumeirah Plaza, near Jumeirah Mosque, **T** 3497111. *1000-2200, Fri 1700-2200. Map 4, D3, p254* The glass-roofed 'Pink Mall' has a very 'residents' feel to it, with plenty of home furnishing stores oozing eastern flair. Upstairs, Melange sells some wonderful

Indian textiles, tableware and the like. Notable is the excellent second-hand book shop, House of Prose, while Planet Jumeirah targets pre-teens with its plethora of arcade games.

Lamcy Plaza, Oud Metha, **T** 3359999. *1000-2200, Fri 1000-2230. Map 2, G4, p254* A vast, five-storey monster of a mall, serving up pretty much everything on a more budget-oriented footing, with particularly good lines in children's clothes, shoes, perfumes and sports equipment. Outlets include Bhs, Indigo Nation, Mexx for less, Mr. Price (next to which there's a great place selling raw silks), Peacocks, KFC, Mothercare, Hush Puppies, Nine West, Shoe Mart, City Sports and Swatch. With 16 play areas in the children's activity centre, LouLou Al-Dugong's is very popular with the kids.

Mercato, Jumeirah Beach Rd, **T** 3444161. *1000-2200, Fri 1400-2200. Map 4, G1, p254* Another one of the better malls vying for popularity with Deira City Centre and BurJuman Centre, Italian renaissance meets Walt Disney in this pure fantasy, cake-like building with its raft of upmarket and specialty shops, including Armani Junior, Barbie (that's right – an entire shop dedicated to the doll!), Damas Jewellery, Diesel Jeans, Gianfranco Ferre, Milano, Miss Sixty, Nine West, Triumph and Virgin. Cinemas, big murals and posing tourists are part of the charm in this extraordinary place.

Oasis Centre, near Ace Hardware, Sheikh Zayed Rd, **T** 3395459. *1000-2200, Fri 1400-2200. Map 1, C6, p248* A good family mall, with decent play areas (Fun City remains a hit with the kids, with its two-tier maze, bouncy castle, video games and even bumper cars) and general entertainments (including bowling). Shopping-wise, Shoemart pulls in the crowds with its designer brands at excellent prices, while the range of other products is fairly limited.

Tall is beautiful
The enormously elegant
Emirates Towers shrouded
in early morning mist.

A day at the races
The much revered camel is still a crowd pleaser at the races.

Golden daze
One of Dubai's greatest draws, the Gold Souk has the biggest concentration of goldsmiths in the world.

Palm Strip, opposite Jumeirah Mosque, **T** 3461462. *1000-2200, Fri 1700-2200. Map 4, B4, p254* This breezy, open-fronted mall is unusual in that it is not housed in a vast, air-conditioned complex. With fairly ritzy clothes shops including Armani Jeans, Karen Millen and a decent swimwear outlet, it's a great place to meander around, stopping either for coffee or a typically Jumeira-esque manicure at Nail Bar. Smart Discovery is a retail and activity store for children offering a wide range of original activities, and Jeff De Bruges choclatier is a rather good place to succumb to temptation!

Town Centre, Jumeirah Beach Rd, **T** 3440111. *1000-2200, Fri 1700-2200. Map 4, off H1, p254* This small, sweet little mall has a few good shops that make it a decent stop on a tourist itinerary: paint your own pots at Café Ceramique over a bagel or other quick bite, pick up some mouthwatering dates at Bateel, or indulge your passion for perfume in any of the numerous perfume outlets. La Caffete does excellent Belgian waffles and proper hot chocolates.

Twin Towers, near InterContinental Dubai, Deira, **T** 2218833. *Daily except Fri 1000-1300, daily 1700-2200. Map 2, A4, p250* Rising up beside the Creek and one of the most photographed sites in Dubai, Twin Towers is geared mainly towards clothes and accessories, jewellery and leather products.

The Village, Jumeirah Beach Rd, **T** 3449514. *1000-2200, Fri 1400-2200. Map 4, D3, p254* A new kid on the Jumeirah block, this place is brand new yet already has a great atmosphere, with a central food court, a baker, and a decent range of upmarket and trendy clothes and accessories outlets. You'll find a great range, from imported Thai silks at Jim Thompson to books to a good collection of beachwear outlets. Many of its shops weren't yet open at time of publication, but it's definitely one to watch.

Wafi Mall, Oud Metha, **T** 3244555. *1000-2200, Fri 1630-2200.*
Map 2, H6, p250 A Mecca for designer shoppers, this ferociously
air-conditioned place is everything smart, luxury and expensive.
Betty Barclay, Caresse, Chanel, Giordano, Givenchy, Goodies,
Marina Rinaldi, Mont Blanc, Osh Kosh B'gosh, Paris Gallery,
Patchi, Petals, and Tag Heuer are just some of the big names
you'll find here. And it's not even that crowded thanks to the
array of attractions a stone's throw away in Wafi City. Plenty to
amuse the kids (both young and adult!) in Encounter Zone with
its raft of entertainments, and try Elements for a novel eaterie.

Music

Music Box, Al-Ghurair City, **T** 2210344. *1000-2200, Fri 1600-2200.*
Map 2, A6, p250 Sells a wide range of both English and Arabic music.

Music Master, Palm Strip, Jumeirah Beach Rd, **T** 3451753.
1000-2300, Fri 1600-2300. Map 4, B4, p254 Has a decent range.

The Music Room, Beach Centre, Jumeirah Beach Rd, **T** 3448883.
Daily except Fri 1000-1300, 1600-1900. Map 4, E3, p254 Seller of
musical instruments and sheet music.

Virgin Megastore has branches at: Deira City Centre, **T** 2958599,
1000-2200, Map 2, D9, p251, and Mercato, Jumeirah Beach Rd,
T 3446971, *1000- 2200, Thu-Fri 1000-2300. Map 4, G1, p254*
Stocks the usual wide variety you expect of Virgin.

! Stronger and spicier than western scents, Arabic perfumes
traditionally served the double purpose of smelling attractive
and disguising the smell of grubby bodies in the days of little
air conditioning and limited access to water for washing.

Bargain basement

As natural to Arabs as breathing, bargaining is a fundamental part of all transactions made in the souks, and even some of the shops. It's expected, and can be as entertaining as it is profitable, with vendors slashing the prices considerably for worthy haggling opponents and cash sales. The trick is first to decide how much you'd be prepared to pay for an item (so do your research in other shops), and then to try and wheedle the price down. Good humour and a polite manner are the best ammunition for success, and you're usually on to a good thing if you manage to knock the price down by a third.

Outdoor and leisure

Ace Hardware has branches Sheikh Zayed Rd, **T** 3381416, *0900-2100, Map 1, C6, p248*, and BurJuman, **T** 3550698, *1000-2200, Fri 1600-2200, Map 2, D3, p250* A good place to stock up before heading off to do any camping. From tents to barbecues, you'll find it all here.

Perfumes and cosmetics

Passionate about perfume and mad about make-up, such is the demand out here that most malls are sprinkled with shops capitalizing on Dubai's booming beauty market.

!
•   *Amouage*, with its enormously elegant scent, is the most expensive perfume in the world, more expensive per ounce even than gold (Dhs600 for 50ml!). Available at Paris Gallery, City Centre, T2955550.

BurJuman Centre, Trade Centre Rd. *Map 2, D3, p250* In this mall you'll find: Areej, **T** 3522977; Crabtree & Evelyn, **T** 3525425; Lush, **T** 3520222; Paris Gallery, **T** 3517704; and Rasasi, **T** 3512757.

Deira City Centre, Deira. *Map 2, D9, p251* This mall hosts: Ajmal Perfumes, **T** 2953580; Body Shop, **T** 2945101; MAC, **T** 2957704; The Nature Shop, **T** 2954181; and Red Earth, **T** 2951887.

Notables include: Faces in Al-Ghurair City, **T** 2234302, *Map 2, A6, p250*; Jashanmal, Wafi Mall, **T** 3244800, *Map 2, H6, p250*; and Make Up Forever, Wafi Mall, **T** 3244426, *Map 2, H6, p250*.

The Perfume Souk, just east of the Gold Souk on Sikkat Al-Khail Rd. *Map 3, C8, p253* This is the best place to shop for Arabic perfumes. Beware, though: they're oil based so can stain clothes, and a small dab is usually potent enough to last a full day.

Souks

Covered Souk, off Al-Sabkha Rd, unfurling behind the bus station towards the Gold Souk. *0900-1300, 1600-2200. Map 3, D10, p253 See also p35* A startling array of goods spills onto the winding pavements and alleyways that constitute the Covered Souk. From household goods to beautiful Indian textiles, from colourful shishas to novelty paperweights, from mind-bogglingly kitsch bedding to anything brightly coloured and plastic – you're likely to find it here. It's therefore a child's retail heaven, packed with impossibly fluffy, frilly hair bands, and oodles of plastic toys that may or may not be battery powered. One particular show-stopper is the ubiquitous waterfall picture, lit from behind, that comes complete with sound track of gurgling brooks and twittering birds!

Fish Souk, near Shindagha Tunnel, Deira. *0700-2300. Map 3, off A7, p253* Even if you're not staying nearby it's worth making the long haul to see the big haul. Hundreds upon hundreds of different type of fish, shark and crustaceans fill the iced display tables with vendors expertly cleaning, gutting and chopping. Great photo opportunities abound, and watching the pros haggling over prices is a treat. The morning constitutes the busiest part of the day and is the best time to visit.

● *Attached are the meat and vegetable souks, brimming with variety and colour.*

Gold Souk, off and around Sikkat Al-Khail Rd, Deira. *0930-1300, 1600-2200. Map 3, C7, p253 See also p35* Famed the world over, the Gold Souk is a major reason why so many women with ulterior motives put Dubai on their holiday hit list! With its enormous collection of shops, its remarkable variety of goodies and its exceptionally reasonable prices, there's no better way for jewellery lovers to drool away their time and eventually emerge with their ideal trophy. Window upon window is crammed with racks dripping with bracelets, necklaces, rings, diamonds, emeralds, rubies, sapphires and more, making the Gold Souk one of the most popular tourist stops in the Middle East. Barter hard!

Perfume Souk, east of the Gold Souk on Sikkat Al-Khail Rd. *0900-1300, 1600-2200. Map 3, C8, p253* This is the best place to shop for Arabic perfumes, sold by the *tolah* (12 ml). The quality of the perfume is reflected in its price, with some of the cheaper scents selling at about Dhs10 per *tolah* while the most exclusive can set you back a staggering Dhs1,500 for the same amount. It does last longer, though, as it's enormously concentrated stuff (often smelling utterly revolting in the bottle, so it's worth applying a bit, letting it settle and only then wafting it under your nose in order to appreciate the true fragrance). Beware though Arabic perfumes are oil based and can stain clothes.

Spice Souk, off Old Baladiya St, Deira. *0900-1300, 1600-2200.*
Map 3, E6, p252 Meandering through this maze of stalls, it's easy to
feel transported to another era. The air seems seasoned by these
great sacks packed with every spice under the sun. This is the best
place in the world to buy expensive spices, although the
competition now provided by Dubai's bigger supermarkets does
seem to have brought about a dwindling in the number of stalls.

Textile Souk, near the Creek, Bur Dubai. *0900-1300, 1600-2200.*
Map 3, H4, p252 See also p44 A true tapestry of colour, the Textile
Souk is a rainbow world of stalls crammed with hundreds of bolts
of material. Although there's a distinct lack of decent drill cottons,
you'll find delicate voile, sleek satins and the most elaborate silks
shipped in from all over the world. With almost unlimited choice
it's best to shop around to see the full range. Prices are negotiable,
and there are good sales during the major holidays.

Karama Shopping Centre, near the junction of Qataiyat and
Umm Hurair Rds, Karama. *0830-1400, 1600-2200.* *Map 2, G3,
p250* A souk in everything but its name, Karama's shopping
centre/market is another exciting place to rifle for bargains. Two
streets of verandah-covered shops burst with cheap (and often
cheap-looking) goodies including T-shirts, trousers, shoes, sun-
glasses and souvenirs. A bit of patience will often pay dividends,
as there is the odd gem to be found. If… 'designer' bags are your
thing, the best ones are to be found by following the whispered
promises of Gucci and Prada off the main drag, and then plunging
into a bit of hectic haggling. Green Coast Fashion shop is
particularly recommended for reasonable prices.

Souvenirs

Streets, souks and even shopping malls are generally awash with
shops sporting possible mementos of a trip to Dubai, although

many of the 'traditional' items are now in fact manufactured overseas. Favourite souvenirs include coffee pots and cups, incense and perfume, elaborate *khanjars* (daggers), pictures depicting traditional aspects of local life, shisha pipes, wooden wedding chests, Omani jewellery and coffee-table books packed with snaps.

Al-Arsah Souk, Heritage Area, Sharjah, is one of the best places to hunt for Arabic souvenirs. Competitively priced and offering an excellent variety of items from *kandouras* (*dishdashas* – item of clothing worn by men in the UAE) to necklaces to the usual assortment of goodies, it's well worth a browse.

Antique Museum, Al Quoz Industrial Area, Intersection 3, Sheikh Zayed Rd, **T** 3479935. *Sat-Thu 0930-2030.* A real treasure trove of goodies, from pashminas to trinket boxes, furniture to textiles, this place is definitely worth a visit if you're on a souvenir haul. With prices that compete even with Karama (see below), shopaholics can fritter away a few happy hours rifling through the tat to find some ingenious bargains. Great textiles.

Arabian Treasures, Deira City Centre, Deira, **T** 2951010. *Map 2, D9, p251* There really are some fabulous treasures to be found in this pocket of five or so shops on the first floor, but with a prime location in the emirate's favourite mall, the prices aren't as competitive as you might find elsewhere.

Central Market (or Blue Souk), King Faisal Rd, Sharjah. *Sat-Thu 1000-1330, 1630-2200, Fri 1600-2200. See also p73* A great spot to pick up Omani jewellery at very competitive prices.

Creative Art Centre, between Town Centre mall and Choithrams, Jumeirah Beach Rd, **T** 3444394, Arabian@arts.com. *Sat-Thu 0800-1800. Map 4, off H1, p254 See also p56* Displays a wonderful range of Arabian prints, antiques and gifts.

Heritage Village, Al-Shindagha. *Map 3, C2, p252 See also p45*
The Heritage Village contains a motley selection of little shops selling everything from carved chests to coffee pots to camel padlocks and other interesting knick-knacks. Barter hard to get a good deal.

Showcase Antiques, in a villa opposite Dubai Municipality, Jumeirah Beach Rd, Umm Suqeim, **T** 3488797. *Sat-Thu 0900-2100, Fri 1700-2000. Map 1, B5, p248* Sells everything from old Arabian and European maps from to antique English and Omani furniture to old watches and a host of prints and frames.

Karama Shopping Centre, Karama. *Daily 0830-1400, 1600-2200. Map 2, G3, p250* This stretch is bursting with curios and souvenirs, most of which, because of its souk-like atmosphere, are very reasonably priced.

Tailoring

Satwa, with its proliferation of good tailors, is the place to go to have material speedily and cheaply run up into clothes.

Coventry, in the alleyway next to Neha Textiles, off the main Satwa drag near Deepak's, **T** 3447563. *Map 4, C8, p255* The chap here is subject to some pretty grumpy mood-swings, but there's no disputing the quality of tailoring he offers.

Khalid Al-Attar Tailoring, Khalid Al-Attar Tower, Sheikh Zayed Rd, **T** 3326500. *Sat-Thu 1000-1330, 1600-2200. Map 4, G9, p255* This is an excellent outfit, with four tailors brought over after trials in India. Good at accommodating perfectionists.

Tailor Works, Al-Hudaiba Rd, **T** 3499906, tailorworks@hotmail.com. *Map 4, C5, p255* The manager, Marcia, is fabulous – you can tell her what you want and she'll go away, find the material and rustle up something spectacular.

Textiles

Fabulous textiles abound in Dubai, usually thanks to the huge number of resident Indians. From the dirt cheap to the dizzyingly expensive, the best places to get them include those listed here.

Damas Textiles, Al-Ghurair City, Al-Rigga Rd. *1000-2200, Fri 1400- 2200. Map 2, A6, p250* Not cheap, but excellent quality and decent range, too.

Deepak's, on the main drag in Satwa, **T** 3448836. *Map 4, D8, p255* Deepak's wide assortment of materials feeds the full gamut of couture requirements levelled its way from the residents and tourists who flock to have outfits made up cheaply in Satwa.

Covered Souk, Deira. *0900-1300, 1600-2200. Map 3, D10, p253 See also p35* Sells an excellent variety of well-priced materials.

Meena Textiles, Lamcy Plaza, **T** 3352570. *0900-2230. Map 2, G4, p250* A popular place with residents looking to have clothes made. Stocks good lines in various types of silk as well as Chantilly lace.

Textile Souk, Bur Dubai. *0900-1300, 1600-2200. Map 3, H4, p252 See also p44* A magnificent array of materials from India, Indonesia, Japan, Korea and Thailand, and it's certainly the most atmospheric place to purchase your fabrics.

Sport in Dubai embraces the widest range of activities imaginable from a desert location. And, refusing to allow little things like geography and climate to scupper plans for world tourism domination, there's even talk of shipping in a mammoth snow dome to ensure a slice of the booming snow sports market. As things stand, there's still more than enough to satisfy the whims of most, whether you're bent on trialing Dubai's truly awesome array of watersports, hell-bent on hell-raising in desert buggies, or determined to let the pros do all the work at one of the numerous spas around town. The most comfortable time of year for outdoor pursuits is winter, as searing summer temperatures make the sea piping hot and the idea of outdoor exertion something to balk at. That said, there's no curbing the year-round enthusiasm of golfing aficionados flooding in to enjoy one of the world's top golf destinations.

Armchair sportsmen are also well catered for with highlights of the season including the Tennis Open, the Desert Classic, the fabulously fashionable Dubai World Cup and the wildly popular Rugby Sevens.

Beaches

Jumeirah Beach Park, Jumeirah Beach Rd, **T** 3492555, www.dm.gov.ae. *Map 1, B6, p248 See p54* A long, thin stretch of sand, grassy areas and barbecue sites. Always busy.

Mamzar Park, Al-Mamzar, **T** 2966201, www.dm.gov.ae. *Map 1, off B12, p249 See p39* A quiet alternative to the busy beaches along the Jumeira strip, it has plenty of facilities and so good for families.

Dubai Ladies Club, Jumeirah Beach Rd, **T** 3499922. *Map 1, B7, p249 See p54* This ladies only club is a relaxing place to come for a spot of 'time out'. With a beautiful beach frontage and spa, etc.

Wollongong University, Jumeirah Beach Rd. *Map 1, B5, p248 See p55* The public beach near the university is a popular haunt with kite-surfers, especially on Friday afternoons.

Jumeirah Beach Corniche, Jumeirah Beach Rd. *Map 1, B8, p249 See p55* Showers, toilets, loungers, parasols and refreshment stands – all that you need for lying and frying.

Birdwatching

Khor Dubai Wildlife Sanctuary, **T** 0506503398. *Map 1, E8, p249 See p25* Special permission is needed to visit the country's largest bird sanctuary, located a stone's throw from the city.

Camel racing

Nad Al-Sheba *Map 1, E6, p248* Not to be missed if you're here in the winter, the camel racing season runs from September to March, with races held three or four days each week at this venue. Races start early in the morning, at about 0700, so be prepared to dust down your alarm clock before waking up to the extraordinary sight of countless camels thundering down the tracks, their tiny jockeys clinging on for dear life, with parties of crazed emirates hanging out of their 4WDs as they take off in hot pursuit. The sight causes a few raised eyebrows over how rigorously the 1993 legislation stating that all jockeys must be 45 kg or more is upheld. Certainly in the past, the demand for the lightest of jockeys meant that frighteningly young Bangladeshi and Indian boys were stuck or bound to the saddles to improve the camel's chances of winning. During the summer there's still plenty of activity out on the tracks, with daily practice sessions that have no fixed time, although 0730 is generally a good time to tip up, before it gets too hot. Free.

Camel Racing Office, **T** 3372068, keeps a copy of the season's schedule, but have little more information than race times.

Camel riding

Most tour operators offer camel rides as part of their desert safari packages, see p27, and these rides are the most exciting and authentic. There are various other places to hop on board these ships of the desert, especially during DSF (Dubai Shopping Festival) when you'll find be-saddled camels at various locations throughout the city, including Heritage Village.

Canoeing

Desert Rangers, Interchange 3, Sheikh Zayed Rd, **T** 3402408. *Sat-Thu 0900-1800*. *Map 1, C5, p248* The only tour company in Dubai currently offering canoeing, to groups of at least six people. The mangroves at Khor Kalba's Nature Reserve is the venue, so timings depend on the tide. It's a good spot from which to get up close and personal with the UAE's varied bird and marine life. The five-hour round trip from Dubai costs Dhs300 with transportation.

Climbing

Climbing is pretty good in the Emirates, with Wadi Bih in Ras Al-Khaimah being a decent spot for traditional climbing, and Wonder Wall, 40 km out of Al-Ain on the Soha road in Wadi Hamad area, offering some bolted climbing opportunities. For more information on climbing, talk to John Gregory **T** 0506477120.

Cycling

Dubai Roadsters, **T** 3394453. These resident cycling devotees get together regularly to hare along the flat roads of Dubai, and are more than happy to swell their numbers with tourists. Call for details.

Wolfie's Bike Shop, Sheikh Zayed Rd, near Ace Hardware and the Harley Davidson shop. *Map 1, C6, p248* They only have three bikes for rent, but are also on hand to answer queries and offer advice. The shop's owner, Wolfgang Hohmann, knows all about the cycling and mountain biking scene in Dubai.

Diving

Al-Boom Diving, Al-Wasl Rd, **T** 3422993. *Sat-Thu 1000-2000. Map 4, C6, p254* Dive locations vary depending on the weather, and may be in Dubai or along the East Coast. Two morning dives a day (Dhs280 each), and a full-day Musandam trip for more experienced divers at the end of the month (Dhs425).

Maku Dive Centre, Holiday Beach Motel, 8 km south of Dibba, the East Coast, **T** 092445747, maku@emirates.net.ae. Run by a fabulous Swiss couple, Kurt and Margrit, they know the area like the backs of their hands and offer a wide variety environmentally friendly trips.

Pavilion Dive Centre, Jumeirah Beach Hotel, Umm Suqeim, **T** 4068827, www.jumeirahinternational.com/diving. *0900-1800. Map 1, B4, p248* On offer are wreck dives on the west coast (Dhs275 full equipment and two tank trips), dives around the East Coast's natural coral reef (Dhs350-400) and the full range of PADI courses.

Dune bashing

If you decide to venture off-road for a spot of dune bashing, be aware that it's wise to do so with plenty of water and at least one other vehicle. There's a real art to sand driving, and even the most experienced of drivers will get stuck and require a tow.

Al-Badayer Motorcycle Rental, on the road to Hatta near Big Red (see p84), **T** 0507365533 (mob). *0830-sunset.* Wide range of bikes and buggies 50-400cc, between Dhs60-250 per hour.

Al-Ramool Motorcycle Rental, on the road to Hatta, on the left near Big Red (see p84), **T** 0504534401. *0830-sunset.* Have a variety of motorcycles available for rent (Dhs80-200 per hour), as well as desert bikes and 4x4s (Dhs120 for 15 minutes, complete with driver).

Desert Rangers, Interchange 3, Sheikh Zayed Rd, **T** 3402408. *Map 1, C5, p248* Many tour operators organize forays into the desert, but Desert Rangers is unique in that it has one- and two-seater buggies especially adapted fordesert conditions. They're lower and have roller bars, making them safer. Safaris are available from their campsite in Al-Awir, the round-trip lasting four hours and costing Dhs350. Dhs150 more for an evening barbecue and belly dancing.

Fishing

Club Joumana, Jebel Ali Hotel, Jebel Ali, **T** 8048050. Deep-sea fishing trips leave for the Arabian Gulf twice daily (weather permitting) at 0800 and 1400, with a maximum of seven people per boat. Four- and eight-hour trips are available, costing Dhs1,200 and 2,200 respectively. Likely catches include barracuda, hammour, kingfish and lemonfish. All equipment is provided along with tea, coffee and pastries. Advance booking is essential.

Dubai Creek Gold & Yacht Club, opposite Deira City Centre, Al-Garhoud, **T** 2956000. *0630-1900. Map 2, F9, p251 See also p211* The club's fully equipped 32' Hattaras carries a maximum of six people, and can be chartered any time between 0700-1800, weather-dependent. A four-hour trip costs Dhs1,875, and it's Dhs250 per additional hour. The main season runs from October to January, and you're likely to catch barracuda, hammour, kingfish, queenfish and sailfish.

Le Meridien Mina Seyahi Beach Resort & Marina, Al-Sufouh, **T** 3993333. *Map 1, B1, p248* On offer is a variety of fully equipped fishing trips from four to 10 hours costing from around Dhs1,900-2,660. Water and soft drinks are provided, but additional arrangements have to be made if you're wanting lunch. The tag and release scheme is adhered to for the larger prizes.

Yacht Solutions, Jumeirah Beach Hotel, **T** 3486838. *Map 1, B4, 248* A 31' Gulf Craft Walkaround and a 34' Blackfin can be chartered for between four to eight hours (from Dhs1,600-2,600 and Dhs2,400-3,600 respectively). Trips depart from Jumeirah Beach Hotel Marina, and can take a maximum of six people off in search of sailfish, shari and the like.

Football

The 'official' football scene in Dubai is small, but on the way up. Opportunities are mainly for residents, although the Jumeirah

Beach Football Clinic is excellent and runs for three weeks from May to mid-June, with professional footballers shipped in from the UK for the benefit of tourists. There are also coaching sessions and matches organized by the UAE English Soccer School of Excellence. Ring James Masterman on **T** 0504764877 (mob) for more info.

Golf

Dubai is rich with opportunities for golf enthusiasts, and it's wise to book tee times well ahead, either by contacting the individual golf courses, or the central reservation service, **T** 3903931. Courses vary hugely, and costs average out at about Dhs375 per round. Prices are higher at the weekends. For keen golfers, becoming a member (Dhs200) of the UGA, **T** 2956440, www.ugagolf.com, entitles you to reduced fees at UAE golf courses.

Al-Badia Golf Course, Festival City, is due to open March 2005. *Map 2, H11, p251* Word on the street is that this Robert Trent Jones course looks like an American sculpted affair: immaculate greens and fairways, and lots of water.

Al-Awir, Dubai Country Club, **T** 3331155. *Map 1, E8, p249* Prior to the grass courses, this is how golf was played – on sand. It's a tough track; the greens are called 'browns' and are a mixture of sand and diesel. If it were grassed, people say it would be one of the best courses in the area, but the management wonderfully wants to keep it as it is. An entrance fee of Dhs65 must be paid at the gate, and you can play either 9 or 18 holes for no extra charge. Buggies cost Dhs50 for nine holes or Dhs75 for the full 18. Advance booking is advisable Thurday to Saturday. The original Dubai open – the Dubai Amateur Open – is still held here.

The Desert Course, Arabian Ranches, Emirates Rd, **T** 8846777, www.thedesertcourse.com. *Map 1, G2, p248* This 18-hole desert style par 72 course, designed by Ian Baker-Finch and Nicklaus Design, is a real challenge. It's an interesting course, but comes in for considerable criticizm because there are too many blind spots. Rates range from Dhs475 Thursdays to Saturdays and Dhs380 Sundays to Wednesdays. Golf pros are available for lessons.

Dubai Creek Golf & Yacht Club, Al-Garhoud, **T** 2956000. *Map 2, F9, p251 See also p38 and p209* December 2004 is the date set for the reopening of this course as part of the first 18-hole golf resort in the GCC. Having hosted the Desert Classic, the course came in for some criticizm, hence the current redevelopment.

Emirates Golf Club, Emirates Hill, **T** 3802222, www.dubaigolf.com. *Map 1, C1, p248* A great favourite, with perhaps the best clubhouse in Dubai both in terms of originality of design and atmosphere. There are two 18-hole par 72 championship courses: the much-loved Majlis (first grass course in Dubai and venue for the Desert Classic) and the Wadi. Both have been sculpted out of the desert, and the terrain has been ingeniously used to create interesting, challenging holes. Players must produce a valid handicap certificate.

Montgomerie Golf Club, Emirates Hills Estate, **T** 3801333, www.themontgomerie.com. *Map 1, D1, p248* This 18-hole par 72 course was designed by Colin Montgomerie and Desmond Muirhead. It is unique in a way that some think daft, others quirky. It boasts the world's largest green – 58,000 sq ft and shaped like the UAE – and there are huge distances between the greens and the next tee. It does however have a determined band of followers. Rounds cost Dhs560 Thursdays to Saturdays, or Dhs425 Sundays to Wednesdays. The facilities are good, including an extensive teaching academy, a floodlit par 3 course and swing studio.

Nad Al-Sheba Club, Nad Al-Sheba, **T** 3363666, www.nadalsheba club.com. *Map 1, F7, p249* Golfers tee off as late as 2200 on the only floodlit 18-hole golf course in Dubai (just think of the cost!). Centred around the famous Nad Al-Sheba Racecourse, there is a spectacularly situated nine-hole links course with 90-odd pot bunkers, while the outer nine holes some say are very unexceptional. Judge for yourself at Dhs220 Saturday to Wednesday or Dhs295 Thursday to Friday and at other peak times. Coaching is available from British PGA pros, and the Dhs525 'Learn Golf in a Week' which runs from September to May has gone down a storm. Book early.

The Resort Course, Jebel Ali Golf Resort & Spa, Jebel Ali, **T** 8048058, www.jebelali-international.com. This wonderful nine-hole course, designed by Peter Harradine, is best known for the eighth hole from where you can see the desert and panoramic views of the Arabian Gulf. Landscaped with exotic trees, desert shrubs, with the odd peacock roaming the freeways, it's a tough, narrow course. It's also home to the best respected golf pro, James Williams. The Challenge Match, where six of the world's top golfers compete, is hosted here annually as the curtain-raiser before the Desert Classic. Golfers have to have an official handicap to play.

Dubai Desert Classic, at either Emirates Golf Club or the Dubai Creek Golf & Yacht Club, is held in March. The US$2 million championship attracts many of the world's top players . See p174.

Hiking

There are plenty of hiking opportunities around Dubai: the Hajar Mountains, Wadi Bih, the East Coast and Al-Ain are all home to some great routes. You can't do much better than referring to the Off-Road Explorer (available in all bookshops) for directions.

Desert Rangers, 2nd floor, Dubai Garden Centre, Interchange 3, Sheikh Zayed Rd, **T** 3402408. *Map 1, C5, p248* Your best bet if you want to go on an organized tour. With 10 years of exploring the surrounding area already under his belt, Saif knows just where to go to find abandoned settlements, wells and ancient *falaj* systems.

Horse racing

Dubai Racing Club, Nad Al-Sheba Racecourse, **T** 3322277, www. emiratesracing.com. *Map 1, F7, p249* From November to April, race nights are held on Thursdays and one other evening kicking off around 1900. Parking and admission are free. Single-day membership costs Dhs60 giving you access to the Millennium Grandstand. There are also a variety of dinner packages available, see www.dub airacingclub.com. In a country where betting is strictly taboo, 'horseplay' competitions encourage spectators to predict the runners and winners in return for cash prizes or souvenirs. Dress code: casual for the general grandstand, formal for the other two.

Dubai World Cup, Nad Al-Sheba Racecourse, **T** 3322277, www.nadalshebaclub.com. *Map 1, F7, p249* The world's richest race meeting takes place on the last Saturday of every March.

Horse riding

Club Joumana, Jebel Ali Hotel, Jebel Ali, **T** 8048058. *Tue-Sun 0700-1200, 1600-1900, 1 Oct-31 May.* While soaring summer temperatures rule out riding from June to September, a variety of desert hacks are possible during the cooler winter months. Beach riding is not permitted, thanks to the nearby stretch being designated an conservation area. Advance booking is essential.

Emirates Riding Centre, Nad Al-Sheba, **T** 3361394. *Sat-Thu 0700-1000, 1700-2000, 15 Sep-15 Jun. Map 1, F7, p249* The ERC organizes desert hacks (Dhs130 per hour) for visitors as well as lessons (Dhs175 for 45 minutes, less for group bookings). Book 24 hours in advance. There are also stable tours, see p28.

Jebel Ali Equestrian Club, **T** 8845485. *Sat-Thu 0700-0900 and random evenings.* An approved branch of the British Pony Club, offer lessons or desert hacks (Dhs110 per hour) throughout the year. Booking is essential, especially during the summer when there are fewer instructors and when only early morning or late afternoon/evening rides are the order of the day.

Hot air ballooning

Voyagers Xtreme, Dune Centre, Al-Dhiyafah St, Satwa, **T** 3454504. *Map 4, A8, p255* This is a fabulous way to see the sights, and you can either drift over the city or the desert. City flights (Dhs500 per person) last for 30-35 minutes and leave Nad Al-Sheba Club at 0630, or Internet City, Sheikh Zayed Road at 1630. Hour-long desert flights (Dhs780 per person) depart at 0600 from Fossil Rock and include breakfast. Advance booking is essential.

Jet skiing

Fun Sports, **T** 3995976, various locations including before Burj Al-Arab and Jumeirah Beach Hotel. *Map 1, B3, p248* The use of jet skis along the coastline has been somewhat curtailed by the amount of construction going on but this operation continues. Dhs400 per hour.

Bur Dubai side of Al-Garhoud Bridge, near the Jaddaf dhow building yard. *Map 2, H9, p251* Cheaper and possibly safer, due to less traffic. Dhs100 buys you a full hour's joy-riding.

Kitesurfing

This wild new watersport, devised in 1999, is the stuff of dreams for adrenaline junkies. A cross between surfing, windsurfing and para-chuting, you stand on a board in the sea, grasp a kite and hopefully be propelled over the waves. Pure, unadulterated madness.

Kitesurfing regulations in the UAE dictate that for insurance purposes you must be a member of **Dubai Kite Club, T** 8845912, Dhs150 per annum, and have a license before you can even try it. Licenses and insurance are obtained from **Dubai International Marine Club T** 3994111. Bring along your passport, two passport-sized photos and medical certificate to say you're fit and well, and licenses can be issued on the spot. However, hiring equipment is a no-no (in case of accidents/prosecution). If you don't already have your own, buying it out here is cheaper than anywhere else. Board, kite and harness costs Dhs4500-6000 (the same as a kite in Europe).

Fatima Sport, www.fatimasport.com. *Sat-Wed 1800-2000*. These guys are the premier sellers of kitesurfing equipment in town. They can also arrange IKO-certified instructors for coaching sessions (Dhs200 with their equipment, or Dhs100 with your own). For further information talk to Angelo, **T** 0504555216.

Mountain biking

Tourist demand for mountain biking in the area has been minimal, but plans are afoot to organize proper two- and three-day tours to the mountains of Hatta or Oman, where the terrain is best.

Biking Frontiers, Pete Maloney **T** 0504509401, www.bikingfrontiers. com. Resident cyclists who are happy for tourists to join in.

Wolfie's Bike Shop, see p207, rents out bikes at Dhs100 for 24 hours and offers advice.

Parks

Creekside Park, Umm Hurair, **T** 3367633. *Daily 0800-2300, ladies only on Wed. Dhs5 per person.* *Map 2, F7, p251* A large, sprawling park right next to the Creek. *See p47 for details.*

Mushrif Park, past Dubai Airport on Al-Khawaneej Rd, **T** 2883624. *0800-2300. Dhs10 per car or Dhs3 pedestrians*. *Map 1, H12, p249* A vast park, coated in trees and grass. *See p39 for details.*

Safa Park, Al-Wasl Rd, **T** 3492111. *Daily 0800-2300, ladies only on Tue. Dhs3 per person*. *Map 1, C6, p248* Boredom won't strike here. Bumper cars, ferris wheel, jogging tracks, etc. *See p54 for details.*

Polo

Ghantoot Polo & Racing Club, Dubai-Abu Dhabi Rd, **T** 025629050. The polo season runs from October to the end of April, and is peppered with numerous chukka tourna- ments and the odd international match that visitors are welcome to watch. Taking pride of place in the season's schedule is the HH Sheikh Khalifa bin Zayed Polo Championship in March, attracting high-goal international teams. Ring for details about the schedule.

Rugby

Dubai Rugby Sevens, Dubai Exiles Rugby Club, **T** 3331198, www.dubairugby7s.com. *Map 1, E8, p249* Kicks off the IRB Sevens season each December, for which around 30,000 rugby enthusiasts converge on Dubai.

Sailing

Dubai International Marine Club, Al-Sufouh, **T** 3434870, www.elmundodubai.com. *Map 1, B1, p248* DIMC's fully air-conditioned, 60' catamaran, *El Mundo*, is available for private charter and can cater for a wide range of tailor-made itineraries, from just a few hours locally to a couple of nights in the Musandam. It's fully furnished with fishing, banana boating, snorkelling and wake-boarding equipment. The set 'Friday Fun in the Sun' party package is popular, where for Dhs125 per person you can be part of a 50-strong crowd of revellers enjoying a four-hour sun, watersports and barbecue fest.

Yacht Solutions, Jumeirah Beach Hotel, Umm Suqeim, **T** 3486838, www.yacht-solutions.com. *Map 1,B4, p248* A 53' Roberts Ketch with captain and crew can be yours to charter for pretty much any tailor-made itinerary. It sleeps eight, and costs Dhs1,200 per hour or Dhs15,000 for 24 hours.

Sand boarding

Boarding with a sandy rather than snowy twist, all the major tour operators organize sandboarding jaunts out to the desert, either as part of a multi-faceted tour, or as an excursion in itself. Costs vary, so it's worth shopping around, but expect to pay in the region of Dhs120-185 per person for an 0830-1130 trip.

Spas

The general rule with spas is that the quality of service depends not so much on where you go, but who you get and how busy they are.

Ayoma Spa, Taj Palace Hotel, Deira, **T** 2232222. *1000-2200. Map 2, B7, p251* Ayurvedic treatments, each session starts off with a fabulous foot therapy. The Abyanga massage is divine.

Beauty Connections Spa, Oasis Tower, Sheikh Zayed Rd, **T** 3213553. *Sat-Thu 0900-2100. Map 4, off H8, p255* Real experts in skin treatments, try the Moroccan Bath for fabulous feeling skin.

Cleopatra's Spa, Pyramids, Umm Hurair, **T** 3247700. *0900-2000, Fri 1000-2000. Map 2, H6, p250* A gorgeous place, the skin and facial treatments here are much feted. Monthly special offers.

Givenchy Spa, One&Only Residence & Spa, Al-Sufouh, **T** 3999999. *0930-2000*. *Map 1, B1, p248* The ultimate indulgence, with a huge range of excellent (and pricey) treatments. Facials are wildly good.

Hammam Spa, One&Only Arabian Court, Al-Sufouh,**T** 3999999. *Daily 0930-1300, 1400-2100*. *Map 1, B1, p248* Wonderful Moroccan Hamman. Ring to clarify timings for ladies, couples or men only.

Ritz-Carlton Spa, Marsa Dubai, **T** 3994000. *Daily 0900-2200*. *Map 1, off B1, p248* Lovely place, excellent treatments and a particularly good line in 90-minute facials.

Shanghai Medical Clinic, Sheikh Zayed Rd, near Safestways, **T** 3434811. *Map 1, C7, p249* Awesome acupuncture, massage and Chinese herbal medicine. The Chinese doctor doesn't speak a word of English, but he certainly knows his stuff!

1847, Emirates Towers Boulevard, **T** 3301847. *Sat-Thu 0900-2100, Fri 1300-2100*. *Map 4, H10, p255* Taking its name from the date the world's first safety razor was patented, this is Dubai's first grooming lounge exclusively for men. Manicures, massages, traditional shaves and reflexology, make for a seriously pampersome place.

Snorkelling

The best snorkelling is found on the East Coast, where there's more to see in the waters. Numerous tour operators organize trips to Khor Fakkan, Fujairah and the like, see p75. See also p207.

Speedboating

Fun Sports, various locations, **T** 0504534828. *0900-1700 weather conditions permitting*. Boat hire comes with captain, and costs

Dhs200 for half an hour for up to two people. Fun Sports operates from the beach hotels in the DIMC area.

Tennis

Aviation Club, Al-Garhoud, **T** 2824122, membership **T** 2865303. *0600-2300. Map 2, F10, p251* Only members can use the excellent facilities available here (daily membership is Dhs125 per person). The club has six courts, a 9-hole par 3 golf course, a 25-metre lane training pool, Jacuzzi and two squash courts, and so is a great place to come for an active day in great surroundings.

Dubai Tennis Open, Aviation Club, **T** 2828971, box office **T** 282-9166, www.dubaitennischampionships.com. *Map 2, F10, p251* This tournament takes place every February, attracting top seeds.

Wakeboarding

Dubai Water Sports Association, Jaddaf, end of Dubai Creek, **T** 3241031, www.dwsa.net. *Daily 0900-dusk. Map 1, E10, p249* Arguably the fastest growing sport in the world, it's the aquatic equivalent of snowboarding, only you can do bigger and better stunts thanks to the rope you're attached to. Daily membership is Dhs20, on top of which it's Dhs55 per 15 minutes wakeboarding.

Watersports

Fujairah Marine Club, Corniche Rd, Fujairah **T** 092220060. *0800-1400, 1700-1900 or later. See p78* Opened in 2002, the Marine Club caters mainly for expats, though it's also a popular stop for tourists bent on aquatic diversions, and is generally held to offer amongst the best scuba diving and snorkelling options in the UAE. The variety of activities on offer include snorkelling, scuba diving, fishing, dhow trips, jet skis and plenty more.

● *The in-house restaurant, Armada, 1100-0100, does a good Friday brunch, while Thursday's barbecue nights also go down a treat.*

Fun Sports, various locations including the Hilton Beach Jumeirah, Metropolitan Resort & Beach Club and Ritz-Carlton, **T** 3995976, www.funsport-dubai.com. One of the larger independent outfits operating offering plenty of choice for the fun-seeking, sea-bent tourist. Everything from banana boat rides to wakeboarding, kayaking to windsurfing, parasailing to sunset cruises.

Wild Wadi, Umm Suqeim, **T** 3484444, www.jumeirahinternational.com. *Jun-Aug 1100-2100, Sep-Oct and Mar-May 1100-1900, Nov-Feb 1100-1800. Dhs120 adults, Dhs100 children, 30% discount if you enter after 1600. Map 1, B3, p248 See also p59* You can't fail to have fun here. Hold onto your hats (well, bikinis) on the fast and furious Jumeirah Scierah, show off your surfing skills (or wipeout to the amusement of the crowd) on the two surf simulators, or sit back and relax on a variety of rides where powerful water jets propel you ever upwards to ensure an extended stint in your inflatable raft. Flash floods on the hour, a wave pool, countless sun loungers, a dedicated children's area and several food outlets mean there's something for everyone. And expect everyone to be there. It is one of the biggest crowd pullers in Dubai.

With domestic life featuring high on the list of Arab priorities, it should come as no surprise that there is plenty of family oriented fun to be had. From the teeniest tot to the bolshiest teen, the list of attractions has a range of appeal wide enough to gladden the hearts of any discerning parent. The government's savvy understanding of summer holidays as a prime time for family travel means that even during the unseasonably hot weather there'll be a decent range of mall-based entertainments geared entirely towards the younger generations. Many hotels, especially the beach properties, run children's clubs, allowing parents to relax in peace while their offspring let off steam in secure environments. Equally, the parks all have dedicated play and entertainment areas, as do the shopping malls. Whatever their preferences, a holiday to Dubai should certainly keep your position as all-round ace parent in tact!

Family Explorer, widely available in bookshops throughout the city, contains exhaustive listings of fun-packed family activities. For parks and beaches, see p215 and p205.

Attractions

Al-Ain Zoo and Aquarium, off Al-Nahyan Al-Awal Rd, Al-Ain, **T** 037828188. *Sun-Fri 0730-1730. See p90.*

Children's City, route 81 between Al-Maktoum and Al-Garhoud Bridges, Oud Metha, **T** 3340808, www.childrencity.ae. *Sat-Thu 0900-2130, Fri 1500-2130. Dhs15, Dhs10 children (2-15 years).* *Map 2, H8, p251 See also p48* It's an excellent new educational museum for youngsters, with interactive displays on space exploration, nature, the human body, global culture and more.

Sharjah Desert Park, 28 km out of Sharjah, between Interchanges 8-9 on the Al-Dhaid Rd. *Tue-Sun 0900-1730, Thu 1100-1730, Fri 1400-1730. Dhs 15 adults, free for kids. See p74* This wonderful complex plays host to Arabia's Wildlife Centre, Sharjah's Natural History Museum and the Children's Farm. Recommended.

Wild Wadi, Jumeirah Beach Rd, **T** 3484444. *Nov-Feb 1100-1800, Mar-May and Sep-Oct 1100-1900, Jun-Aug 1100-2100. Dhs120 adults, Dhs100 children. Map 1, B3, p248 See also p59* Patrolled by hoards of qualified lifeguards, Wild Wadi is a safe environment that's a mega-hit with kids. Its interconnected water shoots, lagoons, wave pool, play area, fast-food outlets and shop can easily keep the children happy for a full day.

WonderLand Theme and Water Park, off route 81, near Al-Garhoud Bridge, **T** 3241222, www.wonderlanduae.com. *Map 2, H8, p251 See also p48* Once brightly coloured, the rides and buildings area now all rather faded which is a shame, as the variety of activities is enormous ranging from arcade games to climbing frames and water slides and shoots to bumper cars and power karts. For impatient children, or adults for that matter, this is a great option.

Kids

Mall amusement centres

Encounter Zone, Wafi Mall, **T** 3247747. *1000-2200, Fri 1330-2200.*
Map 2, H6, p250 *See p188* Lunarland caters for the under eights
while Galactica entertains the older children.

Fun City, Mercato, Jumeirah Beach Rd, **T** 3499976, *Map 4, G1, p254*,
and BurJuman Centre, **T** 3593336. *Sat-Thu 1000-2200, Fri 1400-2300*,
Map 2, D3, p250 *See p188* Plenty of activities for all ages.

LouLou Al-Dugong's, Lamcy Plaza, Oud Metha, **T** 3352700.
Sat-Thu 1000-2300, Fri 1100-2300. Map 2, G4, p254 *See p188*
A play and discovery centre for all ages.

Magic Planet, Deira City Centre, **T** 2954333. *1000-2400, Fri 1200-
2400. Map 2, D9, p251* *See p188* A great favourite for all ages.

Smart discovery, Palm Strip, Jumeirah Beach Rd, **T** 3452755.
Sat-Thu 0930-2130, Fri 1200-2130. Map 4, B4, p254 *See also p188*
Original activities for children.

Restaurants

The vast majority of restaurants in Dubai are very happy catering
for children, especially the restaurants at the beach hotels, where
the bulk of the clientele are families. Otherwise, good options
include **Shabestan**, p128; **Noodle House**, p138, where service is
fast and it doesn't matter what mess you make; and **Fatafeet**,
p131, where the traffic plying the Creek and the promenaders
mean there's plenty to entertain but beware the service can be
slow. Other popular options include the North American chowder
served up at Jumeirah Beach Hotel's **Go West**, p62, and the
hugely popular American menu and Family Fridays at **Planet
Hollywood**, Wafi City, p47.

Directory

Airline offices
British Airways, 10th floor, Kendah House, Sheikh Zayed Rd, **T** 3075777. **Emirates**, DNATA Airline Centre, Al-Maktoum Rd, Deira, **T** 2144444. **Gulf Air**, Salahuddin Rd, Deira, **T** 2713111. **KLM**, 9th floor, Gulf Towers, on corner of Oud Metha Rd and 20 St, Oud Metha, **T** 3355777. **Lufthansa**, 2nd floor, Lufthansa Building, Sheikh Zayed Rd, **T** 3432121.

Banks and ATMs
Banks opening hours are Saturday to Wednesday from 0800 to 1300 (some branches may also be open from 1630 to 1830) and Thursday from 0800 to 1200. The numerous ATM machines dotted around town accept all major credit cards and offer decent rates of exchange. Money exchanges often offer better rates than banks.

Car hire
Avis, **T** 2957121, avisuae@emirates.net.ae. **Budget**, **T** 2956667, bracdxb@budget-uae.com. **Hertz**, **T** 2824422, hertz@alfuttaim.co.ae. **Thrifty**, **T** 3370744, thrifty@emirates.net.ae. **United**, **T** 2666286, ucrdubai@emirates.net.ae.

Cultural institutions
Sheikh Mohammed Centre for Cultural Understanding, Bastakia, **T** 3536666.

Dentists
Be aware that the generally high standard of service will come at a cost similar to that of private dentists in the UK. Recommended practices, all on Al-Wasl Rd: **British Dental Clinic**, **T** 3421318. **Dr Michael's**, **T** 3495900. **Dubai London Clinic**, **T** 3446663.

Disabled
Despite a promising start at the airport, facilities for the disabled have a long way to go. While most five-star hotels are the

exception and there are a few adequately equipped Dubai transport taxis, major tourist attractions are woefully lacking in wheelchair accessibility and in the absence of proper wheelchair ramps in town, getting around can be an endurance test.

Doctors

The medical fraternity is based in Jumeirah. Be warned that without insurance, medical attention could cost an arm and a leg. **Dubai London Clinic**, Al-Wasl Rd, **T** 3446663, **General Medical Centre**, Jumeirah Beach Rd, above Magrudy's, **T** 3495959, **Health Care Medical Centre**, Jumeirah Centre, **T** 3445550.

Electricity

The current is 220/240 volts and 50 cycles. British-style three-pin sockets are common and adaptors are readily available either in hotels or in town (especially Al-Fahidi Road in Bur Dubai).

Embassies and consulates

Australia, Emarat Atrium, Sheikh Zayed Rd, **T** 3212444. **Canada**, Al-Hisn St, **T** 3145555. **France**, API World Tower, Sheikh Zayed Rd, **T** 3329040. **Germany**, Al-Mankhool Rd, **T** 3972333. **Italy**, Dubai World Trade Centre, Sheikh Zayed Rd, **T** 3314167. **UK**, Al-Seef Rd, Bur Dubai **T** 3094444. **USA**, Dubai World Trade Centre, **T** 3116000.

Emergency numbers

Police T 999 (Dubai police HQ can be reached on **T** 2292222); **Ambulance T** 998; **Fire service T** 997; **Operator T** 181.

Hospitals

The standard of healthcare is good in Dubai. Hospitals that handle emergencies include: **Al-Wasl Hospital**, Oud Metha Rd, Za'abeel, **T** 3241111; the **American Hospital**, near Lamcy Plaza and Movenpick Hotel, Oud Metha, **T** 3367777, and **Rashid Hospital**, near Al-Maktoum Bridge, off Oud Metha Rd, Bur Dubai, **T** 3374000.

Internet/email

There are plenty of internet cafés in town, often in malls and restaurants, and with wildly varying prices (anything from Dhs5-15 per hour). Some cafés will let you surf for free if you order food.

Language schools

Arabic Language Centre, Dubai World Trade Centre, Sheikh Zayed Rd, **T** 3086036, alc@dwtc.com. **Polyglot Language Institute**, Al-Masaeed Building, Deira, **T** 2223429. **Sheikh Mohammed Centre for Cultural Understanding**, Bastakia, **T** 3536666, sometimes offers language courses.

Left luggage

At the airport, Terminal 1 Arrivals area (Dhs10 per item for 12 hours for hand luggage and Dhs15 for larger items), **T** 2161734.

Libraries

Alliance Francaise, Umm Hurair, **T** 3358712, *0900-1300 and 1600-2000*. **British Council Library**, near Al-Maktoum Bridge, Umm Hurair, **T** 3370109, *0900-2000*. **Juma Al-Majid Cultural & Heritage Centre**, near Dubai Cinema, Diera, **T** 2624999, *0800-1930*. **The Old Library**, International Art Centre, Jumeirah Beach Rd, **T** 3446480, *1000-1200 and 1600-1800*.

Lost/stolen property

Your best bet in recovering lost property will be either **Dubai Police**, **T** 2292222, or the very helpful **Department for Tourist Security**, **T** 8004438. For items left in a bus, **Dubai Municipitys lost & found department** is the obvious first stop, **T** 2850700.

Media

Dubai's three daily English-language newspapers are *Kaleej Times*, *The Gulf News* and *The Gulf Today*. Foreign newspapers can be found in many supermarkets, bookshops and hotel shops, although they tend to be slightly out of date. There's a wide variety of English-language magazines including *Time Out Dubai*, *What's On*. Media sites include: gulfnews.com, khaleejtimes.com, godubai.com, wam.org and dubaiinteract.com.

Pharmacies (late night)
Pharmacies and chemists are dotted all over the city and easily distinguished by shop signs baring the motif of a snake coiled around a cocktail glass. Dubai Municipality operates an emergency hotline offering numbers of 24-hour pharmacies, **T** 2232323.

Police
Police officers in Dubai are generally very helpful, calm, efficient and master of a variety of languages to boot. **Dubai Regional Police HQ**, at the very southern end of Trade Centre Rd, **T** 2292222, dubai police.gov.ae. A dedicated **Tourist Police** has also been set up to cater more specifically for the needs of visitors.

Post offices
Central Post Office, Zabeel Rd, Al-Karama, **T** 3371500, *Sat-Wed 0800-2400 and Thu 0800-2200*. There are smaller offices throughout the city, and malls and petrol stations sometimes have post services. Some card shops also sell stamps. There are also numerous courier companies including **DHL T** 8004004; **Federal Express T** 8004050; and **UPS T** 8004774. Mail posted to the UK/US takes around a week.

Public holidays
Fixed dates include: New Year's Day; 6 August (accession of HH Sheikh Zayed), and 2 and 3 December (UAE National Day). Moveable dates (with their expected 2005 dates in brackets) include: Arafat Day (21 January); Eid Al-Adha (three days, starting 22 January); Islamic New Year's Day (14 February); Prophet Mohammed's Birthday (23 April); Lailat Al-Mi'raj (4 September), and Eid Al-Fitr (three days, starting 6 November).

Religious services

While Islam is the official UAE religion, there are numerous Christian churches including: **Evangelical Community Church**, Jebel Ali, **T** 88466301, **Holy Trinity**, Oud Metha, **T** 3370247, **St Mary's Catholic Church**, Oud Metha, **T** 3370087, and **United Christian Church of Dubai**, Jumeira, **T** 3442509. **Shri Nathje Jayate Temple**, Bur Dubai, see p42. **Sheikh Mohammed Centre for Cultural Understanding**, **T** 3536666, organizes visits to a mosque on Thursday mornings.

Taxi firms

Dubai Transport Corporation T 2080808. **Gulf Radio Taxis T** 2236666. **Metro Taxis T** 2673222. **National Taxis T** 3366611.

Telephone

The UAE's international dialling code is 971 and Dubai's city code is 04 (omit the zero when calling from abroad). All numbers are then seven digits long. Calls from landline to landline within the city are free and there's no need to dial the city code. Mobile numbers here always start with 050. Public telephones tend to be better value than calls placed from hotels, and are easily found in the malls and on the streets. Some accept coins while most take phonecards, which come in a variety of denominations and are readily available at many shops and supermarkets.

Time

GMT + four hours, BST + three hours.

Transport enquiries

Dubai Municipality bus information, **T** 8004848; **Dubai Transport**, minibus (to the Northern Emirates), **T** 2861616 or **T** 2273840; **Flight enquiries**, **T** 2166666.

A sprint through history

3000 BC	Archaeological evidence points to the area having been settled from at least the Bronze Age. Although historical records mysteriously dry up in the second millennium BC.
5th - 7th centuries	Jumeira was a trade route caravan station linking Oman with what is now Iraq. Livelihoods were based on fishing, boat-building and pearling.
16th century	European influence began with Portuguese interest in the area's trade routes.
18th century	Britain developed an interest and a presence in the area thanks to its trade routes.
1793	Sheikh Shakbut of the dominant Bani Yas tribe assumed political power and settled in Abu Dhabi. Dubai later became a dependency. The area was beset with many tribal wars.
1820	Britain, as part of its policy of defending India, negotiated the first of many maritime truces with local rulers that led to the area being dubbed the Trucial Coast.
1833	Maktoum Bin Butti of the Bani Yas tribe settled on the Shindagha Peninsula at the mouth of the Creek in what is now Bur Dubai. He declared the town's independence from Abu Dhabi, sparking two years of fighting.
1835	Britain's intervention restored peace to the area and Maktoum Bin Butti consolidated and subsequently expanded his rule, laying the foundations on which his still-ruling dynasty took root.

1870s	Dubai had become the principal port on the Gulf coast, with pearling the mainstay of the city's prosperity.
1892	The Exclusive Agreements were signed, giving Britain control over foreign affairs and each Emirate jurisdiction over its own internal affairs.
1894	The economy prospered still more when Sheikh Maktoum bin Hasher Al-Maktoum gave tax exemptions to foreign traders.
1902	The welcome migration of Iranian traders and Arab settlers to Dubai following the introduction of heavy taxes on Iran's Lingeh port by Persian Imperial Customs. Dubai's trade has never looked back.
Early 20th century	Overseas and domestic trade was flourishing, and Dubai boasted the largest souks in Arabia.
1912	Al-Ahmadiya School opened on the back of pearl diving wealth transforming the nature of education.
1930s-40s	The Japanese cultured pearl speeds the demise of the pearling industry. But trade in gold, textiles, foodstuffs and other commodities blossomed.
1950s	Oil was discovered in the Trucial States.
1952	The Trucial Council was formed to promote cooperation between the seven Emirates.
1958	Sheikh Rashid succeeds as ruler of Dubai.
1959	Dubai's first school for girls opened. Dredging of the Creek completed, allowing bigger boats to gain access, boosting trade.

1950s-60s	Dubai's trade was oriented largely towards Iran, the strongest economy in the region.
1960s	Indian and Pakistani population of Dubai grew, and new life was breathed into the textile market.
1962	Oil exported for the first time from Abu Dhabi. First bridge over the Creek completed.
1966	Oil discovered in Dubai's Fateh Oil field. Sheikh Zayed Bin Sultan Al-Nahyan succeeds as ruler of Abu Dhabi.
1968	Bahrain and Qatar join the Trucial States, but opposing objectives lead to the disintegration of this union in 1971.
1969	Dubai begins exporting oil. Rich financial pickings enabled the emirate to develope a sound infra-structure and pursue a raft of ambitious plans to secure its future prosperity.
1971	British withdrew from the area and the United Arab Emirates were formed under the leadership of Sheikh Zayed Bin Sultan Al-Nahyan. Sheikh Rashid Bin Saeed Al-Maktoum was elected Vice-President. The federation was established for mutual defence, security, prosperity and social order. UAE joins the Arab League. Dubai International Airport opened.
1972	Port Rashid completed, greatly enhancing Dubai's import and export trade. Ras Al-Khaimah joined the UAE. Federal National Council (FNC) formed – a 40-member consultative body appointed by the seven Emirate rulers.

1975	Dubai's first five-star hotel opened.
1979	Jebel Ali port opened, benefitting Dubai's trading community. Dubai World Trade Centre opened – the city's first high-rise, which paved the way for a string of other ambitious architectural projects.
1981	Arab Gulf Cooperation Council formed, abolishing the double taxation of goods from other member countries, further enhancing trade.
1985	Emirates airline launched. Jebel Ali Free Zone inaugurated, attracting considerable foreign investment for the first time by allowing 100 per cent business ownership exempt of all taxes and duties.
1989	Dubai Commerce & Tourism Promotion Board established.
1990	Sheikh Rashid died and was succeeded by son Sheikh Maktoum Bin Rashid Al-Maktoum as Ruler of Dubai and Vice-President of the UAE.
1996	Dubai World Cup held for the first time. Dubai Shopping Festival launched.
1999	Burj Al-Arab opened and is hailed as the world's only seven-star hotel.
2003	Work began on ambitious developments including an underwater hotel, the world's tallest tower, and 200 man-made islands in the shape of the world.
2005	Sheikh Zayed dies and is succeeded as President of the UAE and Ruler of Abu Dhabi by his son Sheikh Khalifa.

Art and architecture

Circa 1787	Construction of Al Fahidi Fort (now Dubai Museum) with local materials used for building for many years to come: sea rocks, mud bricks, date palm trunks and palm fronds, held together with sarooj.
1890	Heritage House, originally the two-bedroomed dwelling of a local merchant, was a typical dwelling of the time incorporating a wide courtyard surrounded by a number of *barasti* rooms.
1900	Houses were linked by narrow sandy lanes which provided shade. Old houses consisted of a staggered entrance (for privacy) leading to an inside courtyard. The windowed *majlis* was near the main entrance, facing outwards. The courtyard was designed to provide ventilation and light, and the walls were traditionally beautifully decorated with gypsum.
Early 1900s	The rise of the merchant Bastakia district with its traditional wind tower houses that served as an early form of air conditioning.
1912	Al-Ahmadiya School opened. Built around the ubiquitous courtyard, it's also a good example of the traditional layout of Arab houses.
1930s	Extensions and improvements made to Heritage House typify the care taken with architecture at this time, with ornately carved wooden doors, stucco panelling and intricate window screens bearing the hallmarks of Indian stylistic influences. Bait Al Wakeel was the city's first office block, built in 1936.
1940s-50s	These decades saw a real movement towards today's modern infrastructure with more office

buildings, including the first cement building (1948) and the first reinforced concrete building (1956).

1960s	By the end of this decade, most of the city's infrastructure was in place for the making of a modern city. Al-Maktoum Bridge (1964) improved access between the two sides of the Creek.
1970s	With everything set up, astronomical progress took place during this decade: Dubai International Airport (1971); Al-Shindagha Tunnel (1972); Jebel Ali Port, the Free Zone, Al-Garhoud Bridge (1976); the dry dock (1977); the first water de-salination plant and plans for the beautification of the city.
1971	It was proposed that a survey be made of old buildings worthy of preservation and restoration.
1979	Building of the World Trade Centre – Dubai's first tall tower, and the only one until the early 1990's. A first in terms of size, and environmentally sensitive too, with the window wall set back from the outer wall, shading the enclosing walls and reducing direct solar heat gain on the building fabric.
1990s	Greater movement towards conserving Dubai's historic buildings, including Sheikh Saeed's House.
2000s	The architectural firms at work in Dubai are commercial, with no big guns in the design stakes. Buildings of particular note include Burj Al-Arab, Emirates Towers, Madinat Jumeirah, Royal Mirage.
Present	There is no real tradition of art here, but galleries and exhibitions by local artists are on the up.

Books

Al-Murr, Muhammad, *Dubai Tales* (1990) Dufour Editions. Twenty-one short stories delving into the lives and values of the people of Dubai.

Al-Rostomani, Ahmad Hassan, *Dubai and Its Architectural Heritage* (1991), Al Safeer Publishing. For anyone with an interest in Dubai's rather unusual architectural history.

Beardwood, Mary, *The Children's Encyclopedia of Arabia* (2001), Stacey International. The first educational book on Arabia geared for children. Excellent.

Codrai, Ronald, *Seafarers of the Emirates* (2003), Motivate. Charts the last years of an old way of life and a time when the Sheikhdoms were on the threshold of radical change.

Devine, Barbara, *Elvis the Camel* (2001), Stacey International. The true story of a young camel, injured in a road accident and nursed back to health by three young children. Beautifully illustrated by Patricia Al-Fakhri.

Dubai Municipality, *Elements of Traditional Architecture in Dubai* (1996), Dubai Municipality. A recommended architectural work.

Henderson, Edward, *Arabian Destiny* (1999), Motivate. Fascinating memoires of a British colonial official with an extraordinary understanding and love of Dubai.

Holton, Patricia, *Mother without a Mask* (1997), Motivate. Accepted into an Arab family, this is a Westerner's account of how she comes to understand the background to the traditions governing their lives.

Images of Dubai (2003), Explorer Publishing. A visual showcase, sharing the secrets of this remarkable land and introducing newcomers to the wonders of Dubai and the UAE.

Mallos, Tess, *Cooking of the Gulf* (2004), Magrudy's. A collection of delicious recipes from all the Gulf States. From traditonal Arabian dishes to contemporary favourites, these authentic recipes capture the unique flavours of the region.

Raban, Jonathan, *Arabia Through the Looking Glass* (1979), Collins. An entertaining, perceptive account of the character of the region back in the 1970's, including a fascinating chapter on Dubai.

Richardson, Neil & Dorr, Marcia, *The Craft Heritage of Oman* (2004), Motivate. A beautiful tribute to Oman's artisans and the rich traditions they embody, documenting the different types of crafts in all parts of the country.

Dubai, tomorrow's city today (2004), Explorer Publishing. A guided tour of historical highlights, innovative plans and civic wonderments. See what this city has accomplished in a single generation and wonder at its plans for the future.

Language

You really don't need to know any Arabic to communicate in Dubai. Everybody speaks English, to the extent that even if you try a greeting in Arabic (*As-salam alaykum*: peace be with you) most Arabs will give the customary response (*Walaykum as-salam*: and to you peace) before launching off into high-speed English. It's perfectly possible to spend two weeks here and hear no or very little Arabic, and certainly no more than you'll hear Hindustani, Persian or Urdu, but if you want to try the odd word, you may find the list below useful.

Please   *Min fadlak* (to a man); *Min fadlik* (to a woman)
Thank you   *Shukran*
Thanks be to God   *Al-hamdu li-lla*
God willing (hopefully)   *Insha alla*
Yes   *Na'am*
No   *La*
What is your name?   *Shu ismak?* (to a man); *Shu ismik?* (to a woman)
My name is…   *Ismi…*

Glossary

abaya   a long, loose, black, outer-robe traditionally worn by Arab women
abra   a small, motor-powered water-taxi
baclawa   sweet oriental pastries
barasti   the traditional method of building houses or structures of palm fronds, and the name of the structures themselves
Bedouin   desert dweller of Arabia, often not exclusively nomadic
dhow   traditional Arab trading vessel or sailing ship with a triangular sail
dishdasha   the long, loose robe worn by men in the UAE

falaj   ancient irrigation system consisting of a network of tunnels either above or below ground

faloudeh   a popular Persian dessert: a sweet beverage containing starch jelly in the form of thin fibres

GCC   Gulf Cooperation Council. Member countries include: Bahrain, Kuwait, Oman, Qatar, Saudi Arabia and the UAE

jebel   mountain

kandouras   see *dishdasha*

khanjars   traditional dagger, often in an ornate, curved scabbard, traditionally worn by every male Gulf Arab

khor   creek

majlis   formal meeting or reception room where issues are discussed and disputes settled; also council

qalaleef   dhow builders

sarooj   mortar made of Iranian red clay, manure and water

shasha   canoe-like fishing boats made of stripped palm fronds

shawarma   grilled meat, sliced from a roasting spit of chicken, beef or mutton and wrapped with a salad and sauce in Arab bread

shisha   better known in the west as hubbly-bubbly, this is a tall smoking implement with a bulbous glass bottom

sheikh   a chief or head of an Arab tribe. Also a venerable old man and also the traditional term for a religious leader/teacher

sheikha   wife or daughter of a sheikh

Trucial States   Colonial name for the region before it became the UAE

UAE   United Arab Emirates

wadi   a watercourse or riverbed, often dry for much of or all the year, but not necessarily

Index

Credits

Footprint credits
Editor: Stephanie Lambe
Assistant editor: Nicola Jones
Map editor: Sarah Sorensen
Publisher: Patrick Dawson
Series created by: Rachel Fielding
Cartography: Claire Benison, Kevin
Feeney, Robert Lunn

Design: Mytton Williams
Maps: Footprint Handbooks Ltd

Photography credits
Front cover: Alamy, gold bracelets
Inside: Zee Gilmore
Cut out images: p1 Burj Al-Arab,
p5 camel, p17 Grand Mosque
Generic images: John Matchett
Back cover: Zee Gilmore, camel

Print
Manufactured in Italy by LegoPrint.
Pulp from sustainable forests.

Footprint feedback
We try as hard as we can to make
each Footprint guide as up to date as
possible but, of course, things always
change. If you want to let us know
about your experiences – good, bad
or ugly – then don't delay, go to
www.footprintbooks.com and send
in your comments.

Publishing information
Footprint Dubai
1st edition
Text and maps © Footprint Handbooks
Ltd August 2004

ISBN 1 904777 17 1
CIP DATA: a catalogue record for this
book is available from the British Library

Published by Footprint
6 Riverside Court
Lower Bristol Road
Bath, BA2 3DZ, UK
T +44 (0)1225 469141
F +44 (0)1225 469461
discover@footprintbooks.com
www.footprintbooks.com

Distributed in the USA by
Publishers Group West

Publishing stuff

Complete title list

(P) denotes pocket guide

Check out...

www...

100 travel guides, 100s of destinations,
5 continents
and 1 Footprint...

www.footprintbooks.com

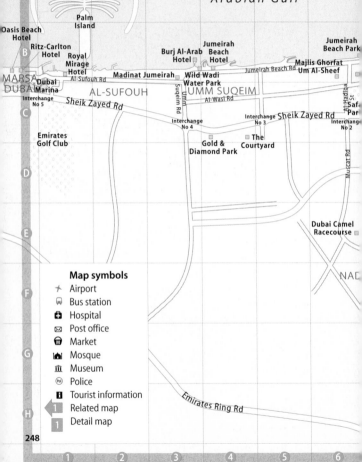

Map 1 Dubai

Arabian Gulf

Oasis Beach Hotel

Ritz-Carlton Hotel

Palm Island

Royal Mirage Hotel

MARSA DUBAI

Dubai Marina

Interchange No 5

Al-Sufouh Rd

Madinat Jumeirah

AL-SUFOUH

Sheik Zayed Rd

Emirates Golf Club

Burj Al-Arab Hotel

Jumeirah Beach Hotel

Wild Wadi Water Park

Suqeim Rd

Jumeirah Beach Rd

UMM SUQEIM

Al-Wasi Rd

Interchange No 4

Gold & Diamond Park

The Courtyard

Interchange No 3

Sheik Zayed Rd

Jumeirah Beach Park

Majlis Ghorfat Um Al-Sheef

Hadiqa St

Saf Par

Interchange No 2

Muscat Rd

Dubai Camel Racecourse

NAD

Emirates Ring Rd

Map symbols

- ✈ Airport
- 🚍 Bus station
- ✚ Hospital
- ✉ Post office
- 🏪 Market
- 🕌 Mosque
- 🏛 Museum
- ⊚ Police
- ℹ Tourist information
- ◀1 Related map
- 1 Detail map

248

PORT RASHID
Hyatt Regency Hotel
Dubai Ladies Club
Shindagha Tunnel
AL-HAMRIYA PORT
Jumeirah Beach Rd
Al-Mina Rd
DEIRA
Al-Khaleej Rd
Jumeirah Archaeological Site
JUMEIRA
BUR DUBAI
Mamzar Park
Al-Wasl Rd
Mankhool Rd
AL-MAMZAR
Al-Satwa Rd
Al-Diyafah Rd
Al-Safa Rd
SATWA
Al-Adhid Rd
Baniyas Rd
Al-Maktoum Rd
Salahuddin Rd
Abu Bakar Al-Siddiq Rd
Abu Hail Rd
Al-Wuheida Rd
Interchange No 1
Dusit Dubai
Zabeel Rd
Al-Maktoum Bridge
OUD METHA
Al-Ittehad Rd
2nd Zabeel Rd
Creekside Park
Oud Metha Rd
AL-GARHOUD
AL QUSAIS
Al-Garhoud Bridge
Dubai International Airport
Airport Rd
Khor Dubai
BUKADRA
Khor Dubai Wildlife Sanctuary
Al-Quds Rd
Al-Nahda Rd
AL-SHEBA
Ras Al-Khor Rd
RAS AL-KHOR
Emirates Rd
Dubai Al-Ain Rd
Nad Al-Hamar Rd
Al-Khawaneej Rd
Mushrif Park
0 km 1
0 miles 1

Map 2 Central Dubai

Al-Mateena St

Hor Al-Anz St

Salah Al-Din Rd

Al-Iwar Rd

Salah Al-Din Rd

Abu Baker Al-Siddique Rd

Al-Muraqqabat Rd

Al-Ittihad Rd

N

0 metres   500
0 yards   500

A

Al-Rigga Rd

B

Clock Tower

Buses to Muscat

Al-Maktoum Rd

C

Ziyad Rd

Baniyas Rd

Deira City Center Mall

Airport Rd

Dubai International Airport

D

1

Al-Maktoum Bridge

E

Airport Rd

Al-Garhoud Rd

Dubai Creek Golf & Yacht Club

Irish Village

Century Village

F

Tennis Stadium

Aviation Club

Creekside Park

AL-GARHOUD

G

201 Rd

411 Rd

Children's City

METHA

Paintball

Al Boom Tourist Village

Al-Qutayeyat Rd

Al-Garhoud Bridge

H

206 Rd

Wonderland Theme & Water Park

UMM HURAIR

Al-Jaddaf Dhow Building Yard

251

Map 3 Deira & Bur Dubai

Al-Shindagha Tunnel

Gold Souk Bus Station

Pedestrian Tunnel

Al-Khaleej Rd

Heritage & Diving Villages

Sheikh Saeed Al-Maktoum's House

Al-Khor St

Old

Baladiya St

Sikkat Al-Khail Rd

Al-Ahmadiya St

Al-Ahmadiya School & Heritage House

AL-SHINDAGHA

Al-Hadd St

Al-Abra St

Al-Ras Rd

Al-Ghubaiba St

Bait Al-Wakeel

Sikh Gurdwara

Shri Nathje Jayate Temple

Textile Souk

BUR DUBAI

Grand Mosque

Al-Suq St

Al Bin Abi Taleb St

Dubai Museum

Al-Ghubaiba Bus Station

Fish, Meat & Vegetable Souk

Al-Khor St
Al-Daghaya St
Al-Soor St
Al-Sabkha Rd

DEIRA

Gold Souk

Perfume Souk

Souk Deira St

Al-Sabkha Bus Station

Covered Souk

Al-Burj St

Deira St

Electronics Souk

Al-Maktoum Hospital Rd

Baniyas Square

Al-Souk Al-Kabeer St

Baniyas Rd

Khor Dubai

The Iwan

XVA Gallery

BASTAKIA

Scenic Rd

Sheikh Mohammed Centre for Cultural Understanding

Al-Fahidi St

Majlis Gallery

N

0 metres   100
0 yards   100

Map 4 Jumeira & Satwa

Arabian Gulf

Dar Al-Ittehad
(Union House)

Jumeirah Beach Rd

Palm Strip

Jumeirah Mosque

Al-Hudaiba Rd

Iranian Mosque

Iranian Hospital

Al-Wasl Rd

Jumeirah Beach Corniche

Jumeirah Beach Rd

Dubai Zoo

Green Art Gallery

JUMEIRA

Al-Wasl Rd

Al-Satwa Rd

Mercato

Town Centre Mall

Creative Art Centre

254

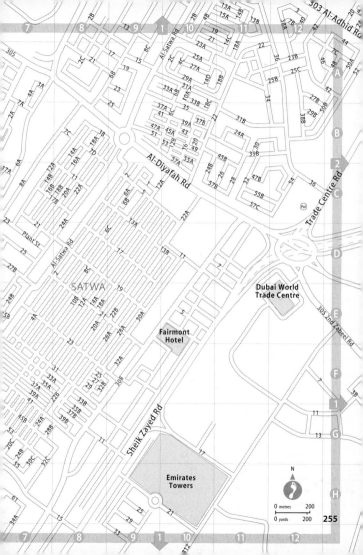

For a different view…
choose a Footprint

Over 100 Footprint travel guides
Covering more than 150 of the world's most exciting
countries and cities in Latin America, the Caribbean, Africa, Indian
sub-continent, Australasia, North America, Southeast Asia, the
Middle East and Europe.

Discover so much more…
The finest writers. In-depth knowledge. Entertaining and accessible.
Critical restaurant and hotels reviews. Lively descriptions of all the
attractions. Get away from the crowds.